SANTHAL FAMILY

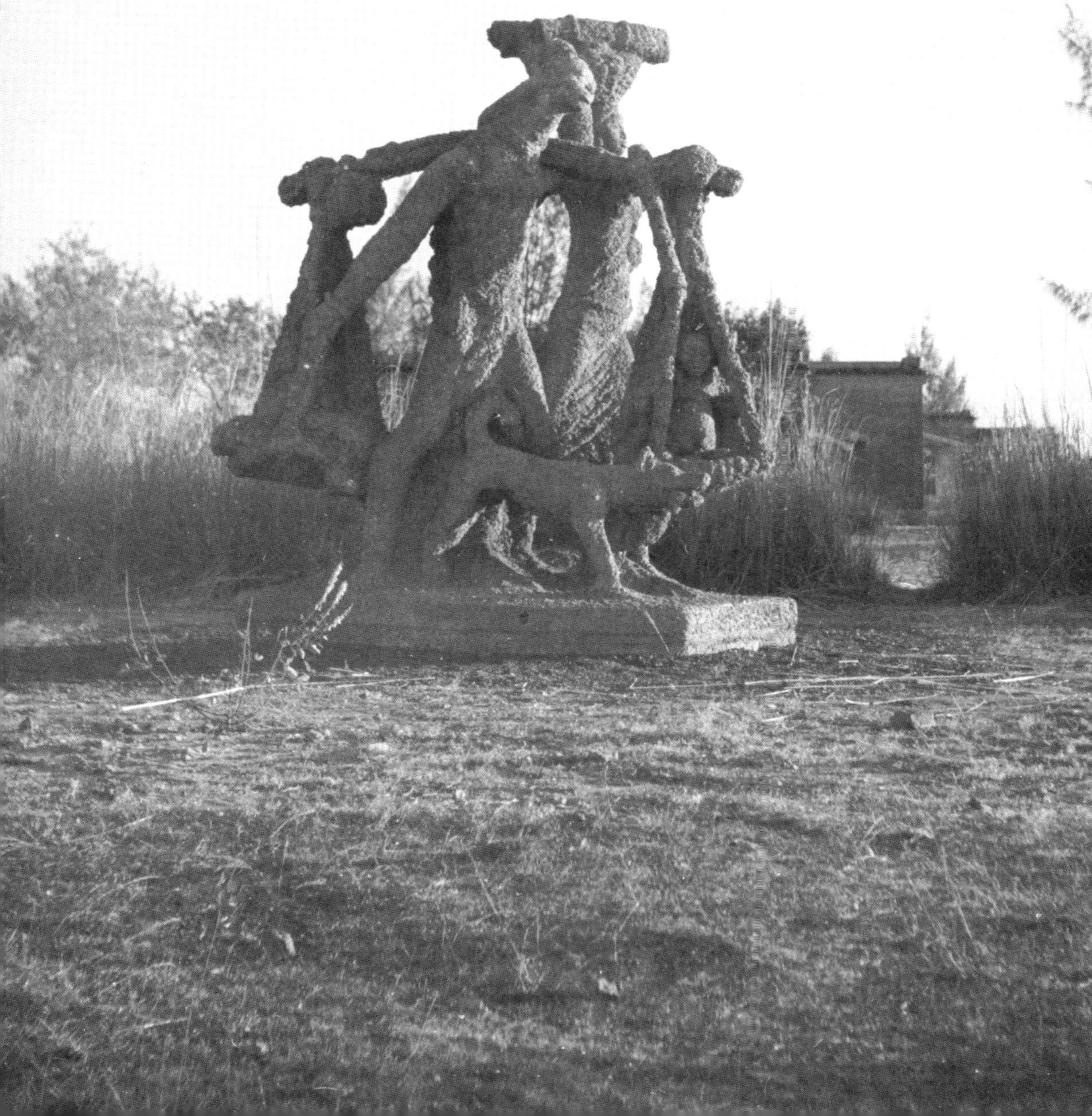

< Ramkinkar Baij, *Santhal Family*, 1938, direct cement concrete, image courtesy Rabindra Bhavan Archive, Santiniketan

SANTHAL FAMILY

When Ramkinkar Baij made the large-scale outdoor sculpture *Santhal Family* at Santiniketan in 1938, he was giving artistic voice to something that was in the air. Baij "grew up at a time, when on the global scene, a kind of deference for primitivism was gaining ground,"[1] and at a local level within the experimental milieu of Rabindranath Tagore's Santiniketan—where a scholarly and cultivated elite sought to find themselves and to effect a cultural renewal in the life-affirming and secluded setting of provincial Bengal—all the different registers of the rural, including the tribal people of the region, were being woven into a progressive artistic and political narrative. Tagore invited two Santhal groups to settle at Santiniketan and within its culture the Santhal were valorised as being in communion with the natural order of things, close to the land and unpolluted by the urbanity and decadence of mainstream society. For the Santiniketan artists, they provided a close-up encounter with an idealised 'primitive' which, unlike the distanced perspective of their modernist European counterparts, allowed for this encounter to be to a certain extent relational. So, Ramkinkar Baij, working out of doors in the college campus of Kala Bhavan, observing the Santhal passing by every day on their way to the fields to work as agricultural labourers, made the artistic decision to monumentalise their presence with this group portrait the *Santhal Family*. If he was picking up on and materialising something that was already present in the Santiniketan ideology, he was also uniquely positioned to avoid the charge of exoticising his subject. Maybe because of his particular class position (he came from a low caste village background) or his personality (which was non-hierarchical, anarchic and connective) or his life-style (which eschewed the manners and protocols of bourgeois society) he was deemed fit to represent this marginalised group.

Ramkinkar's sculpture depicts a mother, a father, a child and a dog, and taking its lead from this fact, one can encounter it as a space to consider the idea of family in a number of different ways. First there is the expansive (and perhaps corny) idea of the 'human family' which appears as a utopian undercurrent in Ramkinkar's work, a suggestion not explicitly stated, but which is nevertheless there, that a particular example of human experience can be generalised to such an extent that it represents the human condition. Then there is another idea (which lends critical weight to the first): that individuals brought together in a collective effort to address something in particular (as they do in this project) can constitute a sort of expanded family group, or a community of the question. Naturally enough, this is not the genetic family, but more like the pseudo families of the counter culture that come together in ad hoc living arrangements, based on contingency, proximity, desire or convenience. Then there is the curatorial question as to whether inanimate objects can be placed in family groups? Traditional museum displays would suggest so, arranged as they are along familial lines, with parent objects and their offspring grouped together in close proximity to uncles, aunts and grandchildren. But contemporary art exhibitions do not necessarily conform to this code. You could say that the big monographic show is the child that has grown up and left home and is now living alone with all of his or her attributes on display but only in relation to each other, and that the various types of group exhibitions (thematic/structural or dealing with place/city/nation/movement) constitute family groupings of traditional and non-traditional kinds. In this project the idea is to break with the regional model (the genetic family) and the sequential one (the family tree) and opt instead for the idea of a grouping based on affinities that cut across generational and geographic divisions (the unconventional family) and then to see how things unfold.

1 Subramanyan, K.G. 2006. 'Remembering Ramkinkar: K.G. Subramanyan in conversation with R. Siva Kumar' in Anshuman Dasgupta (ed.) *Ramkinkar Baij Centenary Exhibition 2006 - 07*. Santiniketan: Kala Bhavana Visva Bharati, p. 15.

ART HISTORIANS DESPAIR

What is the role of art history in a project that takes an artwork from the past as its point of departure? Ramkinkar Baij himself was described as an artist to make "art historians despair".[2] Very much in the Santiniketan spirit—ever suspicious of the mercantile, the professional, the bureaucratic—he gave birth to a great outpouring of work, "produced in the flow of time", without seeming to care much how this would be passed down to posterity. He paid little attention to the durability of the materials he used, abandoned works, erased them, painted on both sides of the canvas, got ripped off by unscrupulous collectors, and regularly gave works away, often to his penniless village friends. Of course, such a casual approach is the artist's prerogative and here there is no wish to play fast and loose with his oeuvre, but then neither is it the intention to organise a retrospective or describe his artistic milieu in great detail. Instead we take as a starting point one work in particular, *Santhal Family*, and reposition it in relation to the present. This is balanced with the knowledge that the contemporary, particularly when it comes to contemporary art from outside of the Western context, is often shown in a void. And so we have been careful to place *Santhal Family* against a backdrop of political and artistic currents which make it legible for a first time viewer. We also give the sculpture a close reading, even if this reading results in a boomerang effect in which the reader is catapulted back into the present. And finally, by inviting artists from diverse backgrounds and cultures to engage with this work, the project positions *Santhal Family* in terms of a world art history, however promiscuous or elusive such a phenomenon might be.

2 Subramanyan, K.G. 2006. 'Moving Focus: Essays on Indian Art' in *Ramkinkar Baij*. Kolkata: Seagull Books, p. 100.

SANTINIKETAN

It is worth recalling that Rabindranath Tagore's ambition for Santiniketan, like his relentless travel itinerary, was global in its reach. He travelled constantly and had considerable exposure to contemporary art in Europe and the United States, South East Asia and Japan. Amongst others, he invited the Japanese artist Arai Kampo to Kolkata in 1919, and in 1921 he invited the art historian Stella Kramrisch to Santiniketan, where she delivered forty lectures on Western art from the Gothic to Dadaism. It is possible that he visited the Bauhaus (Kala Bhavan, the art department at Santinketan, shared some of the basic principles of the Bauhaus school and both were established in 1919), and it is more than likely that he had a hand in the exhibition of work by Bauhaus luminaries that took place in 1923 at the Indian Society for Oriental Arts in Kolkata.

Such was the cosmopolitanism of the place where Ramkinkar studied, tutored and made his most important works; and yet despite the allure of the world and the potential of modernity, the point of departure for the Santiniketan artist was always the phenomenon of what was immediately at hand—"to attend to and participate in the Indian environment where the term is taken to include, in almost equal measure, nature and culture."[3] Tagore's experiment with Indian modernism was thus grafted onto the landscapes and traditions of Bengal:

> I bow, I bow to my beautiful motherland Bengal!
> To your river – banks, to your winds that cool and console;
> Your plains, whose dust the sky bends down to kiss;
> Your leafy mango – woods, where the herd boys play;
> Your deep ponds, loving and cool as the midnight sky;[4]

In Tagore's poems and within his pedagogical system, this natural scene is the basic ground for knowledge. Classes for children were held out of doors and the artists sketched the surrounding countryside, celebrated the changing seasons and tested their intuitions against data provided by the external world. The aim was a 'close tuning'[5] with the natural environment, which, even if it was sometimes at odds with certain aspects of modernity, did not deter these artists from engaging with the cultural/aesthetic forms of modernism, and from being receptive in particular, to the possibilities it held for a national cultural renewal.

3 Kapur, G. 2000. 'Mid-Century Ironies: K.G. Subramanyan' in *When Was Modernism: Essays on Contemporary Cultural Practice in India*. New Delhi: Tulika Books, p. 106.

4 Tagore, R. 1985. *A Half Acre of Land, Selected Poems*, London: Penguin Books, p. 56.

5 Kapur 2000, p. 106.

ON THE CULTURAL FRONT

If this project in part claims artistic license to propose a trans-national and intergenerational reading of *Santhal Family* from the expansive and cosmopolitan Santiniketan model, then it also takes inspiration from the idea that *Santhal Family* can be read in relation to the legacies of communism. Technically Ramkinkar could never be described as a communist and the exact status of his art as a political practice is the subject of debate. Particularly fraught is the question as to whether or not his "human affinities, his being affected by the life world and its calamities—whether manmade, as in the Bengal famine of 1943, or natural—his particular interest in representing life and labour around him almost everywhere he went, and over and above, his concern for the human condition" could be understood as socialist.[6] Ramkinkar himself did not articulate it in these terms, preferring not to theorise his work. However, communist ideology constituted a powerful current in Bengali artistic culture at that time, and his friend the film maker Ritwick Ghatak wrote an entire thesis on this subject in which he states: "Today the task is to arouse, to educate and elevate the masses and to negate the alien influences on them so that they will mobilise into mass organisations. Tomorrow, the task will be to promote these so that they lead to revolutionary actions."[7] No one in the communist party could object to this ambition, but his biting critique of the party that followed saw him falling foul of party discipline and finally being expelled from its ranks a year later.

Ghatak's last film *Jukti, Takko Aar Gappo* (*Reason, Debate and a Story*, released in 1974) is the tale of a disillusioned communist intellectual who, after being abandoned by his wife and child, sets off on a journey and along the way seeks an answer to the vexed question—what becomes of a political praxis, once the vehicle of change in which you once believed has been derailed? Ghatak plays Nilkantha, the principle character, as a sort of mocking self-portrait, leading a motley crew, who have been drawn together by chance, across Bengal. In this role, he draws on his own life experience, as well as on his work as an actor/activist in the Indian People's Theatre Association (IPTA) one of the most significant organisations to come out of the Cultural Front of the Communist Party during the 1940s.

6 Dasgupta, A. 2006. 'Centrifuge: Visual Metaphors for the Modernist Moments' in A. Dasguptra (ed.) *Ramkinkar Baij Centenary Exhibition 2006 – 07*, Santiniketan: Kala Bhavana Visva Bharati, p. 8.

7 Ghatak, R. 2006. *On The Cultural Front*. Kolkata: Ritwik Memorial Trust, p. 28. The publication is a reproduction of a thesis submitted to the Communist Party of India in 1954.

THE TRIBAL INSURGENT

Towards the end of *Jukti, Takko Aar Gappo*, the scene suddenly cuts to a large expanse of open ground where Nilkantha and his gang are confronted by a strange and dramatic scene. A dispute is taking place between a landlord and a group of tribals who stand around in loose formation—sculptural figures silhouetted against the sky—each with a bow and arrow. Later, in the forest, these tribals are felt as a presence, barely audible, easily mistaken for birds or other forest creatures, and later still, they are there, somewhere, in an armed encounter between the police and a group of young rebels, which fills the wood with confusion, gunfire and smoke. And it is with this group of rebels that Nilkantha has his most sustained debate of the kind alluded to in the film's title. Present here in fragmentary form and coming in and out of visibility, is a political practice at odds with the communist administration which ran the state of Bengal from the 1970s onwards—instead we find a Maoist insurgency rising up from the lower classes, including the tribal cultivators, who have been betrayed by the party and consequently resort to an armed insurrection.

The story of the Naxalites is chronicled in the many novels, short stories, plays and newspaper articles that the Bengali writer Mahasweta Devi has written on this subject, a body of material which constitutes a sort of unofficial history of the movement or what Gayatri Spivak has described as a "history imagined into fiction".[8] In these writings, Devi articulates with an acerbic precision, the life experience of those caught up in Naxalite struggles, their grinding poverty, the injustices they face and their fight back, which takes the form of guerrilla warfare wherein a knowledge of the land plays its part, along with propaganda, mythmaking and the confrontation of power with bare life. Devi's *Bashai Turdu* is a case in point. A tribal leader is killed in an armed encounter with the police, his body is identified and exhumed, only for him to appear again at the centre of an armed insurrection when the landlords have pushed the agricultural labourers to despair. Killed four times between 1970 and 1976 Bashai Turdu becomes a mythic figure who, according to revolutionary tradition, gives his name to the oppressed—striking fear into the heart of the authorities, who see him as an elusive figure beyond their reach.

8 Spivak, G.C. 1998. 'A Literary Representation of the Subaltern: A Woman's Text from the Third World' in *In Other Worlds: Essays on Culture and Politics*. New York and London: Routledge, p. 336.

COMMUNISM OF THE SENSES

Ramkinkar also planned to make a public monument of a tribal insurgent, though from an earlier period, and produced preliminary sketches of the warrior Sidhu who led the 1855-7 uprising against the British, but he never completed this work. The tribals he depicted tended to be workers rather than warriors and in another of his large-scale environmental sculptures, *Mill Call* (1956), which stands close to *Santhal Family* in the grounds of Santiniketan, Baij depicts tribal women on their way to the mill, this time running not walking, alerted to the start of the shift by the siren which sounds a shrill note across the fields. Looking like a Socialist Realist monument, but not quite, these women's faces are full of joy, not it seems at the prospect of the hard graft ahead as factory hands, but instead because of the physical sensations that they feel as they run. Startled by the sound of the mill call, they leap up and, putting on clothes which are still wet, run in the open air letting the sun do its work. This explanation for the sculpture comes in a conversation with Ritwick Ghatak, in the documentary about Ramkinkar that Ghatak started in 1975, but never completed. If Ghatak's last film *Jukti Tacco Aar Gappo* is a tragedy, then this unfinished film sounds a final rhapsodic note. Here Ramkinkar is shown in the rural idyll of Santiniketan, conversing with his friend, the two of them regularly stumbling drunk. In its shots of Ramkinkar intermittently sketching or standing before his outdoor sculptures, with the backdrop of Santiniketan as community and beautiful natural setting, we see how these various elements can be synthesised in the creative life of the artist and mirrored back so that the sensuous and object-making processes of art become an "interface between man's individual creativity and his collective sociability."[9] After all, Marx in his early writings saw the sensuality of man and his attachment to things not as inherently wrong, but as detrimental only when appropriated into forms of private property and object fetishism that alienate him from his natural state of being. In a situation of generic communism, he predicted, there would be no division between the making of art and other types of labour; and in this sense Ramkinkar strikes the figure of the artist as proto-communist, engaged in a non-alienated form of labour which registers the material world in its cadences of pleasure and pain and immediately passes this back to the collective.

9 Toscano, A. 2006. 'Destructive Creation or the Communism of the Senses' in G. Watson, G. Van Noord & G. Everall (eds.) *Make Everything New—A Project on Communism*. London/Dublin: Book Works/Project Art Centre, p. 121.

SCULPTURES THAT BEGIN TO MOVE

Ramkinkar's *Santhal Family* is felt as a gesture, or the fragment of a gesture with a before and an after. A gesture that embodies the continuum of lived experiences and ground-level reality captured for a moment in solid form. So perhaps we can read it, not as the static freeze frame that represents and isolates its subject, but as part of a trajectory that positions its subjects within the complexity of the life world. Agamben describes this liberation of the static into the gestural as being like "the legends in which statues break the ties holding them and begin to move."[10] And maybe this slightly comic metaphor could be used to describe the project that we are proposing. Ramkinkar's sculpture represents people who are on the move (pushed, no doubt by grinding want) and, albeit in radically different circumstances, we are on the move as well—not only in relation to this work, but with a host of others from the sub-continent and elsewhere, that come to populate the exhibition space and the pages of this book. Like the Santhal family (who carry their possessions with them) these works arrive carrying luggage of a different kind—the specific cultural information that they need to bring in order to be understood. How much? This is the complicated curatorial question. Bring too much and you get weighed down, too little and you arrive but you are incomprehensible. In the context of a large group exhibition, it is possible to let the cumulative affect of the works themselves become an accretion of information which allows the process of translation to occur in a non-didactic, non-pedagogic fashion. This is certainly the aim here, where *Santhal Family* is always mediated through other artists, writers, filmmakers and the like.

10 Agamben, G. 2000. 'Notes on Gesture' in *Means Without Ends: Notes on Politics*. Minneapolis/London: University of Minnesota Press, p. 55.

THE HOLE IN THE ARGUMENT

But of all the different elements galvanised here, one thing will remain behind. This is of course the sculpture that gives the project its name, something that is physically unavailable to be shown anywhere other than the place where it was first made. This sculpture-shaped hole in the project opens up the possibility for an increased sociability and play between the other works. The other hole in the exhibition is perhaps a rhetorical one. As is evidenced by the essays in this book, and indeed the whole enterprise, Ramkinkar's *Santhal Family* is a work pregnant with possibility for discursive unpacking—touching as it does on the big questions of aesthetics, modernism, nationalism, marginality, micro politics, public space, globalisation and the ethics of representation—all of which can be marshalled into arguments that can go this way or that. But the sculpture also demands a non-rhetorical response, one that acknowledges its radical sense of being in the world without co-opting it on behalf of discourse, or of anything else, an artistic response that is able to meet like with like. When we look at *Santhal Family*, can we also consider the looks of the figures in the sculpture, in order to make this relationship of looking multi-directional, at least in theory. How does the sculpture look? While Ramkinkar's *Thresher* which stands nearby sees nothing (it has no head or eyes), but simply performs an anguished gesture of labour as brute force, and the figures in *Mill Call* laugh out loud as they run, the gaze of the *Santhal Family* is more ambiguous, particularly when it comes to the figure of the man. The woman looks ahead with an air of quiet resolve as if she can see for hundreds of miles and the child peeps through the ropes that support the sling in which he travels, and alongside a grinning dog keeps pace. But the man's moonlike face is tilted up at an odd angle and his expression is one of absolute receptivity. His gaze is not projective (he is not looking *at* anything) it is absorbed and in correspondence with its surroundings, it implicates him in his environment and makes sense of the group's positioning in an outdoor setting. In the same way, when we consider the sculpture, face to face or through its various mediations, we are also implicated, entangled in its specificity, its history, its extensive catalogue of references, its haptics of place. But we are implicated in other ways as well—ways which produce new kinds of correspondences, that do not depend on these considerations.

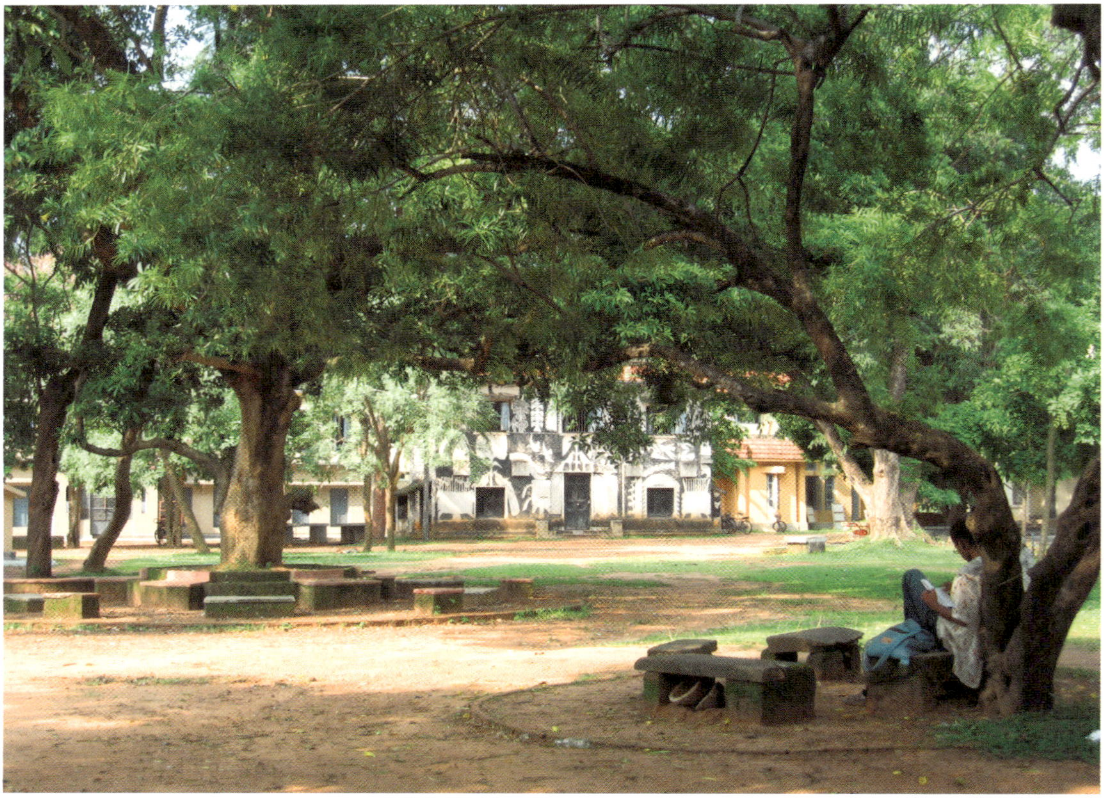

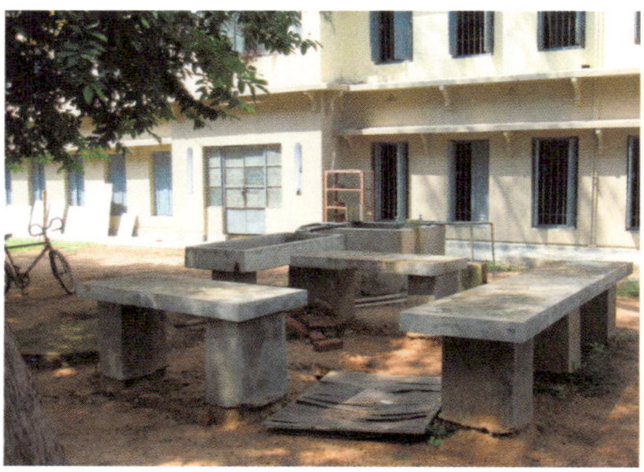

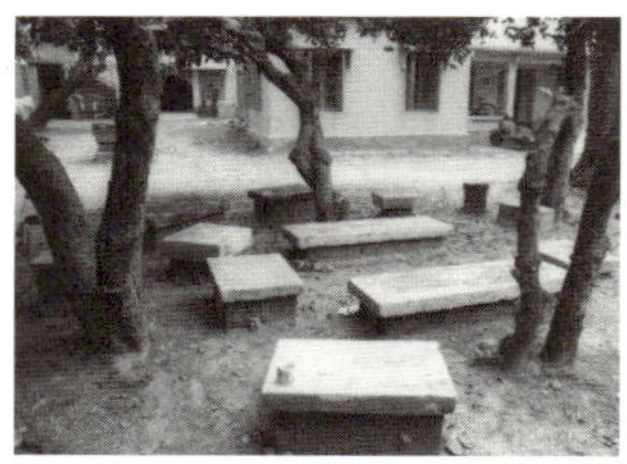

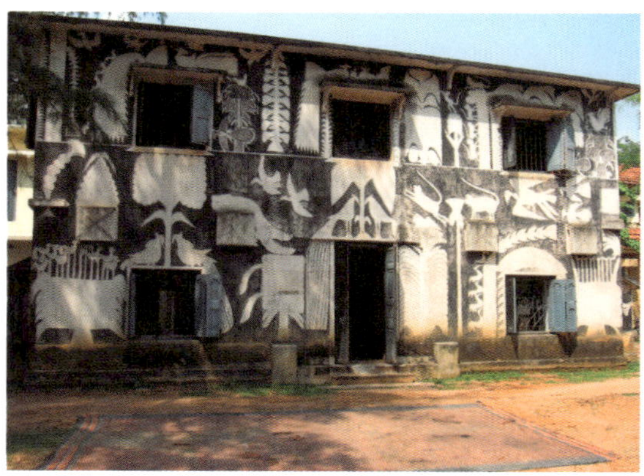

GOSHKA MACUGA
Kala Bhavan Campus Santiniketan

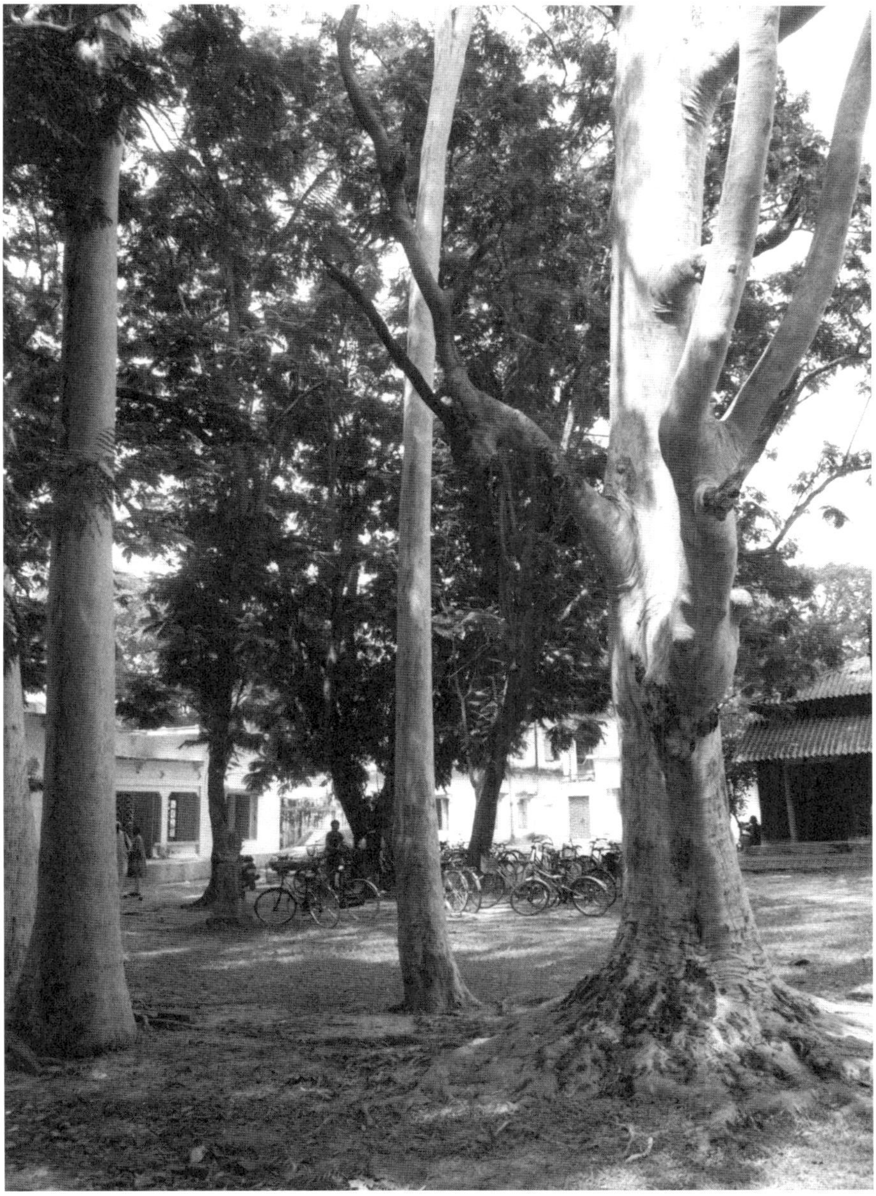

GOSHKA MACUGA
Kala Bhavan Campus Santiniketan

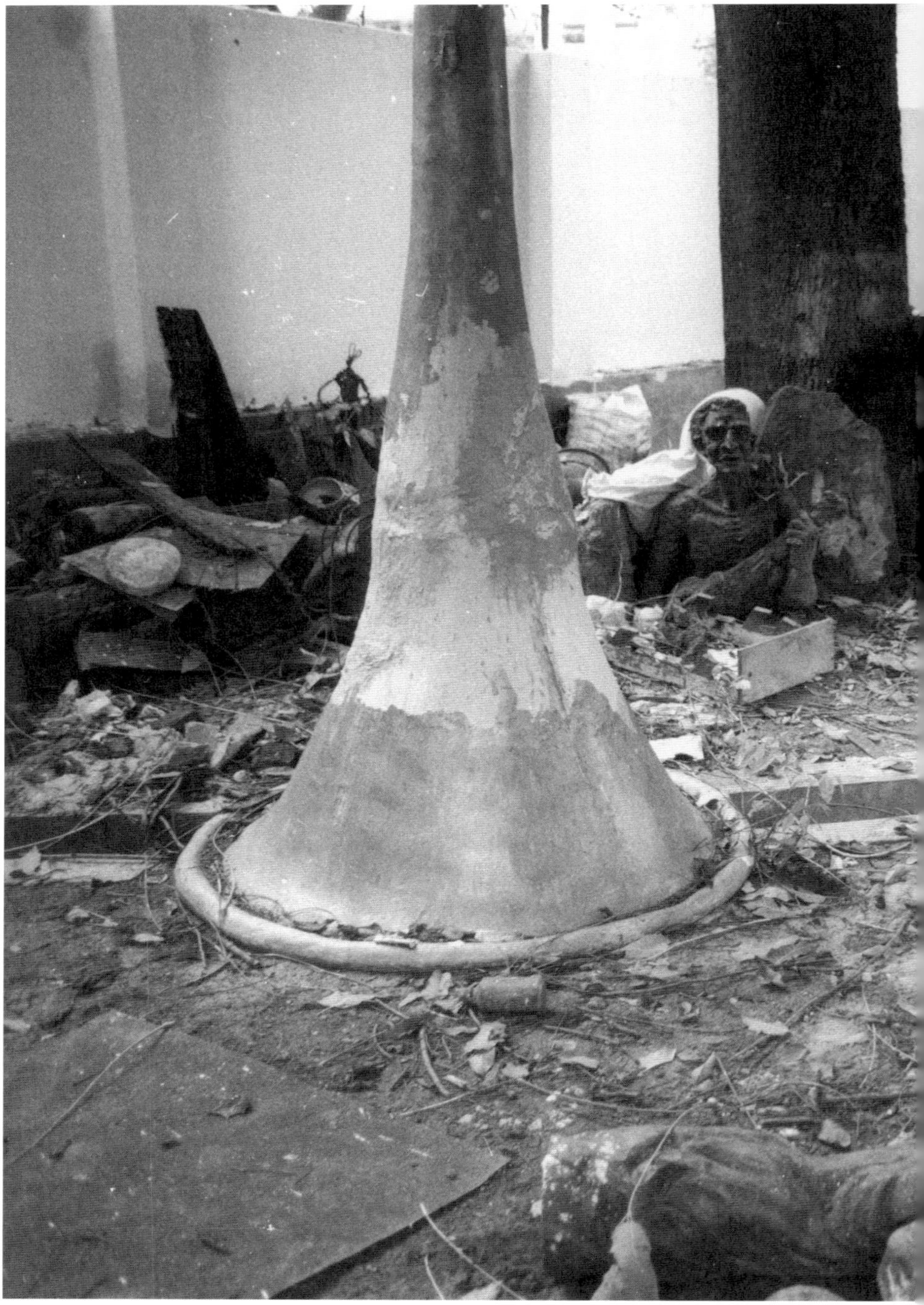

GOSHKA MACUGA
Kala Bhavan Campus Santiniketan

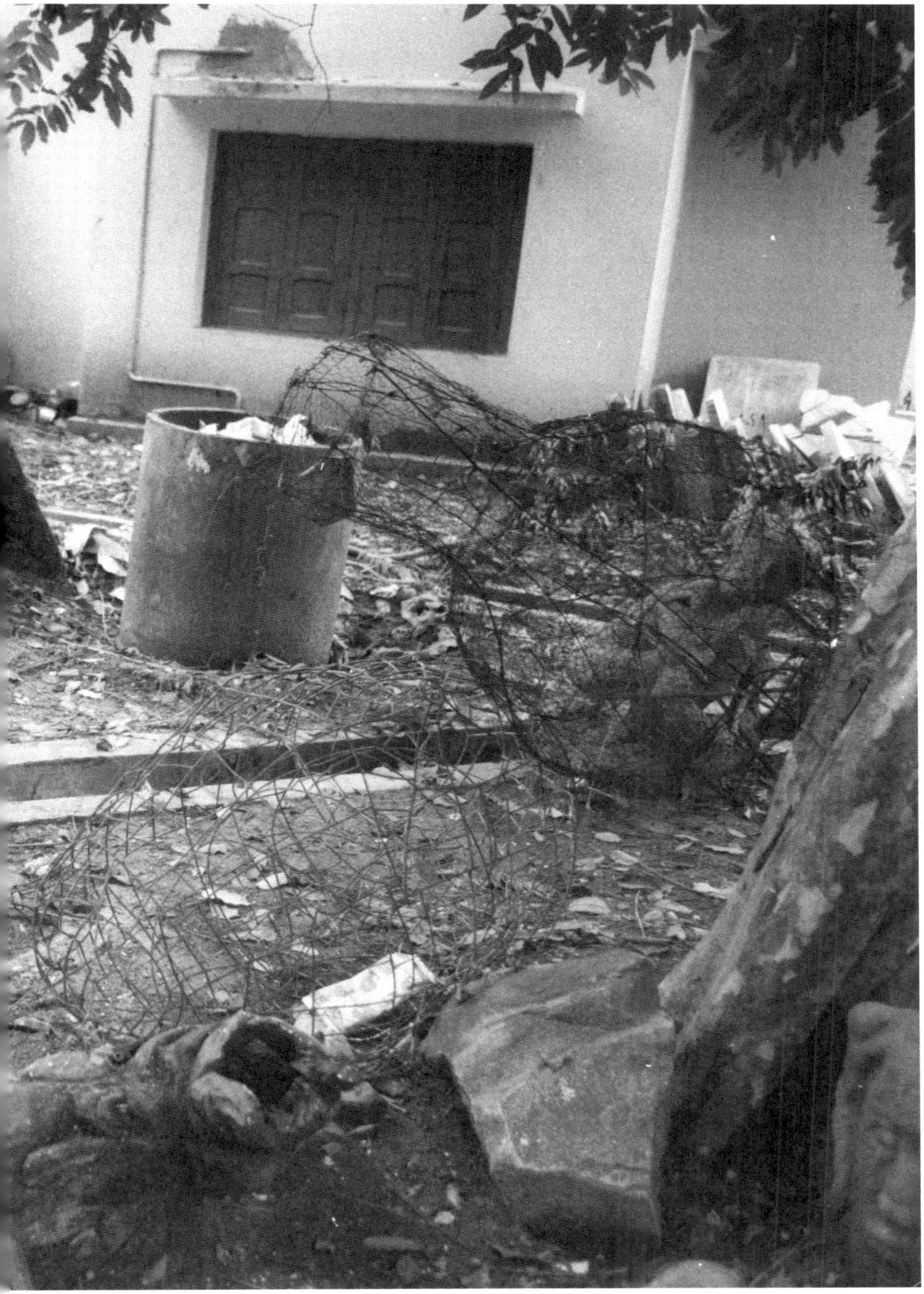

GOSHKA MACUGA
Kala Bhavan Campus Santiniketan

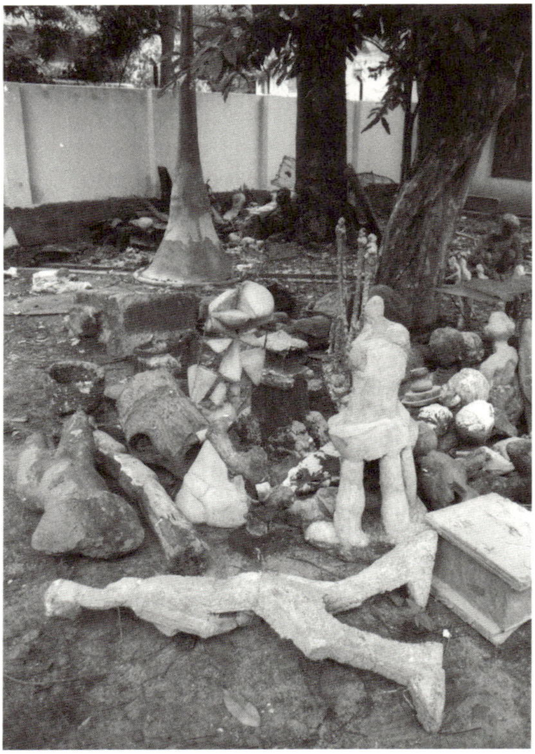

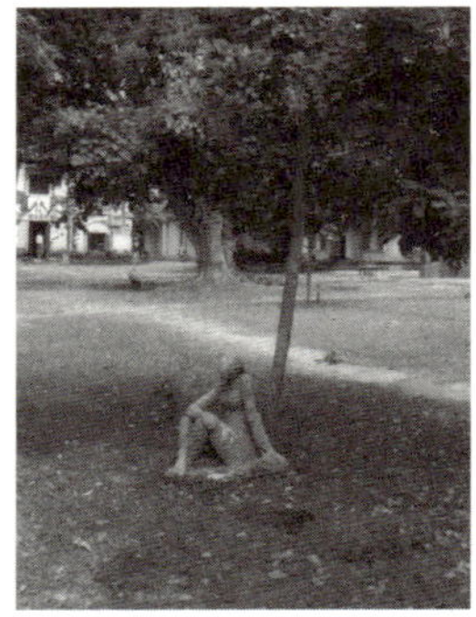

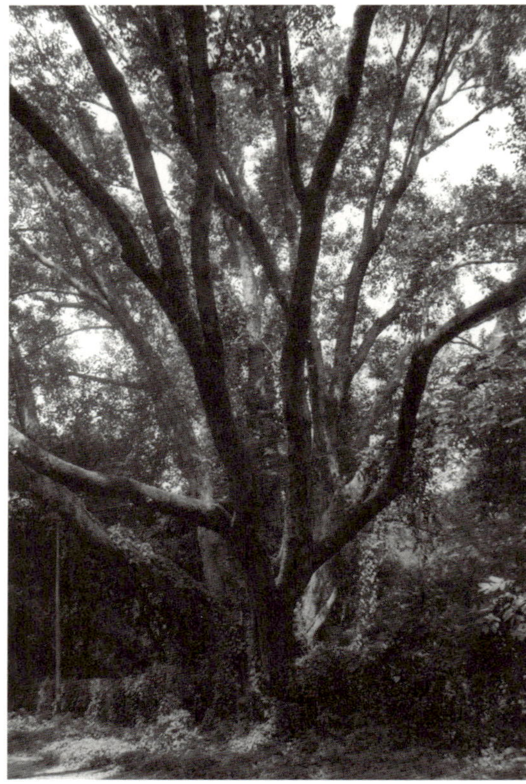

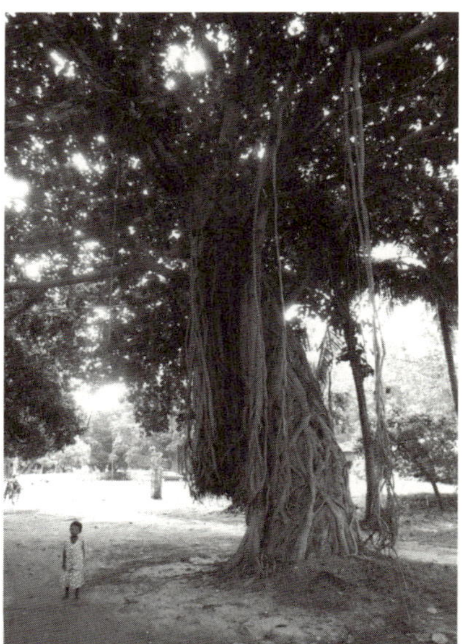

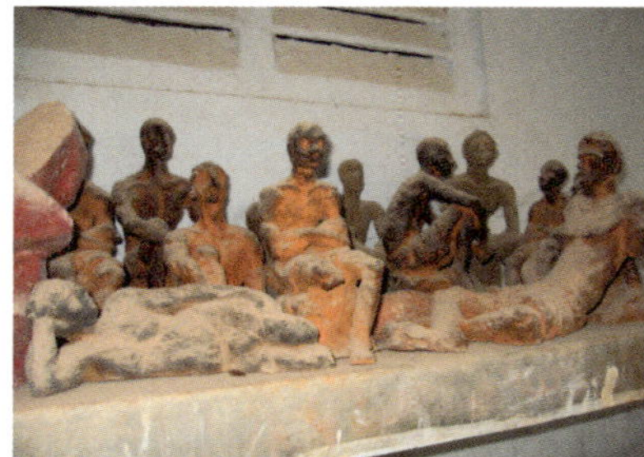

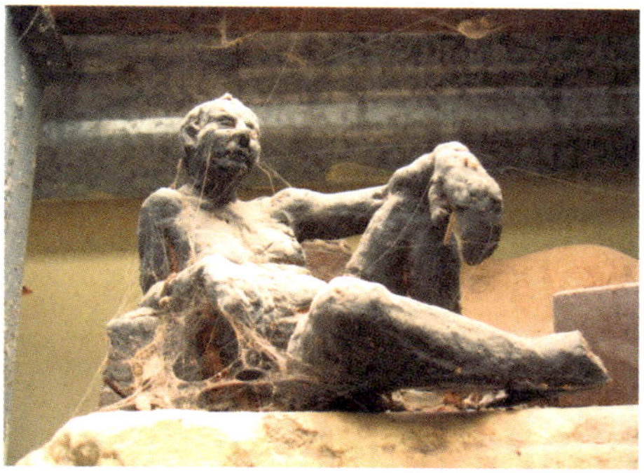

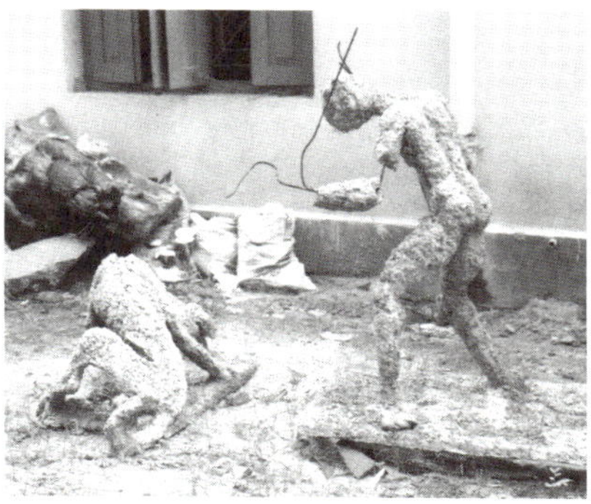

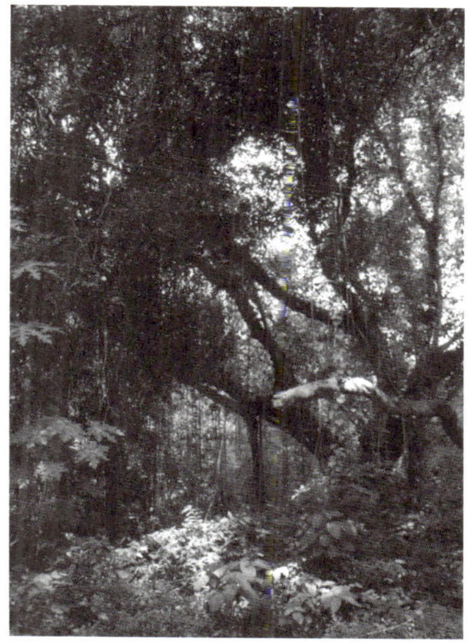

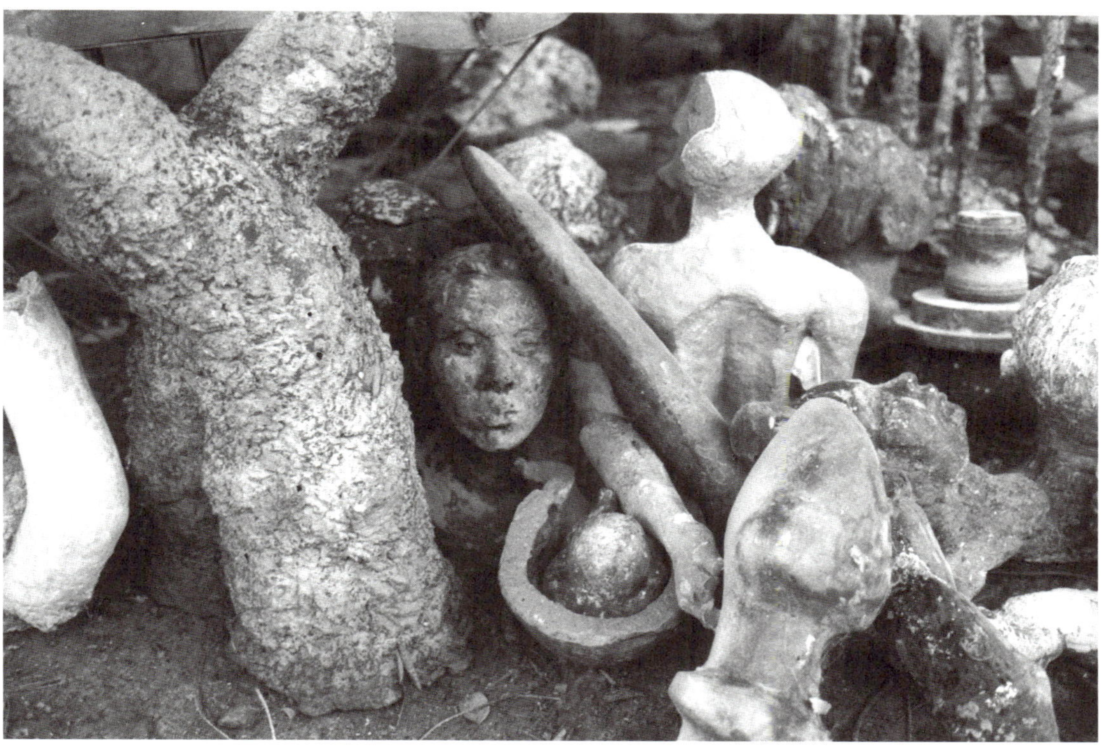

R. SIVA KUMAR

RAMKINKAR BAIJ AND MODERNISM'S DUAL COMMITMENTS

Ramkinkar Baij is a seminal figure in the history of modern Indian art. He is often represented by writers on Indian art as a Promethean figure who brought Western modernism to Santiniketan, the art school and centre for cultural resurgence with which he was associated first as a student and later as one its most charismatic teachers, and who spearheaded the assimilation of Western modernism into Indian art during the 1940s as a gesture of solidarity with the modern world. He is also represented as a subaltern who successfully invaded the preserve of high culture, as one who rose from the lower depths of a colonial society still governed by old hierarchies and grew into a heroic representative of the new humanism of an independent and democratic India. Thus Ramkinkar, like modernism itself, sustains dual commitments: on the one hand, to the exploration of the formal means of expression—the language, processes and art forms—and on the other, to the extension of our understanding of man and life in the light of our experiences—social and subjective. But before we move on to Ramkinkar and try to find out what these commitments meant to him let us try to locate him and Santiniketan within Indian modernism.

Santiniketan and Modernism

The educational and art programmes at Santiniketan were formulated against the background of the Indian struggle against colonialism; and, therefore, the nationalist conception of art as a form of anti-colonialist expression informed its beginnings. In that sense it had certain affinities with earlier nationalist efforts at cultural resurgence. But it deviated from these earlier efforts—especially those initiated by E. B. Havell, Abanindranath Tagore and their followers, or what is collectively called the Bengal School—in that it relinquished historicism as the main plank of anti-colonialist nationalism and of identity building.

In Santiniketan, the quest for a non-historicist anti-colonial art grew into an alternate modernism based on a sense of place and a commitment to local experiential reality. Nandalal Bose—who was the founder of the art school at Santiniketan and Ramkinkar's mentor—and Benodebehari Mukherjee—Ramkinkar's senior at the art school and later his colleague—tried to develop a coherent approach to art practice and an apposite art language based on such an attitude. Rabindranath and his collaborators, however, were anxious to ensure that an art founded on a sense of place should not degenerate into parochialism. Their ideal was not an insular local but a cosmopolitan local. Given their anti-colonial stance, Oriental antecedents were given precedence over Western art. Modernism was thus often subsumed under Pan-Asianism and was read in the light of Oriental antecedents—the West was not kept out but assimilated, even by Nandalal who was the most indigenous amongst them, via the ancient Orient.

Although he had began as a staunch nationalist, in later years, Nandalal conceded that nationalist commitments had prevented him from exploring the possibilities of art as freely as he should have liked, and that, if he had been given another life, he would attempt to do so. From the outset Rabindranath was more clear-sighted in this regard. While he believed that only by being rooted in a culture one gained the power to view the world from one's "vantage ground, and open a vista of thoughts to the world"; he also realised that knowing the 'other' was an absolute necessity for finding oneself fully and anew. Highlighting this he wrote to Sturge Moore (in 1914):

> [The] Literature of a country is not chiefly for home consumption. Its value lies in the

fact it is imperatively necessary for the lands where it is foreign. I think it has been the good fortune of the West to have the opportunity of absorbing the spirit of the East... It has added to the richness of your life because it is alien to your temperament. In course of time you may discard some of its doctrines and teachings but it has done its work—it has created a bifurcation in your mental system which is so needful for all life growth. The western literature is doing the same thing to us, bringing into our life elements some of which supplement and some contradict our tendencies. This is what we need.[1]

Santiniketan and Western Modernism

Ramkinkar came to Santiniketan in 1925. He is generally credited, as we have already noted, with connecting art practice in Santiniketan with Western modernism and of ushering modernism itself into Santiniketan. But from what has been said above it is equally clear that this is a trifle exaggerated; he both benefited from the prevailing intellectual climate and added to it. Let us consider some of Santiniketan's early contacts with Western modernism:

- In 1921 Stella Kramrisch, who trained under Josef Strzygowski and Max Dvorak in Vienna, lectured to the Santiniketan artists on Western art, covering its developments from the Gothic to Dadaism.
- In 1922 an exhibition of the Bauhaus artists was organised in Calcutta under the initiative of Rabindranath. He was also in correspondence with the Bauhaus artist, designer, theorist and teacher, Johannes Itten.
- Between 1921 to 1924 André Karpeles, a painter from Paris who worked in a broadly Post-Impressionist manner, was active in Santiniketan and introduced oil painting and print-making to students at Kala Bhavan (the art school).
- Right from the first decade of the twentieth century Rabindranath took every opportunity that his travels to the West offered him to familiarise himself with the modern art scene in the West and its sources. The exhibitions he saw seem to have included the Armory Show—which was dubbed a harbinger of universal anarchy by its critics in America, but also described by modernists like Stuart Davies as "...the greatest single influence I have experienced in my work."[2]
- Rabindranath returned from these trips with publications on modern Western art and these went into the Kala Bhavan Library, and served as sources for artists like Benodebehari and Ramkinkar.
- The photo archives of world art and craft that Nandalal built up also contained examples of modern Western art.

It is certain that artists at Santiniketan were familiar with modern developments in Western art before Ramkinkar arrived and it is more probable that these antecedents constituted his early access to Western modernism and encouraged him to relate this to his local experiences.

By the mid 1920s Rabindranath, as we have seen, was talking about a definitive need for further expanding the cross-cultural encounters that were already nourishing the art practice at Santiniketan by including the West, and urging artists to enjoy "the freedom to be naturally Indians in spite of all the borrowings that they indulged in."[3] The transformation of Santiniketan in 1921, from a centre of Eastern learning into an international university (or 'Visva Bharati', suggesting an India where the world comes together, or where cultures mingle in order to know and enrich each other) marked the beginning of the institution we know today.

Furthermore, while Rabindranath had played a role in drawing attention of the Santiniketan artists towards Japanese art in 1916 and thus encouraging the Pan-Asian orientation of early Indian modernism, by 1924 he was himself starting to paint, using the linguistic parame-

---

1 Tagore, R. 1997. 'Letter to Sturge Moore, dated 1st May 1914' in Krishna Dutta and Andrew Robinson (eds.) *Selected Letters of Rabindranath Tagore*. Cambridge: Cambridge University Press, p. 146.

2 Davies, S. 1984. 'The Armory Show' in H.B. Chipp (ed.) *Theories of Modern Art: A Sourcebook by Artists and Critics*. Berkley, CA: University of California Press, p. 525.

3 Tagore, R. 1961. 'Art and Tradition' in *On Art and Aesthetics*. Calcutta: Orient Longman, p. 59.

ters adapted by Western modern artists from 'primitive' and children's art. Thus when Ramkinkar arrived in Santiniketan its art programme had already moved through two distinct phases and was on the threshold of a third phase; this one marked by a greater readiness to assimilate the lessons of Western modernism into its art practice.

Just as Benodebehari consolidated the transformation of Pan-Asianism into an instrument for the articulation of local experiences initiated by Nandalal, so too Ramkinkar became the chief—but not only—consolidator of a similar use of Western modernism for the articulation of experiences of the local initiated by Rabindranath, first as a writer and later as a painter.

The Genius of Ramkinkar

The genius of Ramkinkar was ideally suited for this role. Among the Santiniketan masters he probably had more innate talent than the others and was a natural learner. Even before he came to Santiniketan his natural talent (which found expression in nationalist posters and portraits of the leaders he made as a school boy, and the theatre backdrops he did for the local clubs) had caught the attention of the nationalist leader and publisher Ramananda Chaterjee. And this paved the way for his coming to Santiniketan.

When Ramkinkar arrived in Santiniketan and showed his works to Nandalal, he is reputed to have said: "Why you are already there, now what more? Anyway, you may stay on for two or three years."[4] But his natural talent or prodigious skill had two sides to it. On the one hand, it made it possible for him to absorb and appropriate varied styles with great ease; what others had to strive for and cultivate he could master almost effortlessly. On the other hand, it also meant that his oeuvre—like that of Pablo Picasso, an even more celebrated example of prodigious talent—was not marked by a pronounced coherence. While exceptional facility could lead to stylistic diversity, coherence comes more naturally to artists whose careers are guided by the style or language they develop (Nandalal, Benodebehari), or to those artists on whom an idiom is forced upon by the limited skills at one's command (Rabindranath).

In other words, Ramkinkar's prodigious talent made him open to many and contrary influences. His work from the pre-Santiniketan years is marked by the influence of the academic realism he absorbed in an unsystematic and autodidactic manner from the different strands of realist art he saw. In his early years in Santiniketan he assimilated with equal earnestness the style and the skills associated with the Bengal School, which in the colonial context was conceived as a cultural antidote to academic realism, but which an artist like Benodebehari assiduously avoided because of its historicist bias. In the early 1930s Ramkinkar relinquished his affinities with the Bengal School and embraced the tradition of the local as being developed by Nandalal and Benodebehari. But he added a personal twist to it by substituting the pan-Asian inspiration that shaped the syntactic structures of Nandalal's and Benodebehari's art with representational conventions drawn from post-realist Western models. This came about at one level through his contact with Liza von Pott (an Austrian sculptor) and Marguerite Milward, a student of Emile Antoine Bourdelle who introduced him to what may be termed Post-Rodinesque sculpture. Both these sculptors were in India to do ethnographic portraits, and it is therefore possible that they also indirectly instilled ethnic and primitivist awareness into Ramkinkar's perception of the local. But this ethnographic awareness merged in his sculpture with an awareness of the pre- and post-classical sculpture of India that he and Benodebehari learned to admire and drew on in contradistinction to their immediate predecessors. Throughout this formative period in Santiniketan, Ramkinkar was also drawing upon several modernist movements in his paintings, including: Post-Impressionism, Cubism, Futurism, Expressionism, Surrealism, and Abstraction. Several individual artists were particularly important: Paul Cézanne, Auguste Rodin, Jacob Epstein, Henry Moore and above all Picasso whom he

4 Baij, R. 2002. *Mahasay Ami Chakkhik, Rupokar Matro*. Alipurduar: Monchasha, p. 19.

openly admired. And from the 1950s, in an uneven way, he drew on socialist art, towards which he was drawn despite his self-confessed reservations.

Being an outsider and an eclectic, like the other Santiniketan artists, he did not see these as historically grounded styles, but as simultaneous possibilities to be drawn upon and even mixed. Their worth was to him purely contingent upon a given context and thematic. In practice, this meant an overlap of styles which are otherwise considered to have an inviolable evolutionary relationship within Western modernism. Thus during the mid and late 1930s we see him using (still mostly naturalist) Post-Impressionist styles for celebratory representations of the local, on the one hand, and on the other hand, the introduction of exaggerations and distortions to give his subjects vitalistic, primitivist, or expressionistic overtones. This later emphasis led Ramkinkar to assimilate diverse formal means including those of Futurism, Cubism and Surrealism (in that order) during the late 1930s and early 1940s; all the while, his his watercolours of the same period retain a Cézannesque structural quality.

Until the early 1940s, Ramkinkar's assimilation of the formal possibilities of modernism and his engagement with the local coincided unproblematically in his work. *Santhal Family,* which he completed in 1938, is perhaps the finest example of this. On one level, it is an image of the local tribal community, represented on a monumental scale, larger than life but not overtly valorised—stately and slow moving figures that hold themselves well against the trees and the general scale of nature that surrounds them. The monumental effect remains today, and it would have been even more obvious when the sculpture was first made as there were fewer buildings in the vicinity and clusters of tall spear-grass growing around it set the comparative scale, rather than the overarching trees that now surround it. Considering that the peasant and the tribal were either absent from the work of his immediate predecessors and contemporaries, not represented on such a scale, or were represented as ethnic and fringe groups who added some exotic colour to mainstream social life, *Santhal Family* marks a quiet but significant rupture from previous social perceptions. At another level, Ramkinkar ushered the thus far unrepresented or romanticised tribal figure into the domain of high art using the universally accessible trope of the human family, displaying both empathy and familiarity with the people he represented. If, in stylistic terms, *Santhal Family* can be described as a sculptural equivalent of Post-Impressionism, it is also equally permeated by the values of pre-classical Indian sculpture where the earthy materiality of the human body is eminently palpable.

The Bengal famine of 1943 and the Second World War changed the stylistic/social balance, as a critical engagement with the human condition became more pressing. Of course, with the emergence of a leftist cultural movement in the late 1930s Ramkinkar was not alone in making this shift in focus. In the Indian context, the Progressive Movement in literature was an important antecedent to similar developments in theatre and the visual arts. And in the early 1940s, as communist and socialist concerns began to spread gradually into art, Ramkinkar was seen as the artist who came closest to representing such concerns. Perhaps his reading of Rabindranath, of Maxim Gorky and other Russian writers, and of Bernard Shaw had prepared him for this turn. It definitely brought him some attention and encouraged him to move further in this direction.

As there were no local antecedents or contemporary explorations he turned to Picasso's works of the interwar years—whose post-Cubist work of the early 1930s with its mixture of Cubist syntax and Surrealist innuendoes he was already drawing upon—for inspiration. *Guernica* (completed in 1937) with its Expressionist use of Cubism and allegorical framework became an important antecedent for Ramkinkar from the mid-1940s onwards, and under its impact he moved from expressionism to allegorical painting, expressively employing post-Cubist fragmentation.

Yet the events of the 1940s also made things somewhat more complicated. What had been an existential engagement with the local, in which the subaltern figured familiarly and prominently, grew into a more ideologically-loaded engagement with the proletariat; and with this the aesthetics of realism made an intervention into his modernist project. Ramkinkar declared equivocally: "The artist is also a human being—a social animal. And man, with all his material and spiritual perceptions, is also the theme of his art. Thus riots, partitions, famines, and war—every insult to humanity—would surely agitate an artist."[5]

However this did not mean the end of formalist experimentation, as this type of progressive cultural initiative was also an anti-Fascist movement. As the Fascists branded modern art 'Degenerate', with the Nazi state-sponsored exhibition of 1937, and abstraction gained a new vigour and ideological edge in this context in Europe, Ramkinkar gained a new impetus for formalist experiments. He was not only inspired by the Indian Progressive Movement but also marginally linked with anti-Fascist art practices in Europe. He exhibited at the Salon des Réalités Nouvelles in 1950 and at the Salon de Mai in 1951, which in an anti-Fascist gesture carried the legacy of the Abstraction-Création group, founded in Paris in the 1930s, into the post-war period. Like early proponents of abstraction in the West, Ramkinkar also saw a deep connection between music and art. "Music," he wrote, "especially classical recitals, activate peculiar patterns inside my brain. Emotions get activated. Singers like Faiyaz Khan or Amir Khan can erect grand edifices in the brain."[6]

Although Ramkinkar remained committed to formal experiments and was generally critical of Socialist Realism, with his growing commitment to an anti-Fascist and pro-left humanism, he felt that he had to make some kind of materialist assertion. Suggestive allegory as seen in *Shifting Generations* (1947) now gave way to open didacticism as noticeable in paintings, such as *Birth of Krishna* (1950), *Harvesting* (1957) and *In the Castle* (completed some time in the mid-1950s), and eventually to a valorisation of the proletariat as in the painting, *Thresher* (completed some time in the mid-1950s). And despite his reservations about Socialist Realism his art now began to look a little like Socialist Realist art; here a realist critique of human life that had given an incisive edge to his vision began to give way to a popular figurative mode that monumentalised the figures but shed some realism in that very process. Of course, the monumentality and exaggerations were meant to bring the proletariat out of their marginal social existence, to make us see and acknowledge them. But by blowing them up, by turning them into pneumatic giants, Ramkinkar also turned his women and men into less convincingly human figures. In his late works, the Santhali people whom he led like living pagan gods into the arena of high culture were transformed from people into totemic mascots symbolising a cause.

The contradictory forces vying for Ramkinkar's practice during the late 1940s and the 1950s were not unique to him. To see it a little more clearly we only have to look at the art objects which were displayed at the Spanish, Russian and German pavilions of the 1937 Universal Exhibition in Paris, as emblems of the different political positions and values that these nations supported. While *Guernica*, representing the modernist response to war, was displayed inside the Spanish pavilion where, with its fragmented figures, it looked modest and collage-like; Socialist Realism was asserted with Vera Mukhina's heroic *Factory Worker and Collective Farmhand*, placed prominently atop the Soviet pavilion just opposite the Spanish. This contrast in style was further complicated by the evident stylistic similarity between Mukhina's Socialist Realist sculpture and Joseph Thorak's sculpture *Comradeship* (one of Hilter's favourites) in front of the German Pavilion—both employing monumental and didactic figuration to suggest staggering power.

Ramkinkar was perhaps not unaware of the aesthetic and political conundrums implied in his own eclectic practice, yet continuing his dual commitments to formal innovation and to the human and socialist cause, from the 1950s onwards, he could often be seen to waver between them like one caught in a dilemma. At one level, this makes him comparable to artists like Reneto Guttuso and Peter de Francia—who, like Ramkinkar, wanted to reconcile the dual projects of modernism but sometimes got caught between modernism's twin horns. Thus what Timothy Hyman wrote of Peter de Francia's 1959 painting *Bombing of Sakiet* is also applicable to late Ramkinkar: "It is a picture that belongs very much to the fifties with its angry rather hectoring tone, absolutely devoid of the ironic distancing which would sweeten any such bitter pills in the art of the succeeding generation. But I think this kind of direct and explosive political protest comes to us today as a breath of fresh air."[7]

We cannot be certain whether or not Ramkinkar would have used the words 'political protest' so emphatically to describe his own work, but, as he himself said, as an artist he was agitated by insults to humanity and he responded with great passion, directness and without ironic distancing.

---

5 Ibid. p. 52.

6 Ibid. p. 59.

7 Hyman, T. January 1981. 'Peter de Francia' in *Navigating the Void: Essays on the Figurative Painting in the Twentieth Century*. Baroda: Faculty of Fine Arts, M.S. University, Baroda, p. 54. Originally published in *Art Scribe*, No. 9, 1977.

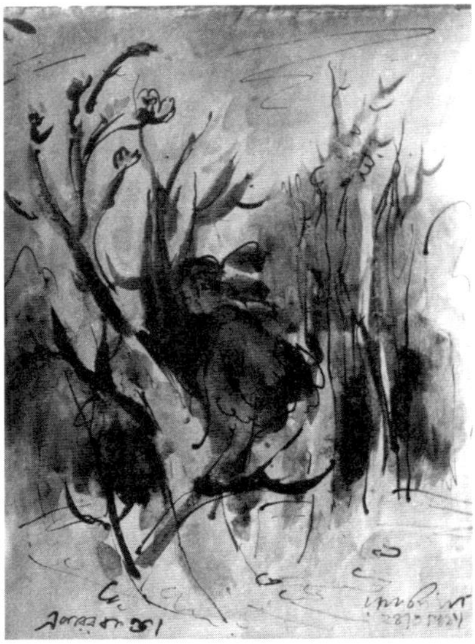

Ramkinkar Baij, *Untitled* (trees),
24 March 1941, ink and watercolour on paper,
image courtesy Anath Nath Das Collection

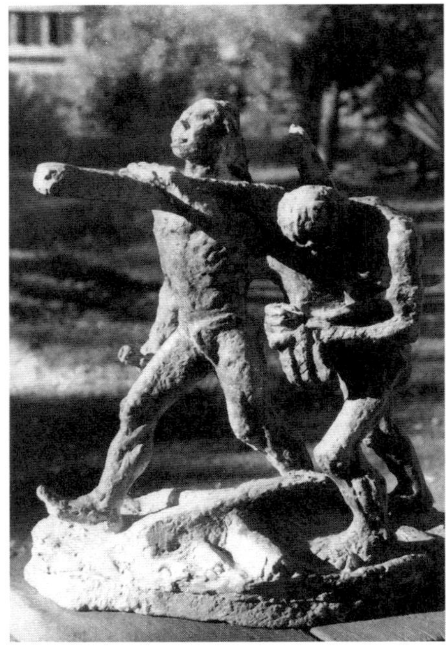

Ramkinkar Baij, *Father and Son*, c. 1940, clay,
image courtesy Anath Nath Das Collection

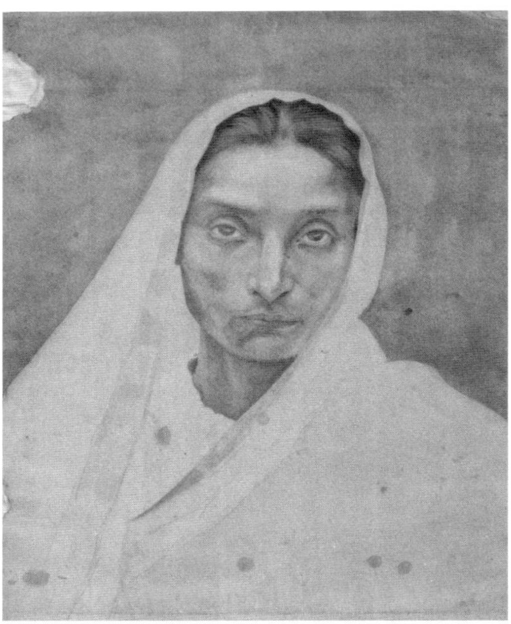

Ramkinkar Baij, *Untitled* (Portrait of Basanta Baij,
Ramkinkar's sister-in-law), c. 1928 watercolour on paper,
image courtesy Kala Bhavan, Santiniketan Collection.

Ramkinkar Baij (1906-1980) grew up in a small district town in Bengal, rife with the nationalist spirit of the early *swadeshi* (indigenism). His curiosity about both contemporary and traditional Indian art as well as Western visual cultures formed his artistic mentality. This curiosity found room for expansion, combination and layering with his arrival in Santiniketan, where he was looked at somewhat comparatively as a westerniser.

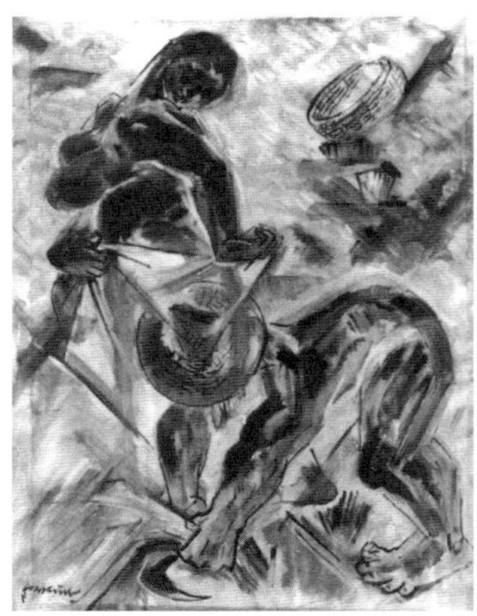

Ramkinkar Baij, *Untitled* (harvesting),
c. 1940, oil on canvas, image courtesy
Anath Nath Das Collection

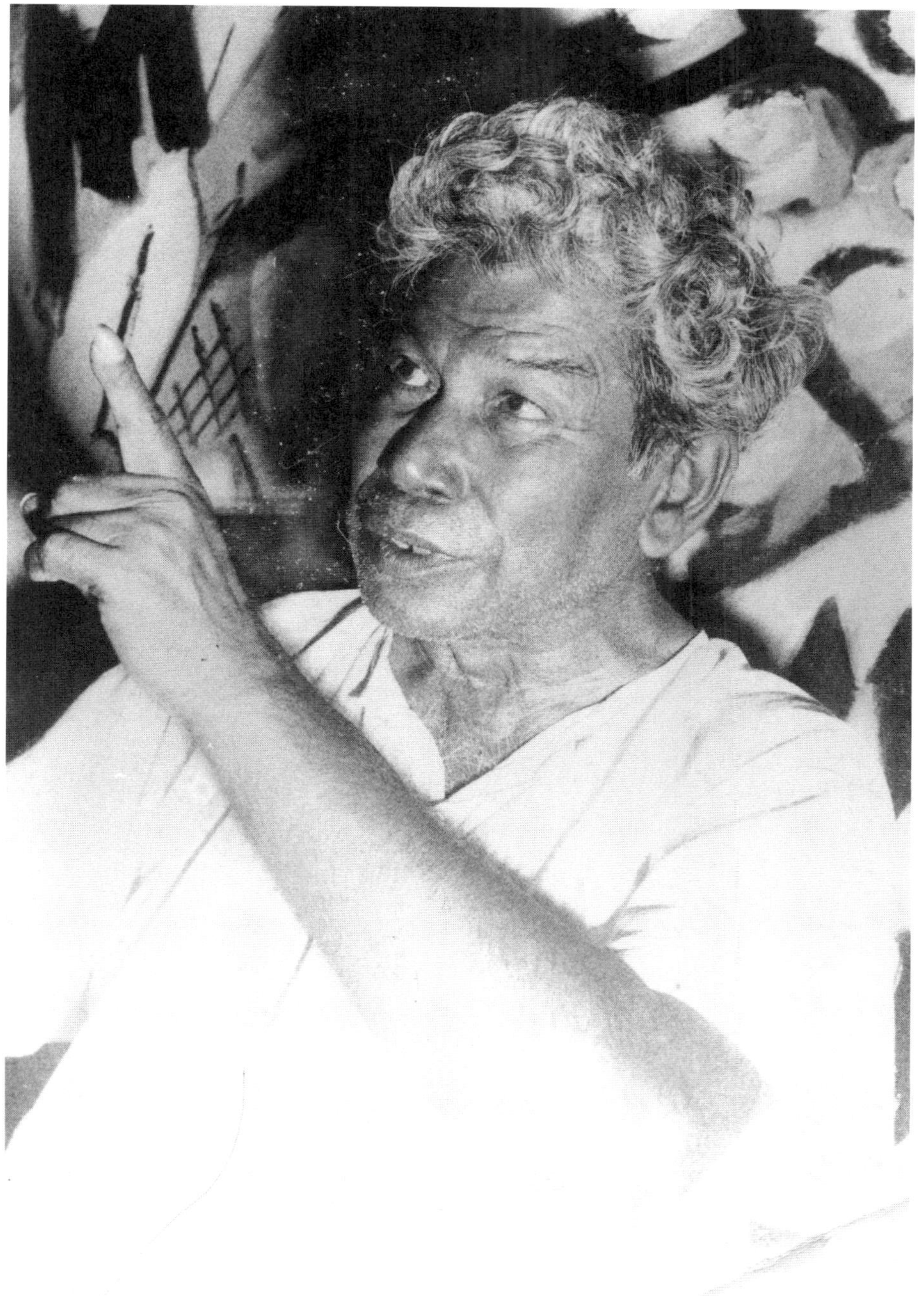

Ramkinkar Baij at work, image courtesy Rabindra Bhavan Archive, Santiniketan

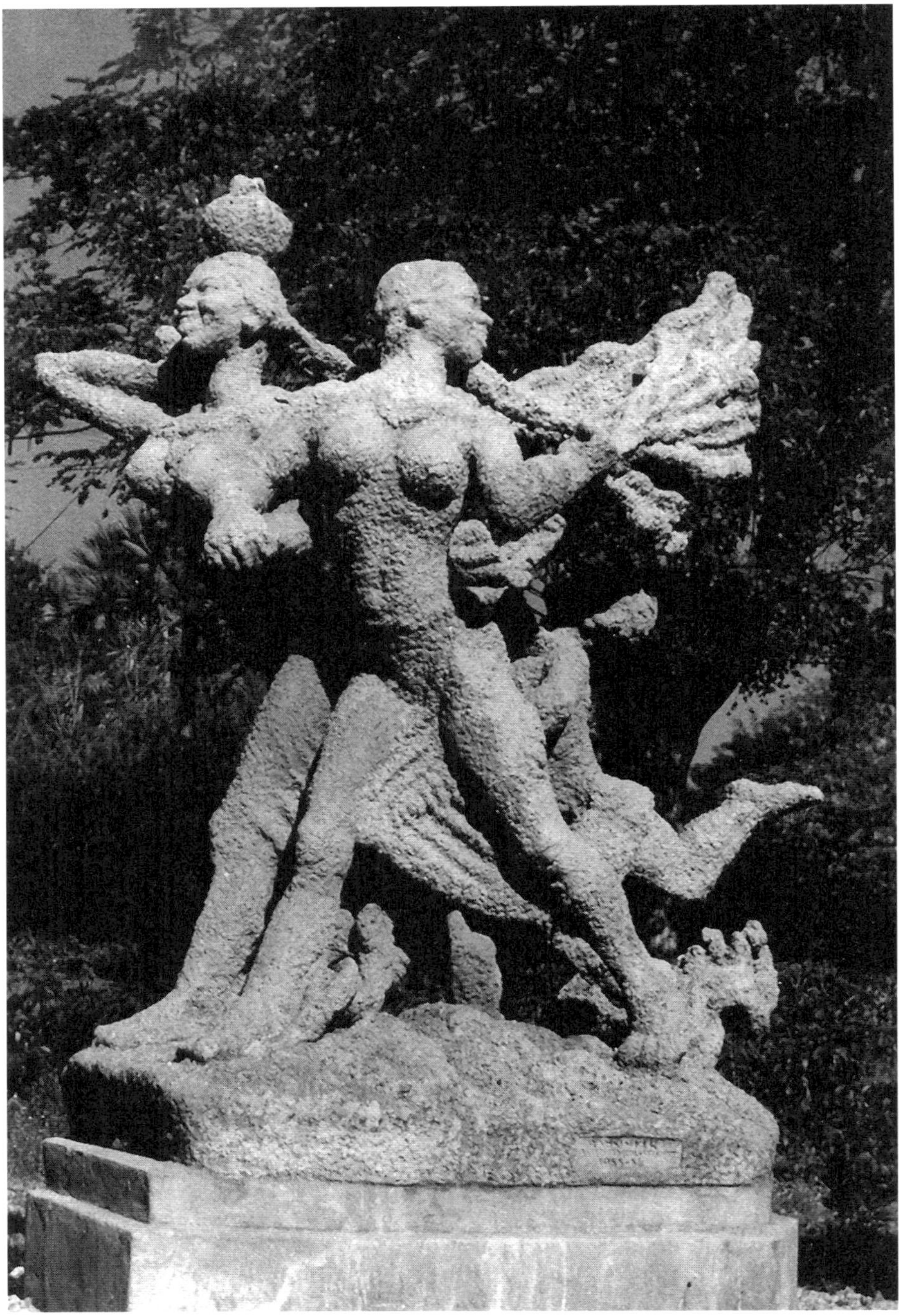

Ramkinkar Baij, *Mill Call*, 1956, direct cement, image courtesy Anath Nath Das Collection

Growing up in Tagore's Santiniketan, he among others imbibed the concept of the double agendas of modernism—the simultaneity of home and the world, the local and the global. As if the local and the immediate were translatable entities in a language that has equal shares of these dualities. Much of what we recognize as meaning(s) in Ramkinkar's works are their accrued meanings, so that his outdoor sculptures, or what are properly called 'public', along with the rest of his practice, have lived within several worlds or interpretive communities that form, unform and reform their existence.

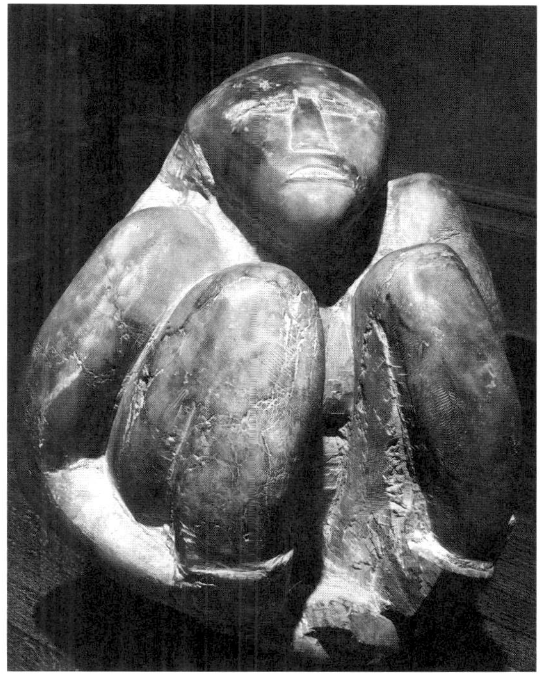

Jacob Epstein, *Elemental Figure*, 1932, alabaster, private collection, image © Courtauld Institute of Art and the Estate of Jacob Epstein

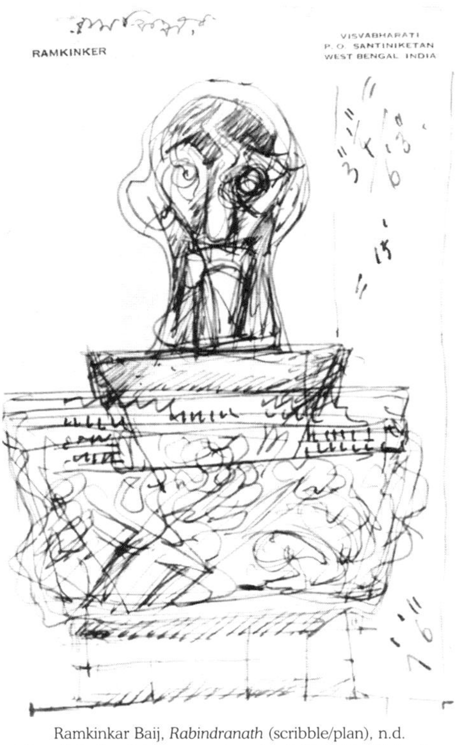

Ramkinkar Baij, *Rabindranath* (scribble/plan), n.d.
ink on letterhead, image courtesy Anath Nath Das Collection

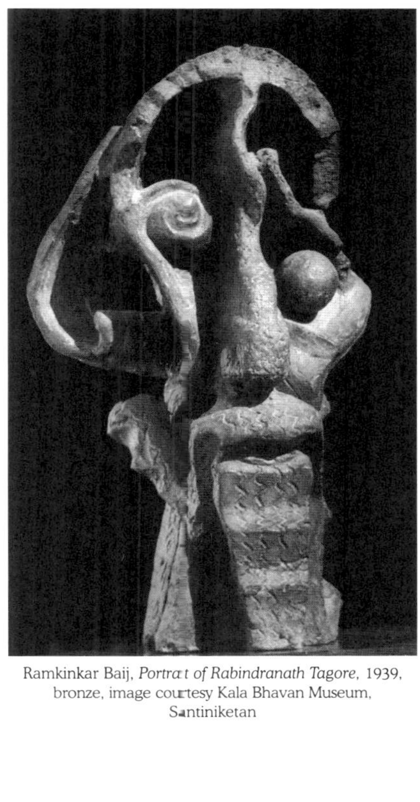

Ramkinkar Baij, *Portrait of Rabindranath Tagore*, 1939, bronze, image courtesy Kala Bhavan Museum, Santiniketan

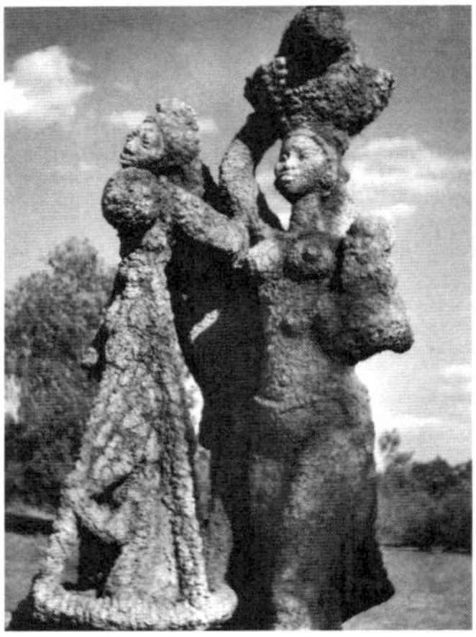

Ramkinkar Baij, *Santhal Family* (detail), 1938, direct cement concrete, image courtesy Anath Nath Das Collection

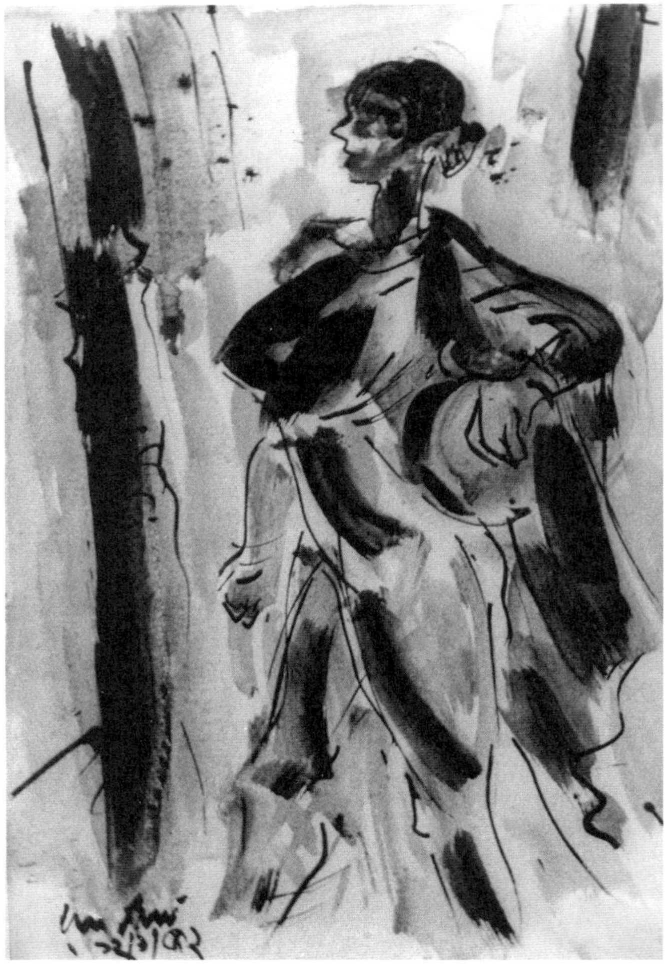

Ramkinkar Baij, *Untitled (Woman fetching water)*, c. 1950, ink and watercolour on paper, image courtesy Anath Nath Das Collection

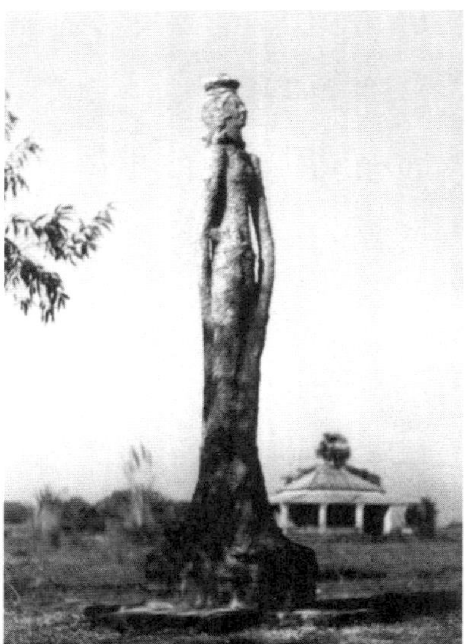

Ramkinkar Baij, *Sujata*, 1935 (photographed c. 1940), direct concrete, image courtesy Anath Nath Das Collection

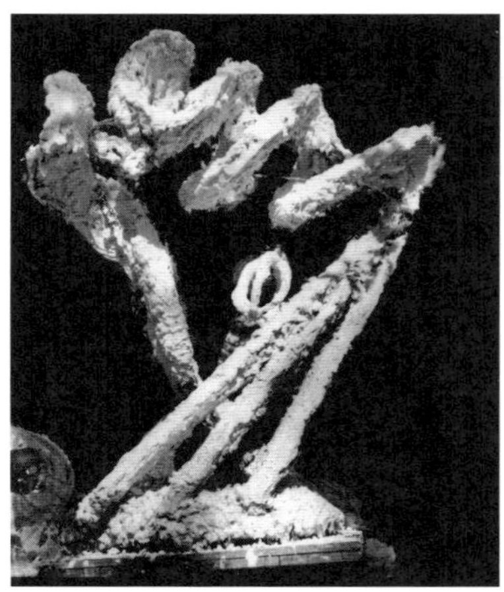

Ramkinkar Baij, *Abstract Sculpture* (under construction), c. 1940, plaster, image courtesy Anath Nath Das Collection

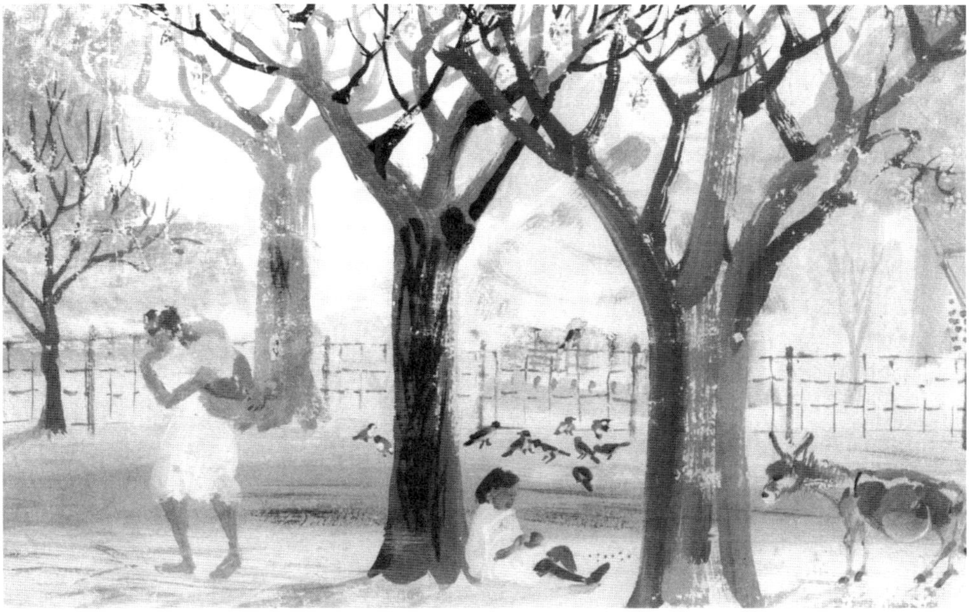

Nandalal Bose, *Ashram*, 1934, tempera on paper, image courtesy NGMA, New Delhi

The prime stress on rhythm imbued in Ramkinkar by his teacher Nandalal Bose was adapted by him and his capable colleagues —among them Binodebehari Mukherjee.

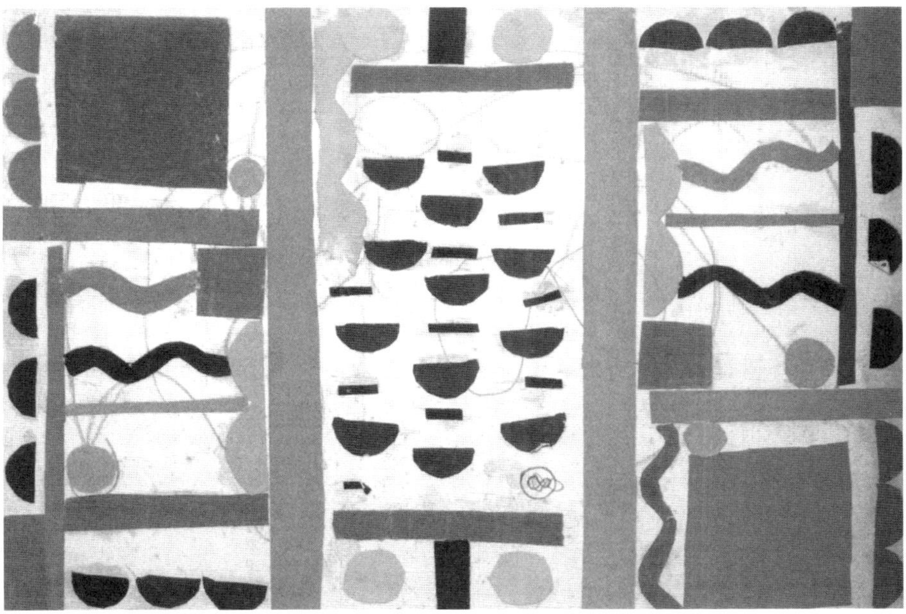

Binodebehari Mukherjee, *Window*, c. 1958, papercut, image courtesy NGMA, New Delhi

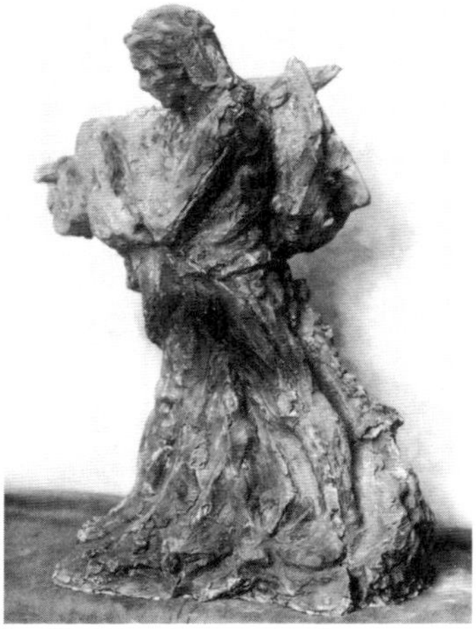

Ramkinkar Baij, *Untitled (Man walking with a sack)*, c. 1928, clay, image courtesy Anath Nath Das Collection

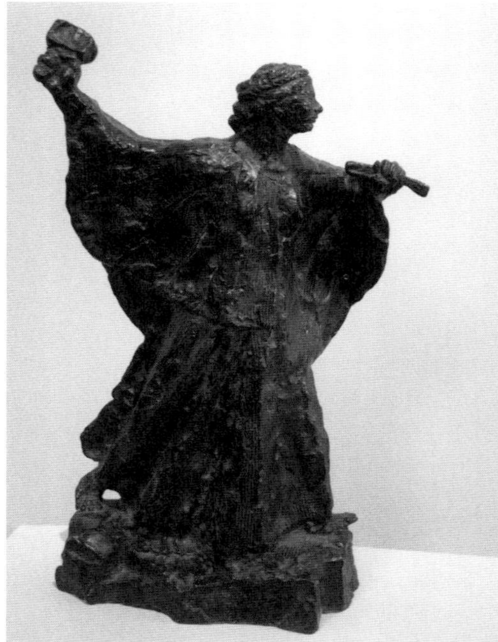

Emile Antoine Bourdelle, *The Sculptress at Work*, 1906, bronze, Alexis Rudier foundry [inspired by Cléopatre Sevastos], image © 2006 David Monniaux, creative commons

His formal sources were many—among the European artists, Auguste Rodin's influence came via Antoine Bourdelle who had in turn been a teacher of Mrs. Marguerite Milward, a visiting artist at Santiniketan who introduced Ramkinkar, among others, to sculpting.

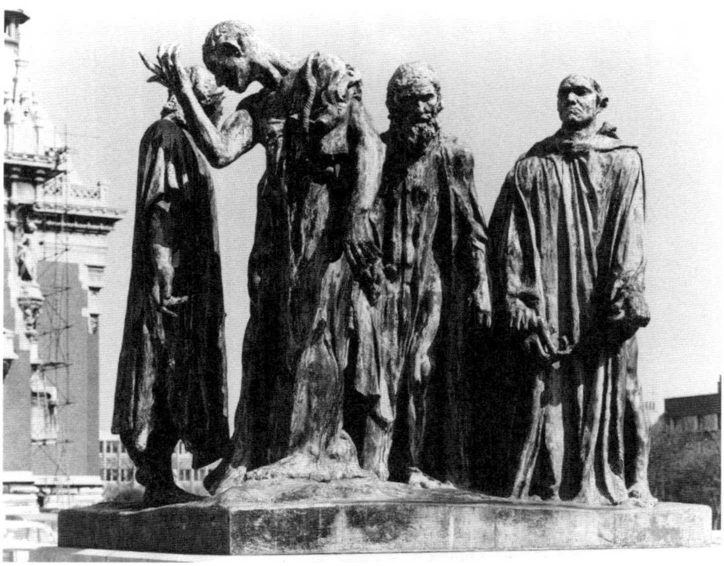

August Rodin, *The Burghers of Calais*, 1884-1889, bronze, situated at Place de l'Hotel de Ville, Calais, Pas-de-Calais, France © Courtauld Institute of Art

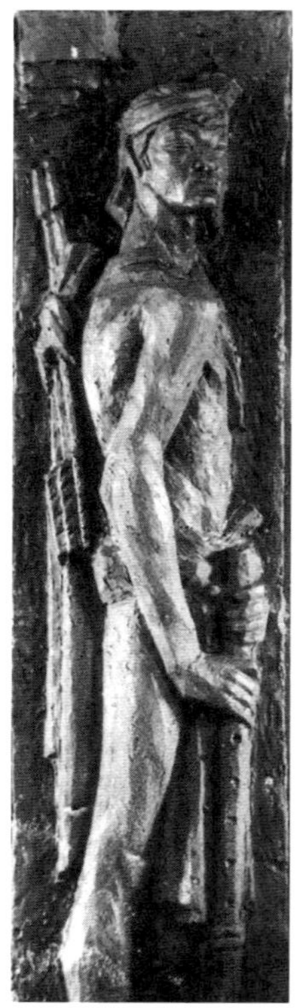

Ramkinkar Baij, *Shyamali doorway* (in construction), 1935, clay relief, image courtesy Anath Nath Das Collection

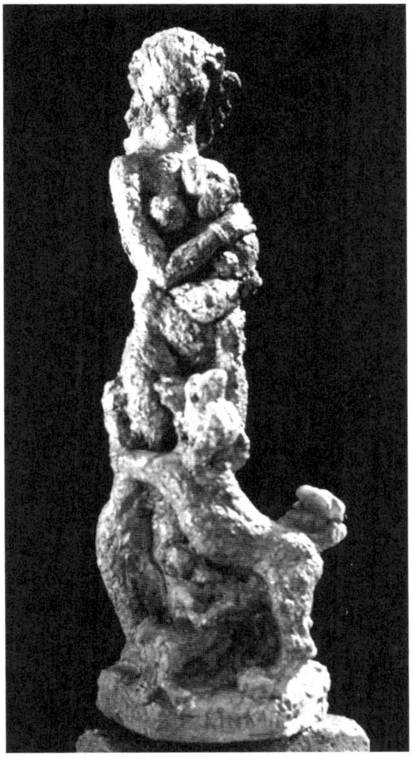

Ramkinkar Baij, *Untitled* (woman with dog), c. 1940, concrete, image courtesy Anath Nath Das Collection

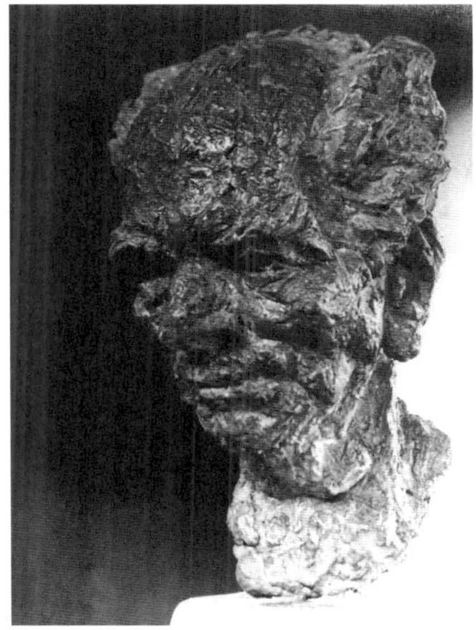

Ramkinkar Baij, *Portrait of Abanindranath Tagore*, 1943, plaster cast, image courtesy Anath Nath Das Collection

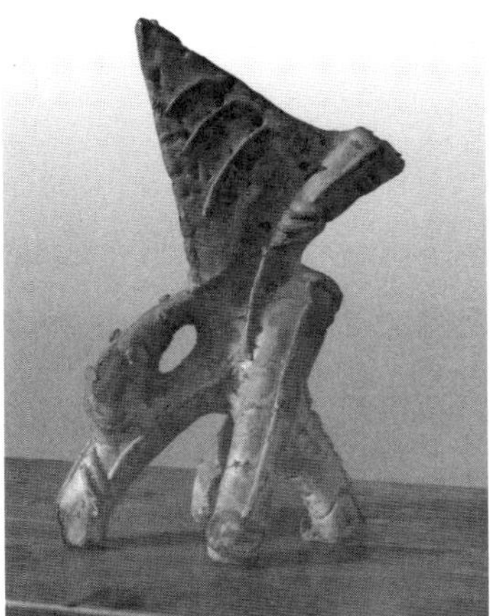

Ramkinkar Baij, *Untitled*, 1943, Dokra cast, image courtesy Kala Bhavan Museum, Santiniketan

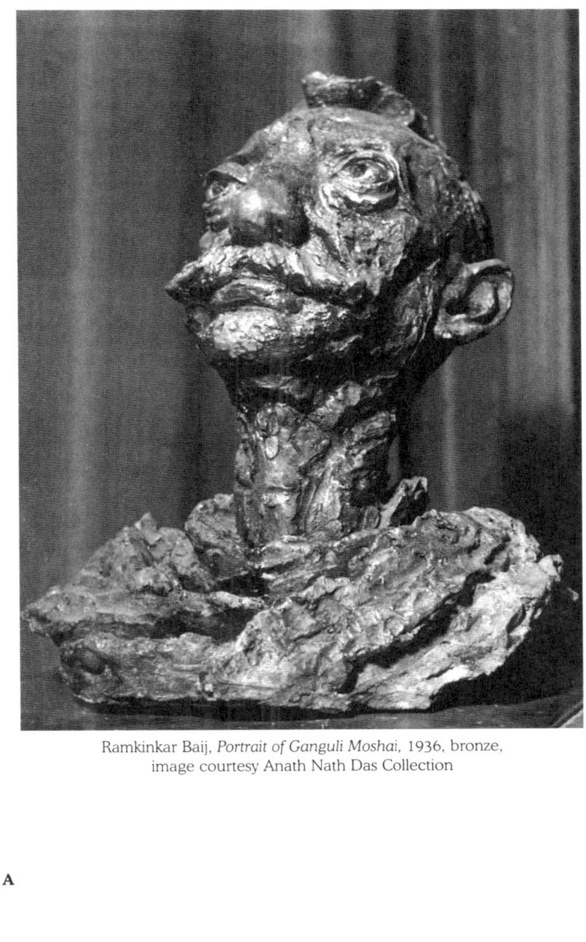

Ramkinkar Baij, *Portrait of Ganguli Moshai*, 1936, bronze, image courtesy Anath Nath Das Collection

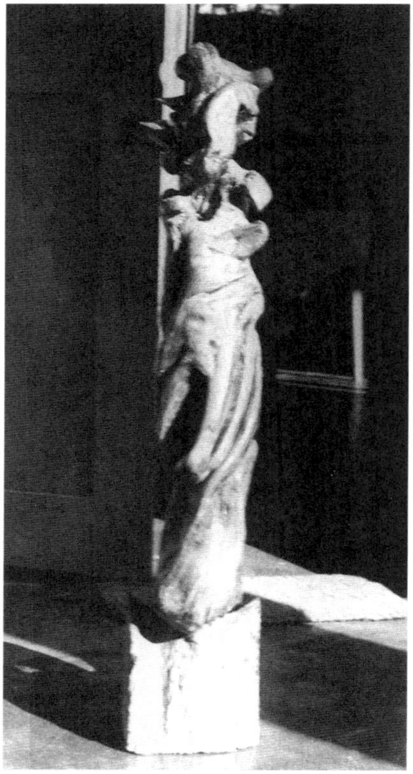

Ramkinkar Baij, *Untitled* (woman with snail head), c. 1940, clay, image courtesy Anath Nath Das Collection

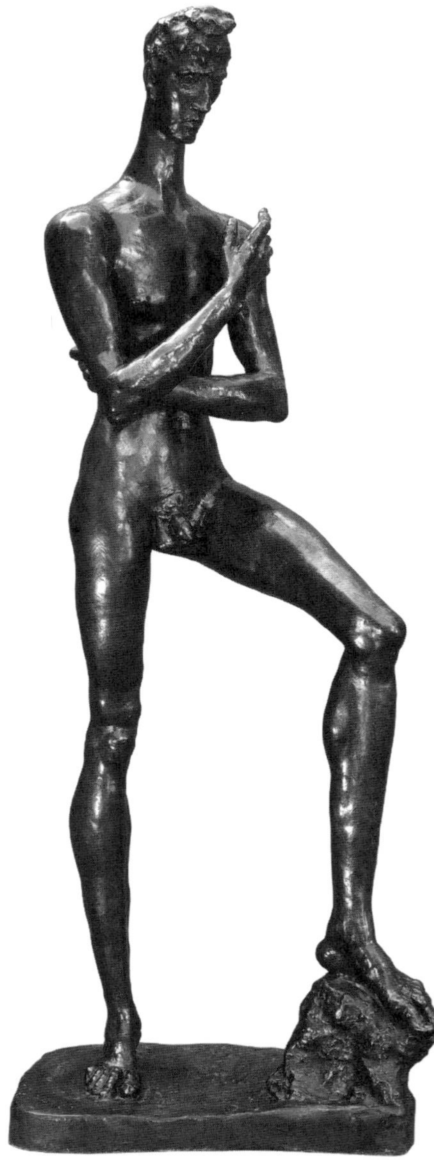

Wilhelm Lehmbruck, *Emporsteigneder Jüngling* (ascending youth), 1913/1914, bronze (cast 1924), Stiftung Wilhelm Lehmbruck Museum – Zentrum Europäsicher Skulptur, photo: Bernd Kirtz

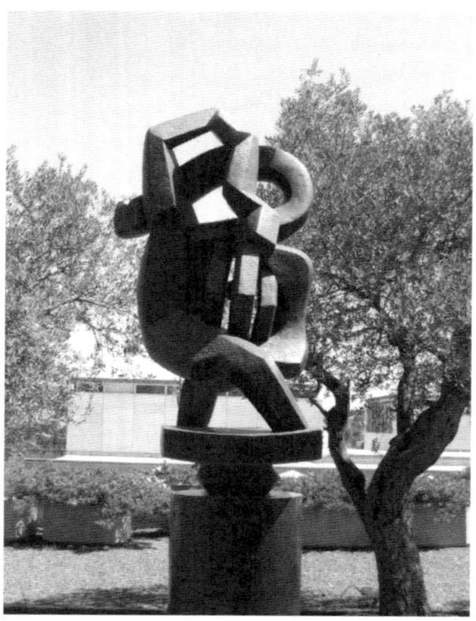

Jacques Lipchitz, *La joie de vivre*, 1927, bronze, installed at Israel Museum, Jerusalem, image © Jair Talmor, creative commons

Apart from Rodin there were many early and mid-century modernists who left their influences on Ramkinkar—Jacques Lipchitz, Pablo Picasso and the Surealists as well as Wilhelm Lehmbruck were appreciated because of their knack for combining figuration and abstraction. The wars and debacles in the world order including colonialism and famine and bondage of various kinds led Ramkinkar to recombine these various sources purposively in order to direct them to an increasingly politicized terrain.

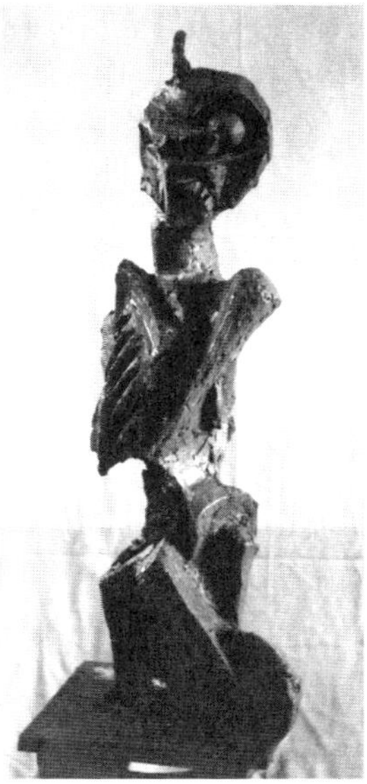

Untitled (semi-abstract figure), c.1940, plaster, image courtesy Anath Nath Das Collection

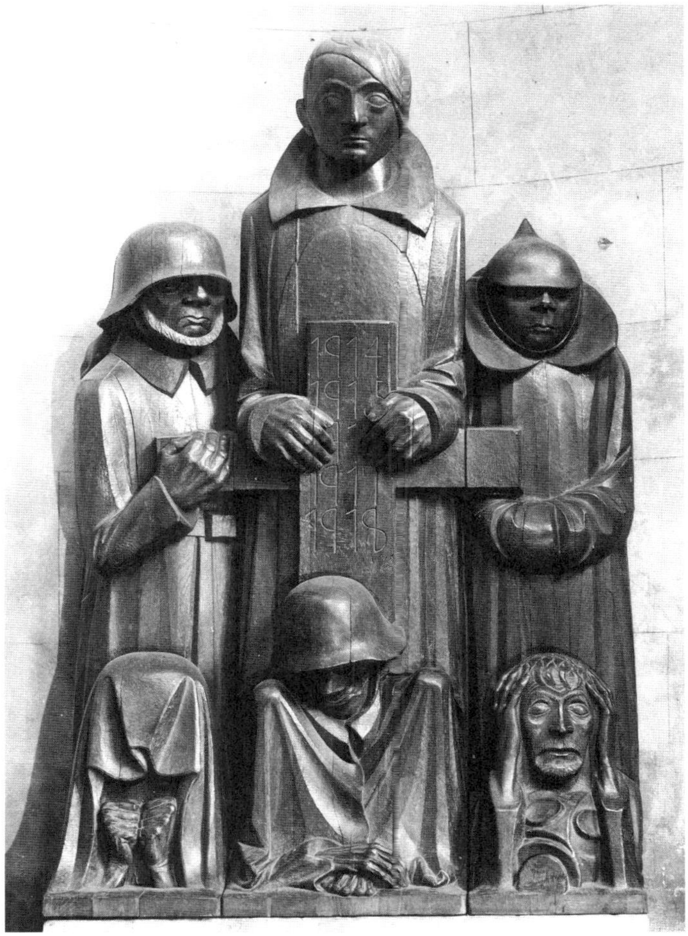

Ernst Barlach, *1914-1918 War Memorial*, 1927-1929, situated in the Cathedral of Saints Maurice and Anne, Magdeburg, Germany © Courtauld Institute of Art

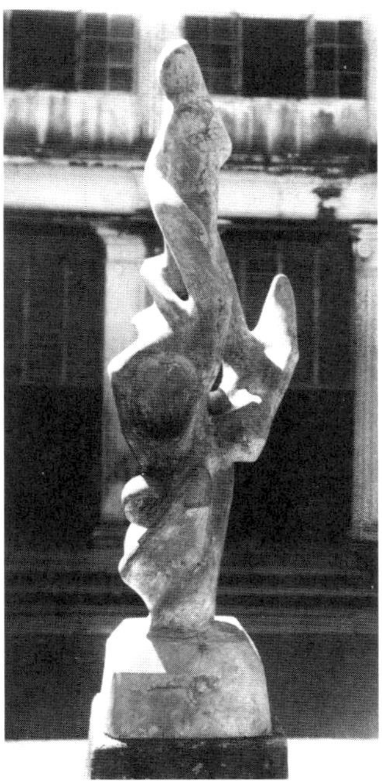

Ramkinkar Baij, *Lamp stand*, 1940, direct concrete, image courtesy Anath Nath Das Collection

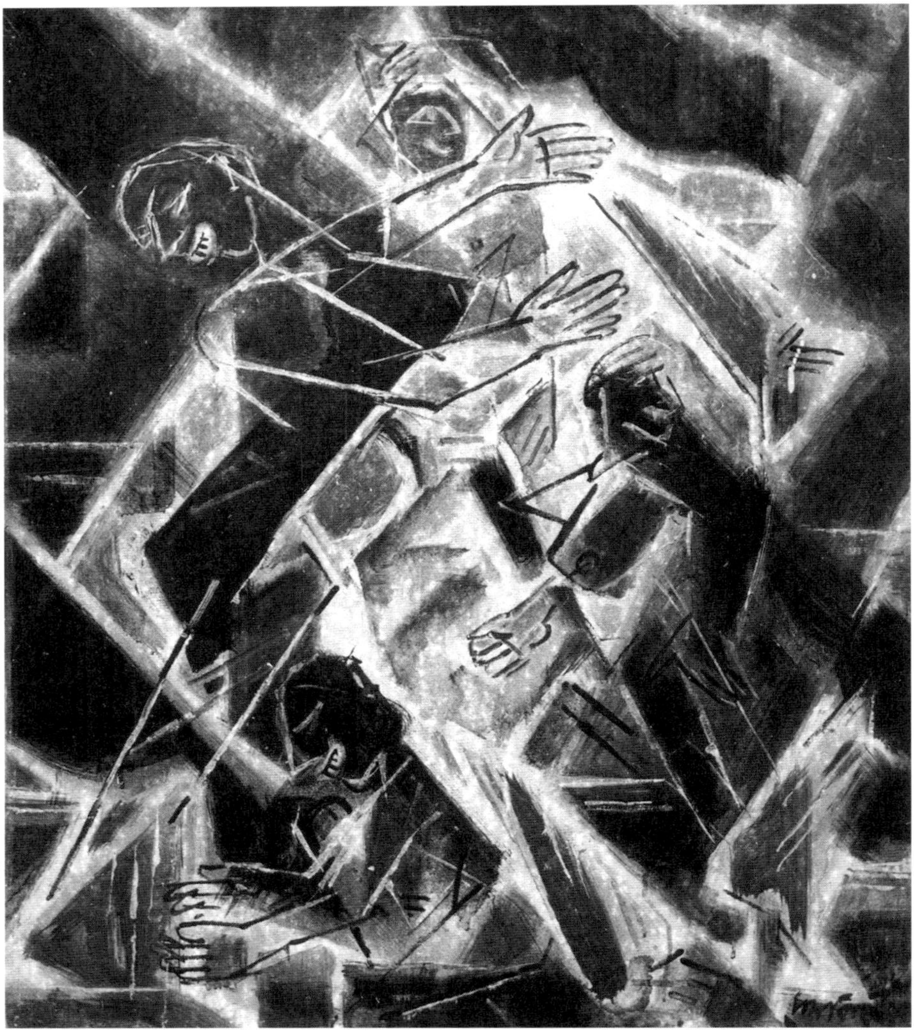

Ramkinkar Baij, *Untitled*, c.1950, oil on canvas, image courtesy Anath Nath Das Collection

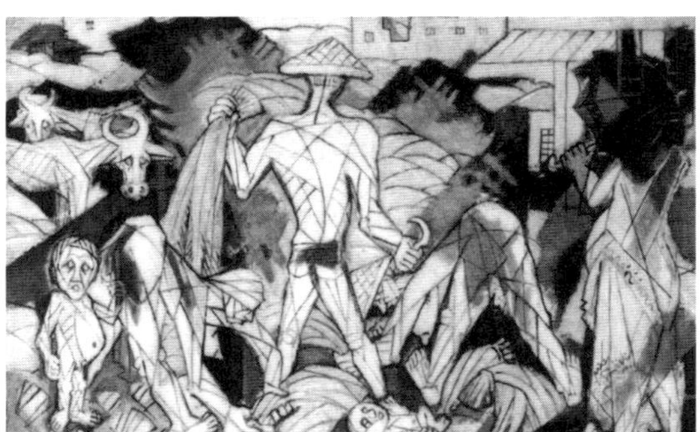

Ramkinkar Baij, *Untitled* (harvesting), oil on canvas, c. 1960,
image courtesy NGMA, New Delhi

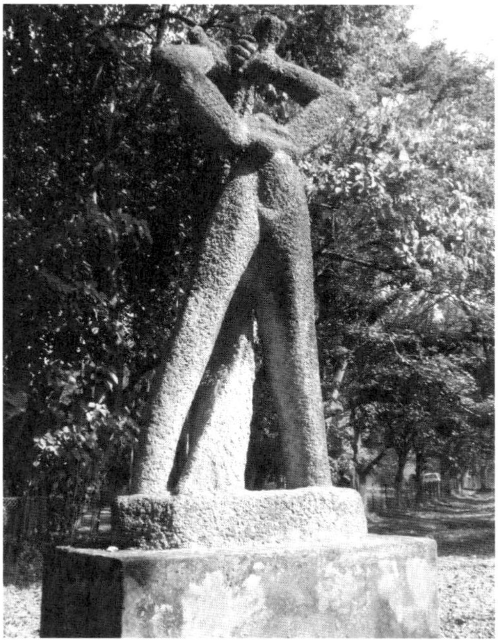

Ramkinkar Baij, *Thresher*, 1945, direct cement,
photo: Grant Watson

Realities like war and famine also brought Ramkinkar close to the international vocabularies of form developed to reflect on the changing life world. Both empathy and reason played their role in the resulting admixture. In *Thresher*, the dynamics of the labouring body under duress projects fragmentation as a predicament of representation. One can see at once: shades of empathy similar to the work of German sculptors Lehmbruck or Barlach; a play of expressive vocabularies also found in Picasso's war series; as well as the frontality and projections of Soviet-style Socialist Realism. The consciousness that emerges has an equal share of inward and outward reflection.

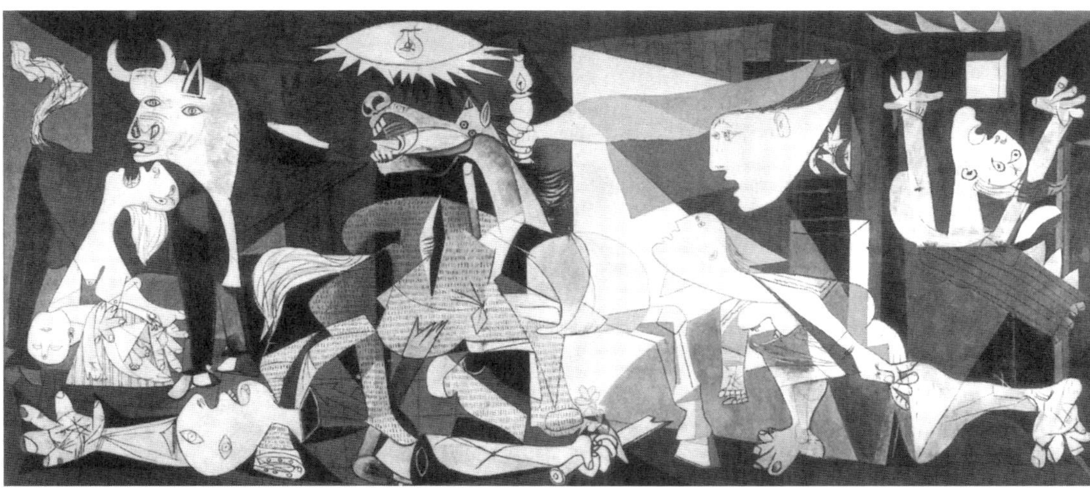

Pablo Picasso, *Guernica*, 1937, oil on canvas, Museo del Prado, Madrid

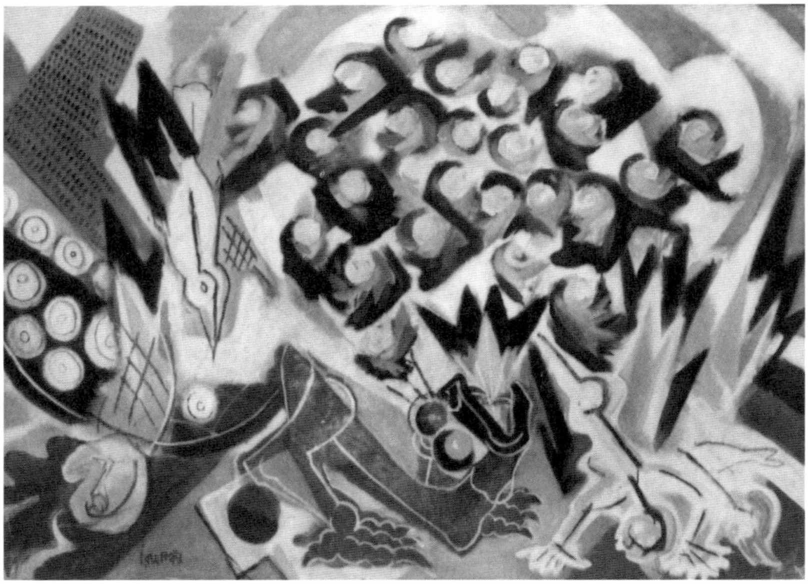

Ramkinkar Baij, Atomika, 1969, oil on canvas, image courtesy NGMA, New Delhi

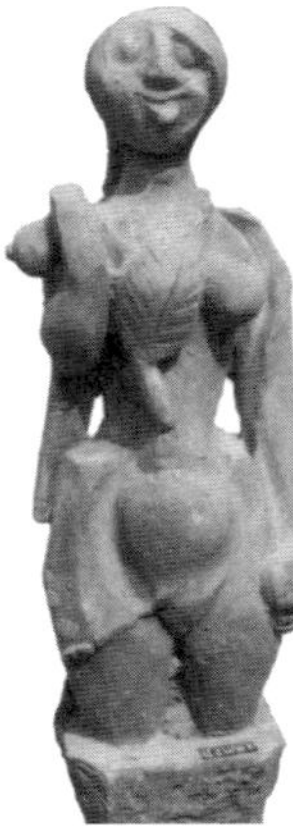

Ramkinkar Baij, preperatory maquette for Yaksha sculpture, c. 1958, plaster, image courtesy NGMA, New Delhi

Many of Ramkinkar's modernist sculptural ideas worked in combination with traditional sources. These were often from the pre-Christian or the early Christian era, the Yakshas/Yakshis and the Mithuna, or erotic sculptures from Hindu and Buddhist temple architecture. Towards the end of his artistic career Ramkinkar Baij revisited the theme of his painting *Atomika* from a decade earlier, an image of destruction that existed in contrast to his large-scale public project Yaksha/Yakshi with its promise of bounty. Ancient tradition and modernity are interlinked in a practice where time is experienced as a cyclical entity.

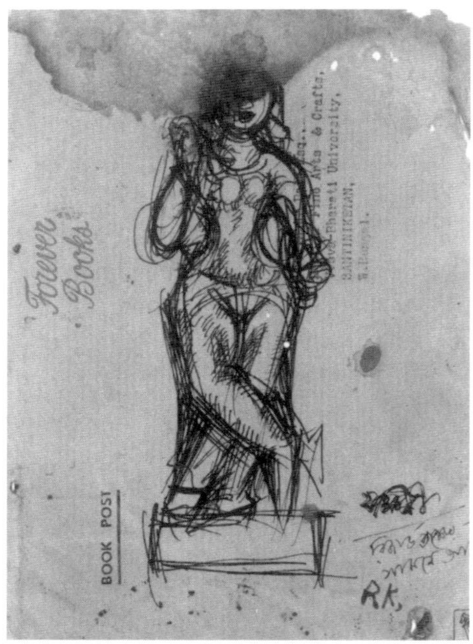

Ramkinkar Baij, preperatory sketch for Yaksha sculpture, c. 1955, ink on paper envelope, image courtesy NGMA, New Delhi

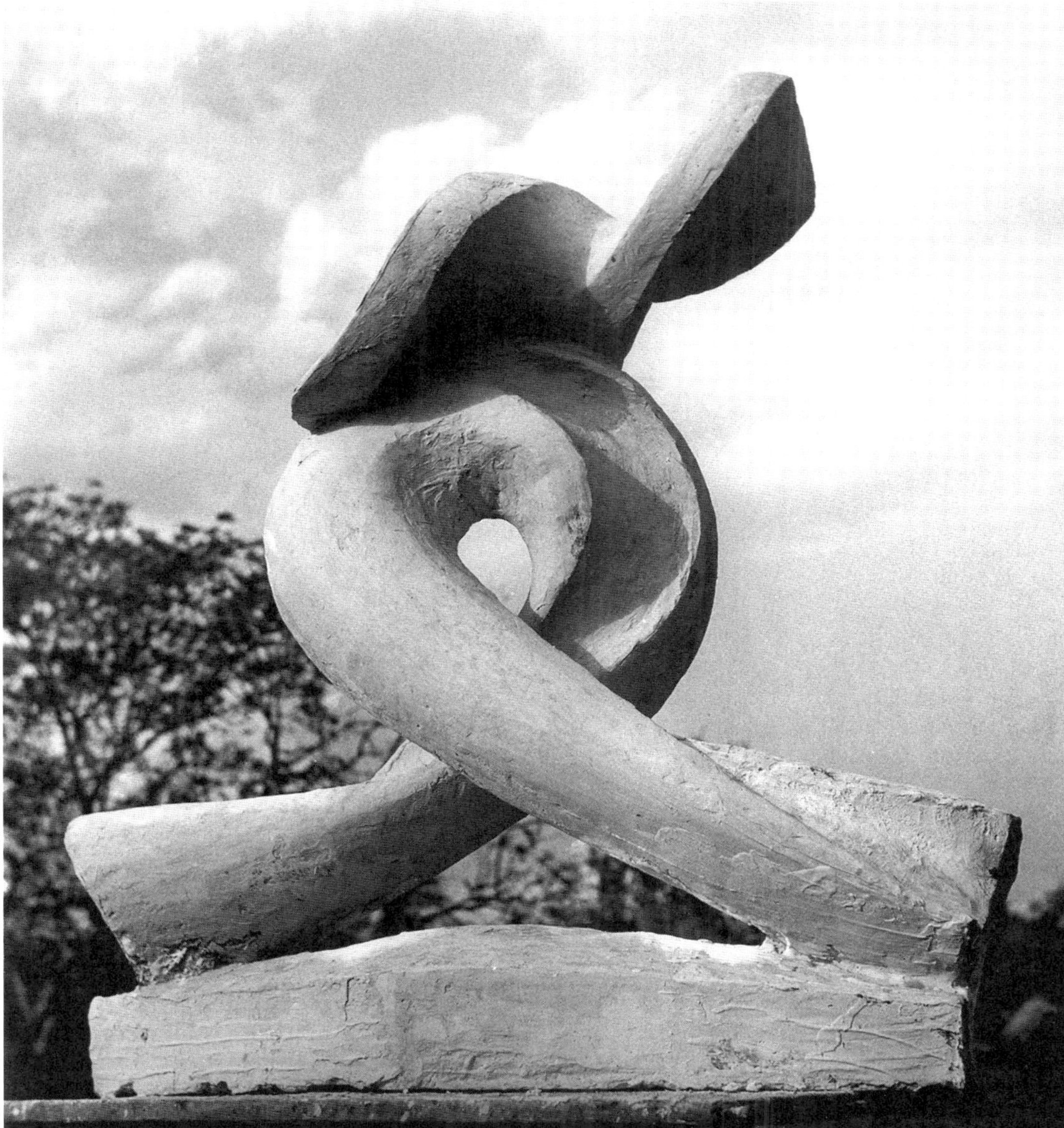

Ramkinkar Baij, *Speed*, 1953, plaster, image courtesy Anath Nath Das Collection

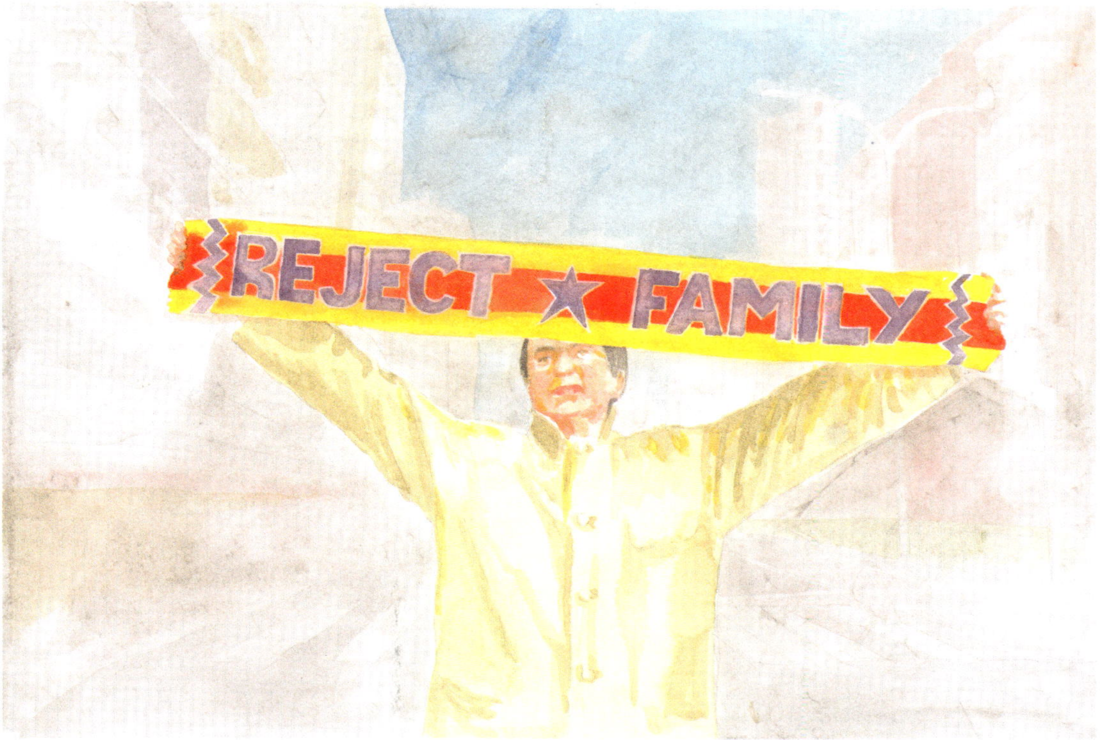
REJECT ★ FAMILY

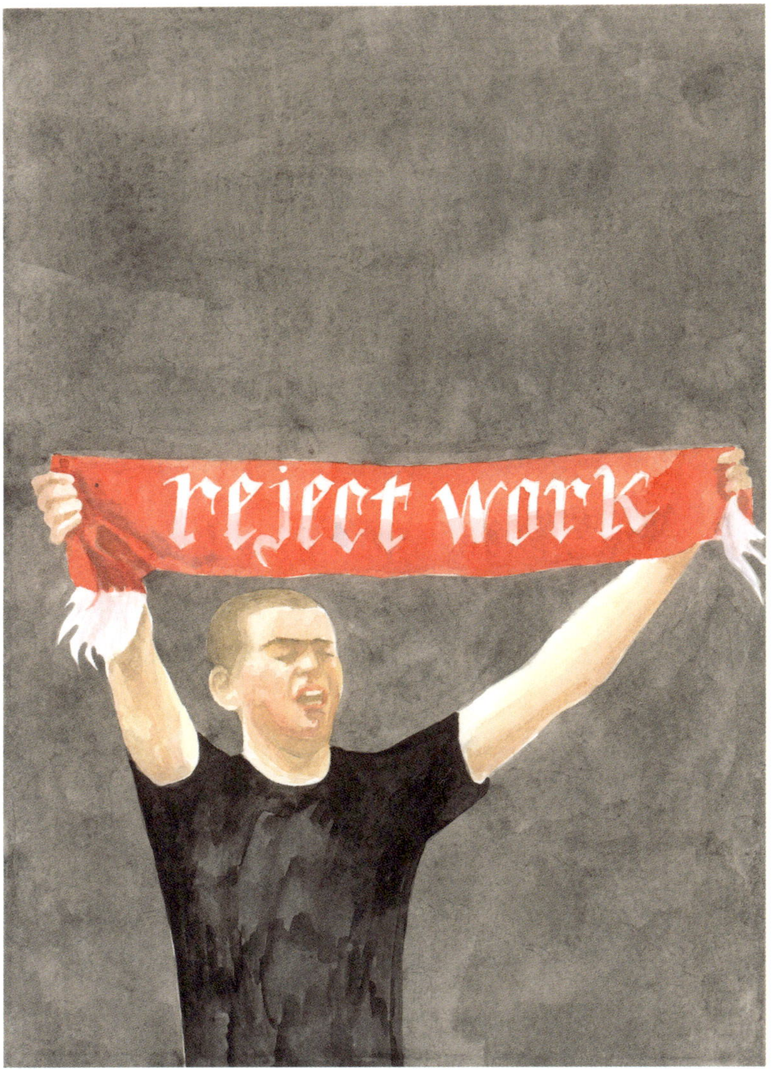
reject work

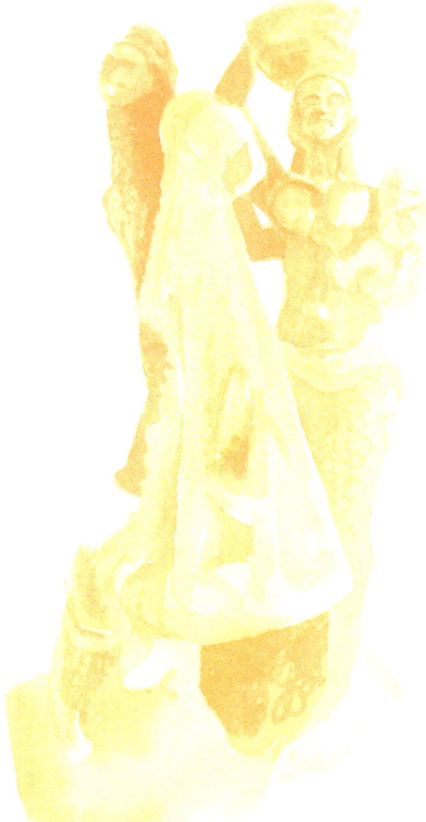

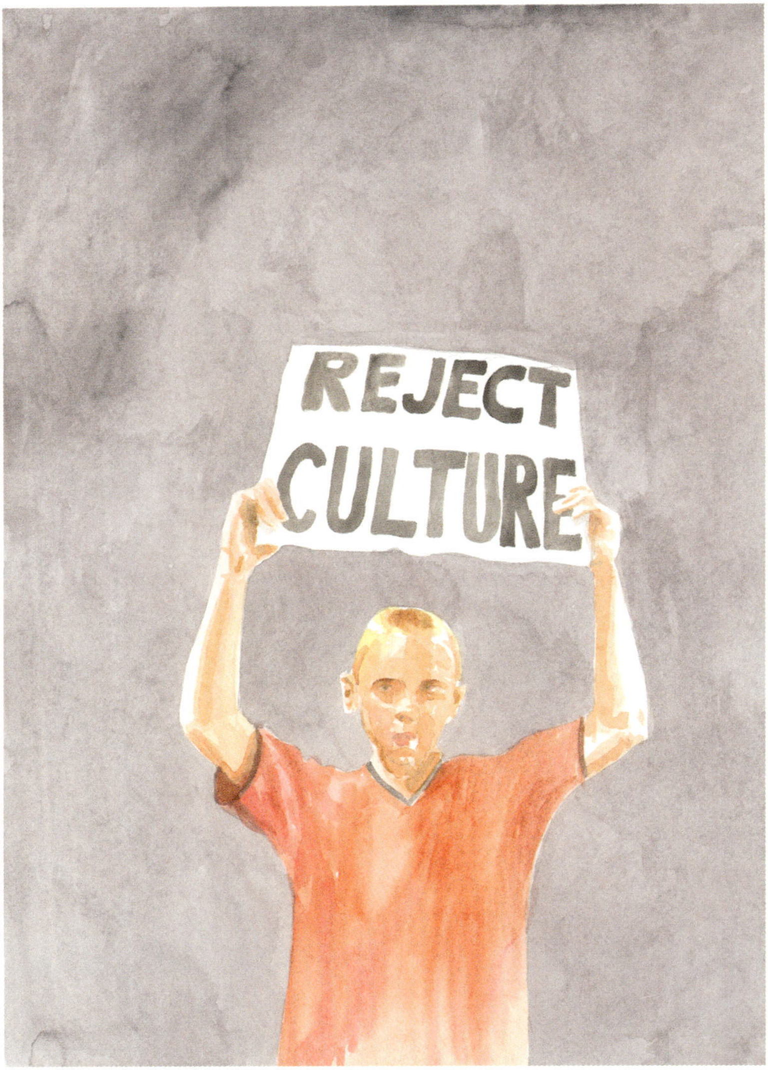
REJECT
CULTURE

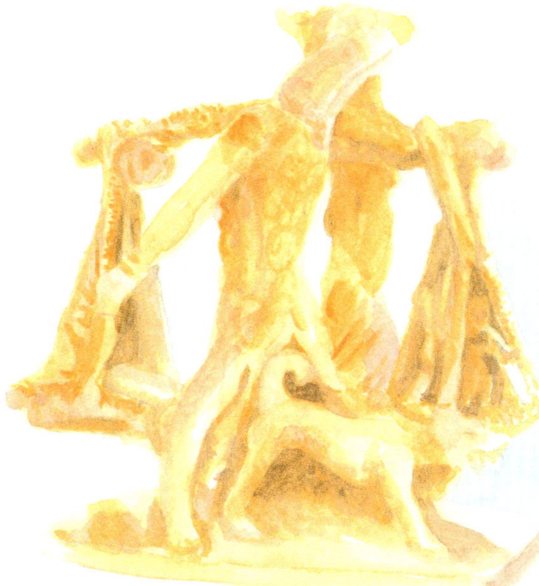

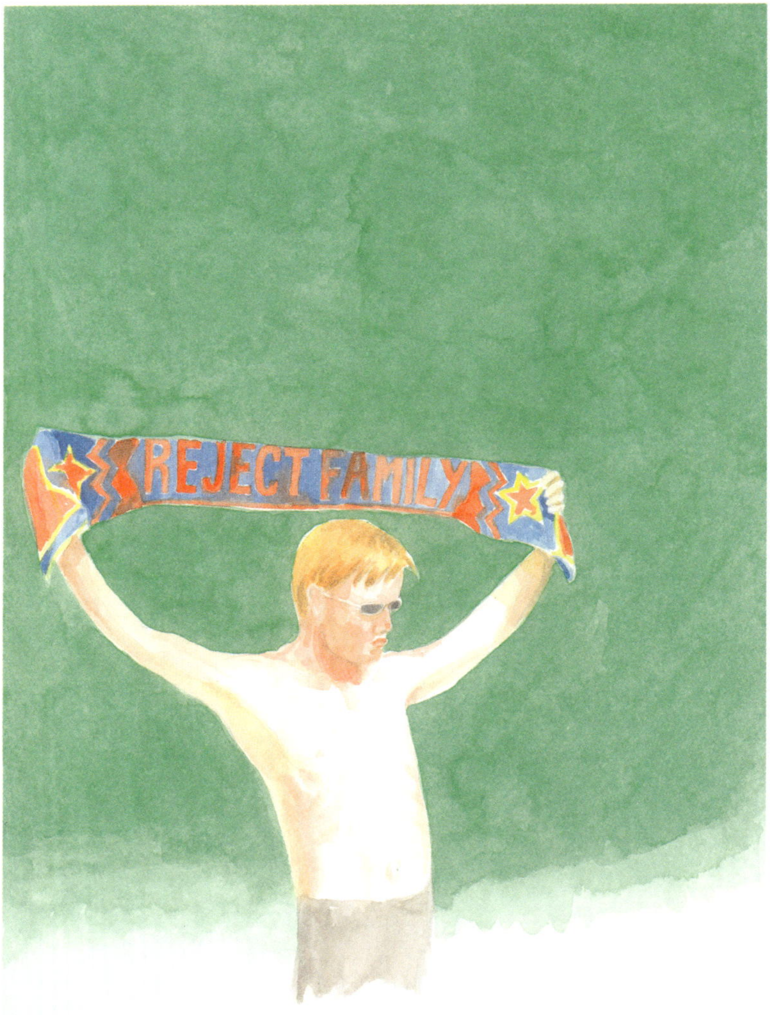
REJECT FAMILY

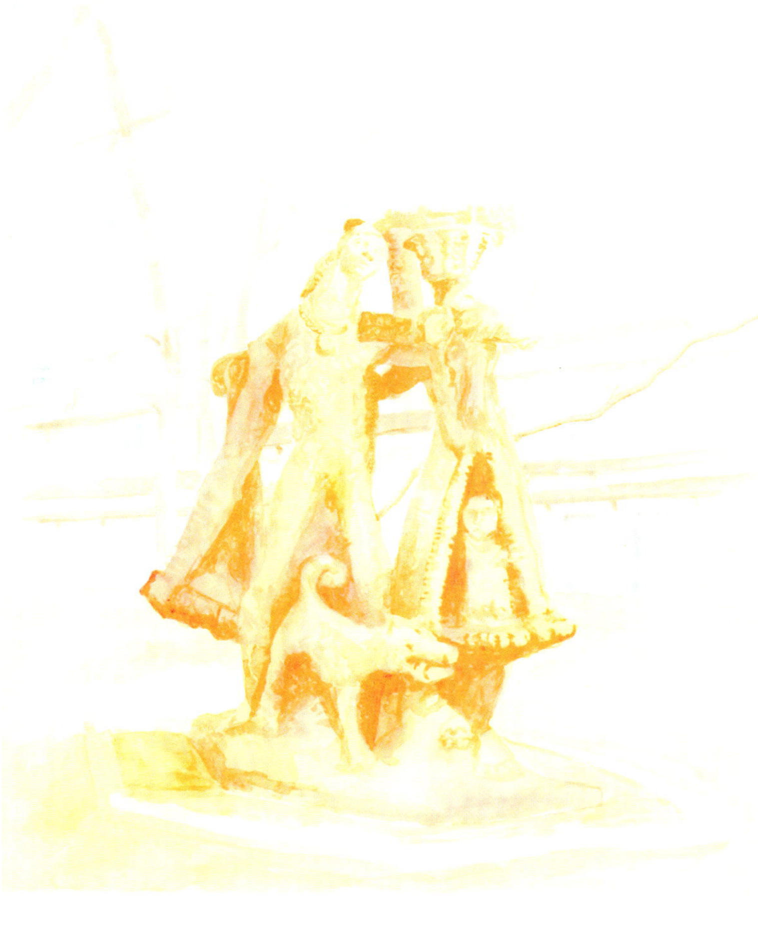

 JUAN PEREZ AGIRREGOIKOA

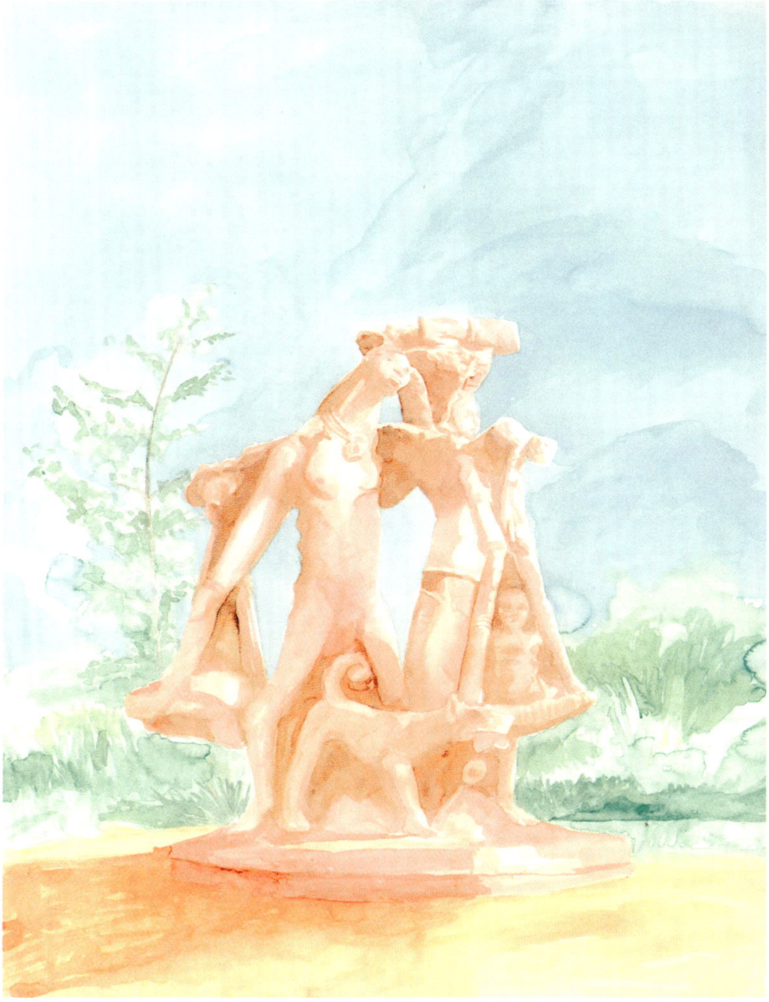

WILL BRADLEY

BURYING LENIN IN BIRBHUM AND PENTONVILLE

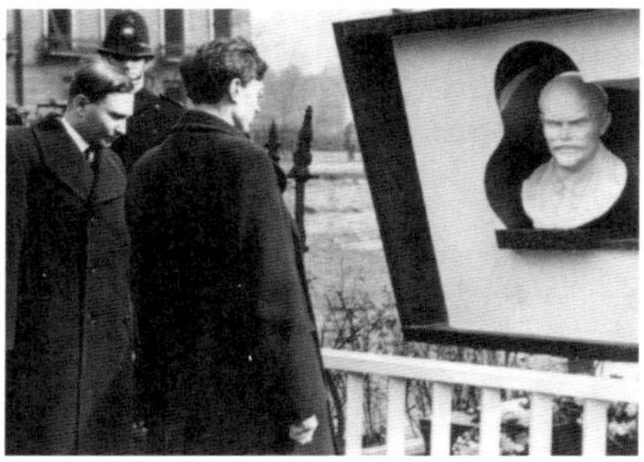

© Marx Memorial Library, London

At the same time that Ramkinkar Baij was completing his sculpture of a Santhali family in Santiniketan, the 1938 Empire Exhibition was taking place in Glasgow. More than twelve million people attended the vast showground in Bellahouston Park, with its Ferris wheel, Crazy House, Midget Town and Stratoship. But the attractions did not end there. You could admire the many national and corporate pavilions, including two—one for Scotland, and one for Imperial Chemical Industries (ICI)—designed by the acclaimed young architect Basil Spence. Later you could take a walk down Colonial Avenue and marvel at exhibits demonstrating the way global trade could bring the world together, then stop off at the Royal Air Force display of eleven Hawker Hind bombers, each powered by a gleaming Rolls-Royce Kestrel V engine. If you were lucky enough to have been there on Empire Day, 24 May, you would even have seen them fly.

In 1923, Le Corbusier had nominated the aeroplane as the pre-eminent symbol of modernity, to be apprehended not as "a bird or a dragonfly, but as a 'machine for flying'." But the moment of the aeroplane as simply a 'machine for flying' was already far in the past, and by 1935 even the techno-optimist Corbu had acknowledged the fact. He suggested that his Radiant City plan, with its dispersed buildings and hardened concrete structures, offered an urban model that would be "capable of emerging victorious from an air war," while, in the context of the introduction to a picture book entitled *Aircraft*, published the same year, his prescription for urban architecture sounds uncomfortably prescient: "Cities, with their misery, must be torn down. They must be largely destroyed and fresh cities built."[1]

Like the Ferris Wheel or the Stratoship, the military aeroplanes' flight was a visual spectacle, a mass public entertainment for a radio age, symbolising the industrial, technological, economic and military power that confirmed not just Western, but British superiority. And though Egypt, Iraq, Canada and the Irish Free State had all achieved independence from Britain in the preceding decade, Empire Day—which marked the late Queen Victoria's birthday—was still marked by street parties that celebrated dominion over Aden, Australia, the Bahamas, Bahrain, Botswana, Bermuda, Guyana, Belize, Somalia, Brunei, Myanmar, Sri Lanka, Cyprus, Egypt, Fiji, Gambia, Ghana, Grenada, Hong Kong, Jamaica, Jordan, Kenya, Kuwait, the Maldives, Malta, Mauritius, New Zealand, Nigeria, Malawi, Oman, Papua New Guinea, Palestine, Zimbabwe, Zambia, the Seychelles, Sierra Leone, South Africa, Swaziland, Tanzania, Tonga, Trinidad, and Uganda in addition, of course, to the Indian subcontinent. But what the 1938 Empire Exhibition—like its ancestor, the Great Exhibition of the Works of Industry of All Nations, at Crystal Palace in 1851—also, not only demonstrated, but unreservedly celebrated, was the intimate relationship between Imperial power and capitalism.

Within little more than a year, Britain, and the occupied territories of the Empire with it, was at war with Germany. Britain's unilateral involvement of India in the Second World War was the final catalyst for the 1942 Quit India movement of anti-Imperialist civil disobedience, and the scale of the war enabled many other independent resistance struggles throughout

1 Le Corbusier, 1988. *Aircraft*. New York: Universe Books, p. 12. First published in London, 1935; in Paris, 1987.

the Empire, as well as public or clandestine anti-British alliances between nationalist movements and the Axis powers, particularly in South-East Asia.

On the home front, and on a micro-scale, the uncertain outcome and altered situation of the war enabled the manifestation of a cast-concrete public art monument that, looking back, appears as a conceptual counterpoint to Baij's *Santhal Family*. In London in 1942, in the aftermath of the height of German aerial bombing of the capital during the Blitz, and with the support of the local council, the architect Berthold Lubetkin erected a memorial to Vladimir Ilyich Lenin in Pentonville, near the address in Holford Square where Lenin had stayed briefly in 1902. The monument, erected as an adjunct to a new housing development, featured a cast-concrete bust of the late Soviet leader alongside a symbolic broken chain, set in a structure best described as equal parts municipal signboard and Constructivist bus-shelter.

Despite the war alliance between Britain and the Soviet Union, poor old V. I.'s bust was repeatedly attacked. At one point in 1943—according to Iain Borden's account in *Strangely Familiar: Narratives of Architecture in the City*—the monument was daubed with graffiti that included the symbol of Oswald Moseley's Blackshirts and the letters 'PJ', for the anti-Semitic fascist slogan 'Perish Judah'.[2] Two years later—the monument having been restored and guarded by police in the interim—Lenin was once again the target of material criticism from the far right, winding up earless and noseless with a swastika painted on his forehead.

The story of the abuse of Lubetkin's Lenin memorial is most often told as a counter to the 'spirit of the Blitz'—one part of the myth of British unity during the war—in order to underline the existence of an active fascist element in London society. But just as significant is the story of the monument's disappearance. If it was protected from fascist attack during the war, it was certainly not immune from the machinations of political exigency afterwards, and, if the exact circumstances of its destruction are somewhat obscure, what remains certain is that the monument no longer exists and that its ultimate fate was inevitable. A copy of the bust of Lenin remains in the collection of the Islington Museum, while a possibly apocryphal version of events has Lubetkin, pre-empting the recorded municipal decision to remove the monument, taking it upon himself to dismount it, with the help of a crane, and burying it nearby.

Post-war Britain, however, was not entirely unsympathetic to the application of certain elements of modernist thought. Though it is doubtful that reconstruction was guided by the claimed military advantages of Corbusier's vision, it was certainly open to its economic expediencies. It found a place for Basil Spence, the architect of the Scottish Pavilion at the Glasgow Empire Exhibition, for example; for his renowned Coventry Cathedral, but also later for his Queen Elizabeth Square tower blocks in the Gorbals area of Glasgow, just a mile from Bellahouston Park, high-rise and high-profile examples of the failure of a nationwide experiment in low-budget social housing that was divorced from a social context and from any functioning or coherent application of an idea of social justice. They were demolished in 1993.

To talk about modernism is to acknowledge a complex of readings of cultural, political, social and economic conditions whose geographic and temporal extension is disputed, and which have neither definite borders nor any fixed system of coordinates. The act of situating any cultural event within the cartography of modernism is never neutral but implies a warping of the interpretative fabric, a privileging of certain forces over others, and necessarily invites a host of antagonisms with the myriad mappings already vying for influence. One alternative approach, which I have tried to take in recounting these somewhat tangentially-related events, is to acknowledge the canonical concepts and technologies of cultural modernism as, in practice, embodied piecemeal, fragmented and adulterated, mutable and contingent and, more importantly, applied in the service of ideologies and exigencies whose relation to their intended cultural or even polemical function is often disappearingly slight.

Ramkinkar Baij's sculpture of a Santhali family is routinely described as the first work

2 See Borden, I. 1996. *Strangely Familiar: Narratives of Architecture in the City*. London: Routledge, p. 16.

of modernist public sculpture to be produced in India, a result of the internationalism of the Santiniketan school. At the same time, it is often suggested that Baij's depiction of members of a tribal family symbolises a productive break with both older Indian and colonial restrictions on artistic subjects, a break made possible in this instance by the coincidence of emerging complex and highly-politicised neo-nationalisms within Baij's rural background.

The *Santhal Family* is an art-historical touchstone, but its implied situation as an originary synthesis can have the unwanted effect of suggesting a singularity, a wormhole through which uncountable traditions and practices somehow must pass in order to enter a new space of Indian modernity. Baij's own later practice suggests a personal unwillingness to conform to the expectations his work had raised, but it is perhaps more useful to consider these expectations as themselves being both produced by and subject to much wider forces.

Dwarkanath Tagore—grandfather of the writer and educationalist Rabindranath Tagore and father of Debendranath who in 1863 acquired the land at Santiniketan where Baij's sculpture now stands—is buried in London, in Kensal Green Cemetery.[3] This is in part because, unlike his more widely celebrated descendants, Dwarkanath was the archetypal capitalist-imperialist collaborator. Aside from his participation in the opium trade and his role in the European exploitation of India's natural resources, he was also the owner and landlord of large estates in Bengal and an enthusiastic supporter of British rule. In an attempt, perhaps, to erase this memory from the family history, Debendranath burnt most of his papers.

It could be plausibly argued that without Dwarkanath's particular entrepreneurial endeavours, neither the Santiniketan school nor Baij's sculpture would exist. It seems likely, however, that a first monument of Indian modernist sculpture would have emerged in any case, called into being by more powerful pressures than the simple details of individual lives. Looking back, it also seems inescapable that such a monument, made at that time, should have something like the character of *Santhal Family*.

In the spirit of internationalism that led his writings to be translated by Pablo Neruda and read by Lenin, Rabindranath Tagore had written: "When in the name of Indian Art, we cultivate with deliberate aggressiveness a certain bigotry born of the habit of a past generation, we smother our soul under idiosyncrasies unearthed from buried centuries."[4] But the processes of nation-building, already well under way by 1938, demanded a contradictory reinvention of tradition that conformed to the unfolding political reality. The creation of a symbolic language free both of colonialist shackles and of the awkward facts of real rural life could act as a bridge between a contemporary folk culture already situated as a lost past, and a future in which the dissemination of the image of that culture would stand in for its empowerment.

To succeed in these very particular circumstances, the embrace of modernism should be decisive, but not traumatic. It should look to a modernist internationalism both in order to refute colonial forms and to demonstrate an independence from classical traditions, all the while counterbalancing that internationalism with an inclusive localism that simultaneously speaks of a coming integrated nationalism. And it should possess an artistic dignity, a stamp of genius, that apparently keeps it above politics, unchanging and outside of time.

Particular concepts of modernism and nationalist symbolism are certainly at stake in Baij's aesthetic, but their embodiment and interpretation is also conditioned by wider political considerations, by social and economic relationships. The question any society asks of its public art is never simply "who is the monument to?" but always also "who is the monument for?" As a self-conscious navigation between mythic truth and realist artifice, between archetype and aspirational image, between Bengali experience and European influence, between an unrepresented traditional culture and an unformed future, the major subject of the *Santhal Family* was not only the

---

3 Debendranath Tagore founded an Asram, or meditation centre, on the land that he acquired, which was later transformed by his son, the famous Rabindranath Tagore, into the Santiniketan school, which is still in operation.

4 Tagore, R. 1996. 'The Meaning of Art' in *The English Writings of Rabindranath Tagore*, New Delhi: Sahitya Akademi, p. 586. The essay was originally published in 1921.

representation of Santhal life or culture, but also the elite discourse of Indian modern art. It left the Santhal experience unchanged, even as it drew Baij's own rural background into the network of supporting narratives that gave the work its cultural power.

Of course, to say this is not to deny the success or significance of Baij's art, but rather to acknowledge it. This continuing public significance also means that the fate of Baij's gesture remains in play and open, in the process of being formed by the still-unfolding conflict between capitalism and its colonised cultures, a conflict that in no sense ended in 1947 and which recognises no geographic restrictions, but whose pressures produce corresponding counter-forces and realignments. And then, there is something that proceeds from other qualities of the work itself, from a relation to a symbolism of the human form that is not universal or eternal, but nonetheless deeply-rooted, something hard to define, but also to displace; something like hope.

The comparison here of Baij's *Santhal Family* with Lubetkin's *Lenin Monument* is intended both to set in relief certain of the conditions under which Baij was working, and, ultimately, to frame a larger question. Lubetkin exploited a moment of historical contingency to realise an unstable, ultimately and unsupportable intervention into the immediate urban fabric. The existence of the Lenin memorial owed a great deal to Lubetkin's personal history, and to the temporary power he had been granted as a working architect, and little to the local social conditions. Baij's sculpture, though disconnected from the Santhal community, was realised as an integrated part of the Santiniketan discourse. Though it was set within a modernist architectural support, Lubetkin's portrait of Lenin was cast from a pre-existing and highly conventional plaster bust, eschewing formal experiment or overt expression and stepping back from any suggestion of artistic avant-gardism into a neo-classical monumental tradition. Meanwhile Baij's formal invention—an expressionist mass of thrown concrete on a figural wire frame—allows his work to be offered the ethical protection widely accorded to individual artistic expression. The unknown Lubetkin also chose to canonise a dead ideologue, to set up an idol to the imagined inevitable outcome of the dialectic of historical materialism in the heart of the Empire, rather than to create a living depiction of a people in search of liberation. With no immediate community to support it against the depredations of the fascists and the antipathy of the state, Lubetkin's monument was condemned, while Baij's sculpture continues to be rediscovered and reinvented.

Lubetkin's memorial represented a symbolic intrusion the Empire ultimately could not tolerate, as it pointed to an ideological and material conflict that would inescapably extend and transform far beyond the immediate war. And it did so in established, iconic visual terms that could not be conveniently resituated and tamed as laudable individualist experiment. In this sense, its success was also exactly its failure, as it disappeared almost without trace. Baij's monument, on the other hand, remains standing, but also subject to cooption under the transformative operation of globalised capitalism. This operation, now freed of the constraints of particular national hegemony, is indifferent to both national or regional identity and to the assertion of historical difference or tradition in opposition to either of these—so long as any emergent identity is able to obscure, for example, the restructuring of local social relations in the formation of a client culture that wears its tradition only as ornament. The intense, lost historical struggles of the Santhal people against colonial domination have not yet been entirely vindicated. The promise, the hope of Baij's sculpture is perhaps encoded in the gestures of the figures, but its ultimate significance remains deferred.

SAKSHI GUDDA SAKSHI GODE

(witness hill witness wall)

For several years now, I have had the idea of working on the theme of 'Sakshi Gudda', the pillars of earth left untouched for measuring the quantity of soil excavated in an earthwork. My interest was in these pillars of earth left behind with the vegetation on the top, their sculptural presence, and of course their meaningful title.

The site that I located in the premises of the University of Agricultural Sciences, on the edge of the city of Bangalore, had more to offer than just land for a Sakshi Gudda excavation. Within its green cover was hidden a semi-circular wall, about 50 feet in length and 15 feet in height, in front of which was a circular pit of 30 feet diameter. It had been a target practice shooting range, which was now elevated to the status of a lovers den encouraged by the trees growing in it, nature here in a subversive role. The pitted wall had over time become a witness to the lovers, with graffiti etched all over it and the stepped shooting trench a silent pit of dry leaves. The approach to this hidden place, its silence heightened by the sound of squealing pigs from the nearby piggery, is also the dumping ground for building debris and garbage, both organic and non-degradable, burnt to ashes or remaining as layers of time.

My intervention acknowledges this landscape, making use of existing materials and visual signs. The entry to this site begins with a walk guided by a surface line leading to the debris. A narrow trench, dug through the burnt dumping ground slices it to reveal its layers, while at its deepest end, red earth flanks the sides. Gunny sacks filled with dry leaves define the exit. Descending into the shady pit, the wall presents itself like a screen, on which my own graffiti, a Kannada folk poem, is engraved: 'Who shall I think of when I rise at dawn, let me think for a moment of Mother Earth, giver of sesame and cumin.'

Sheela Gowda, February 2001

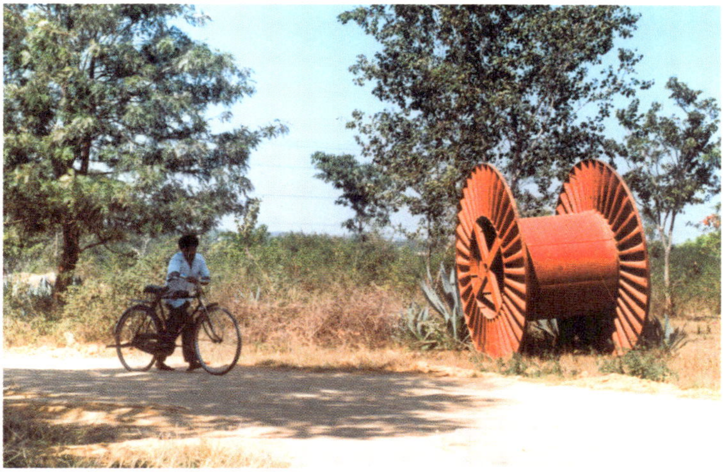

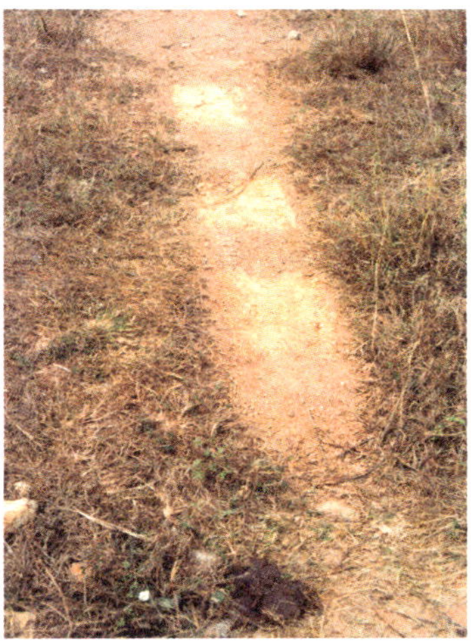

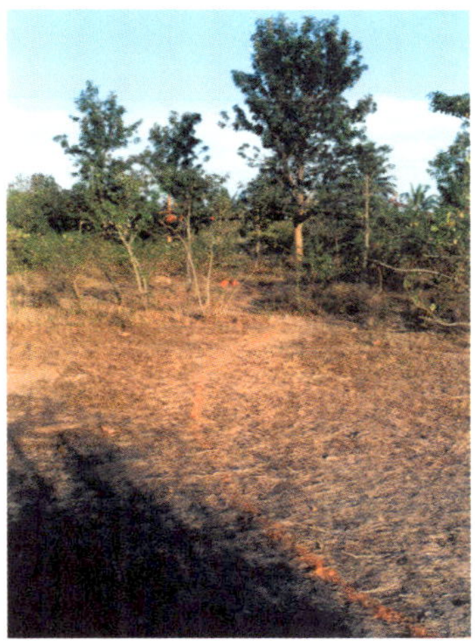

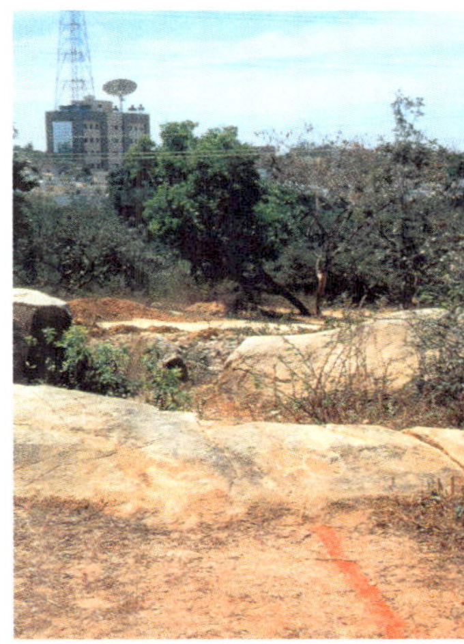

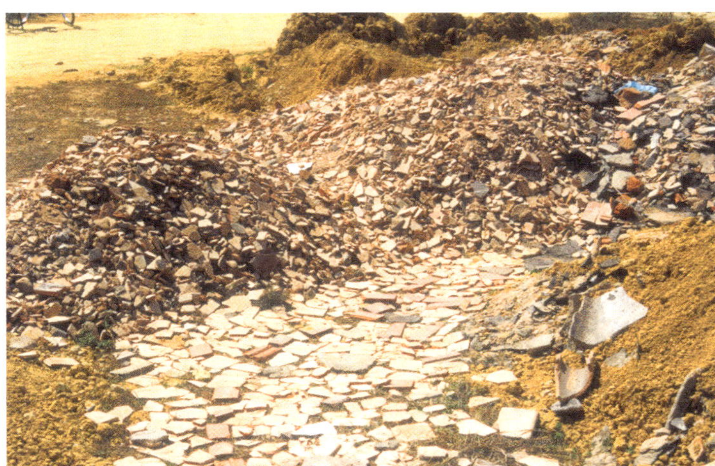

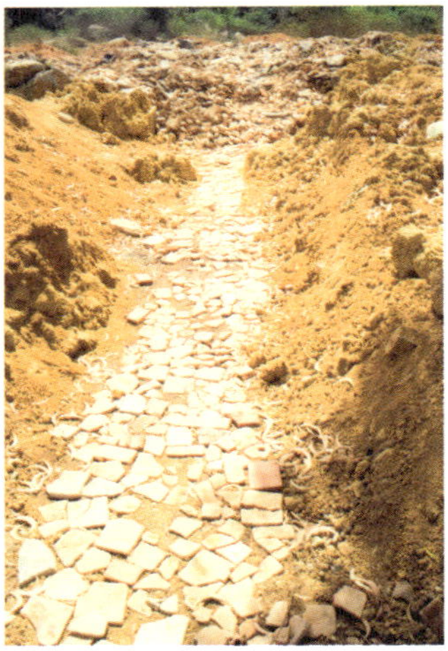

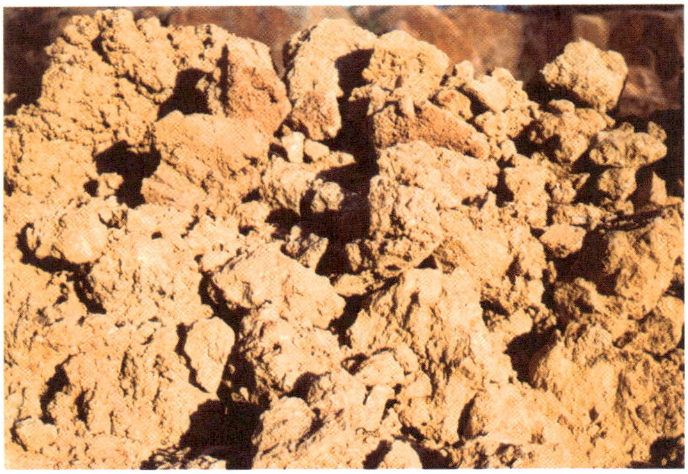

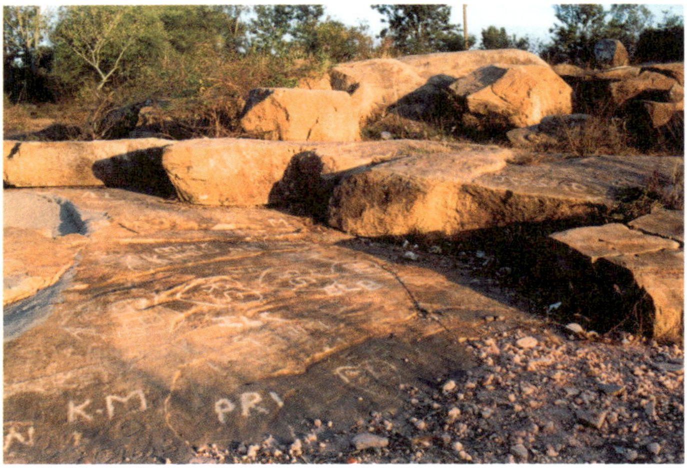
K-M
PRI

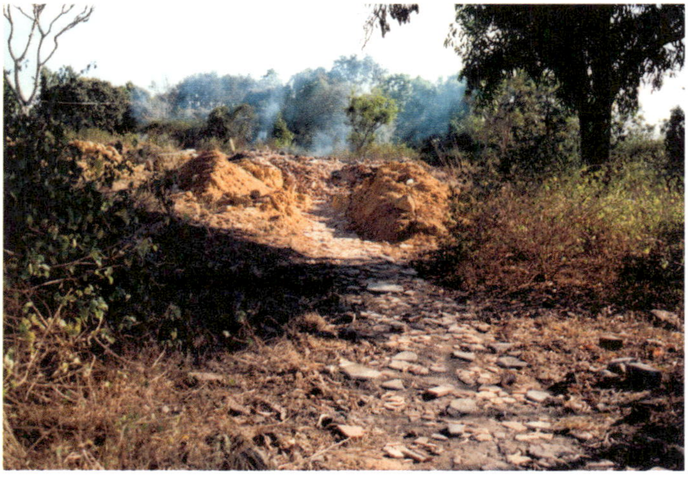

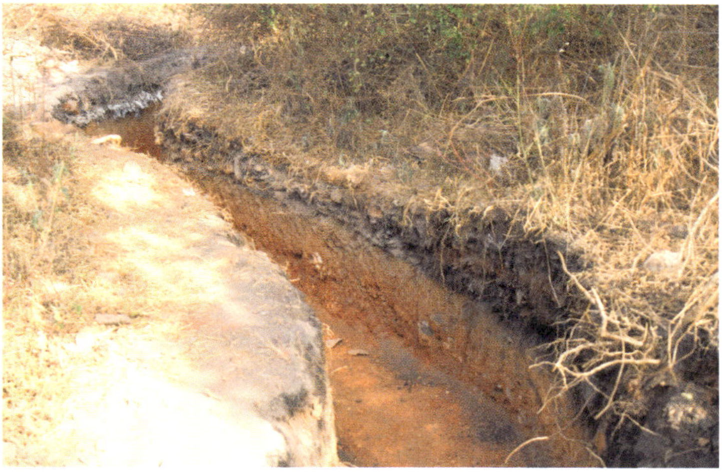
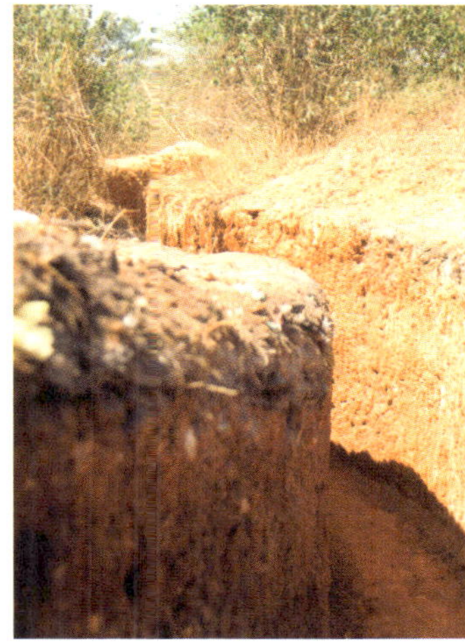
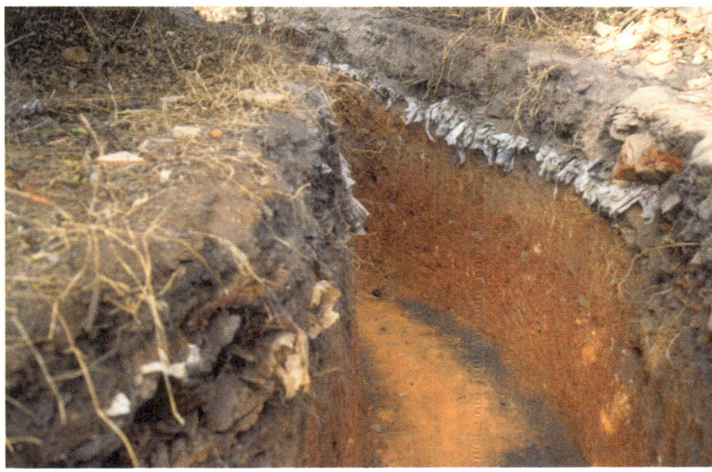
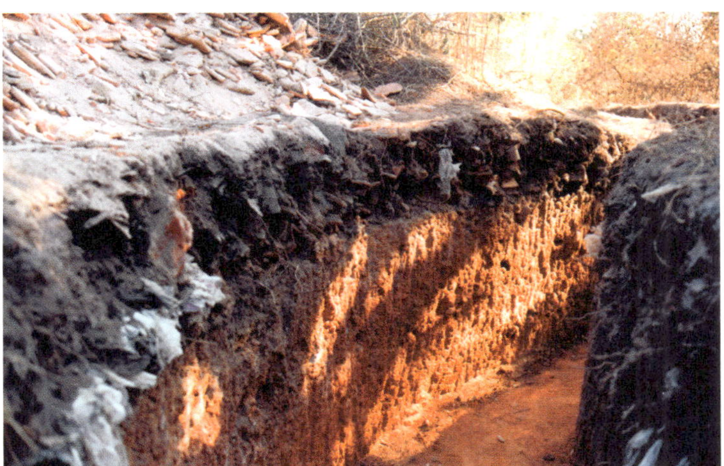
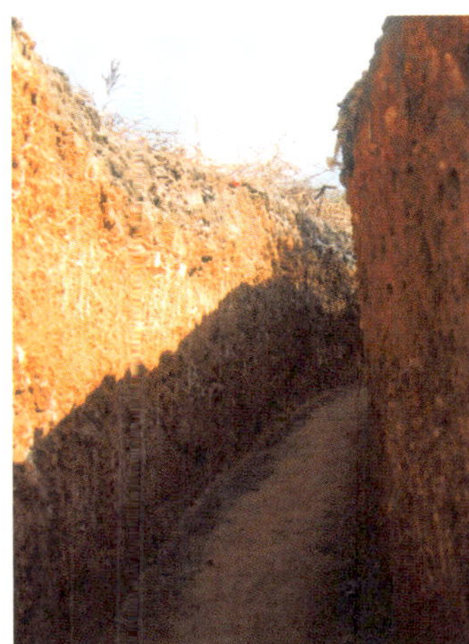

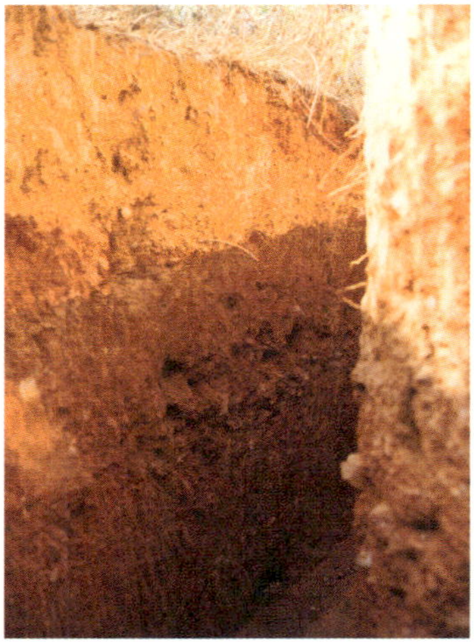
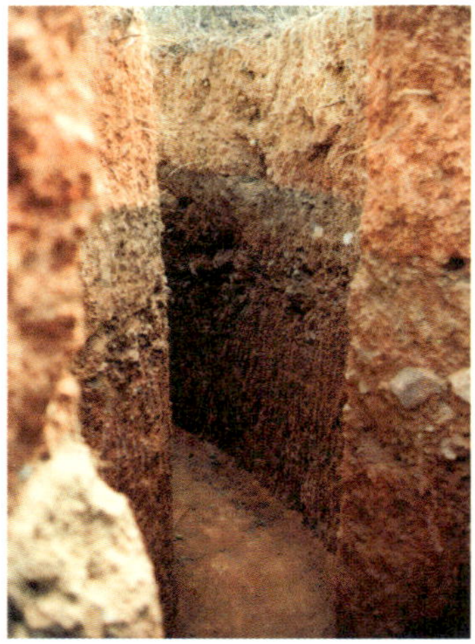
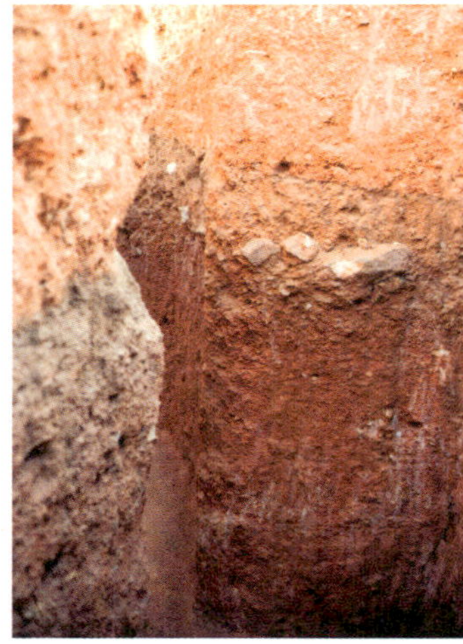
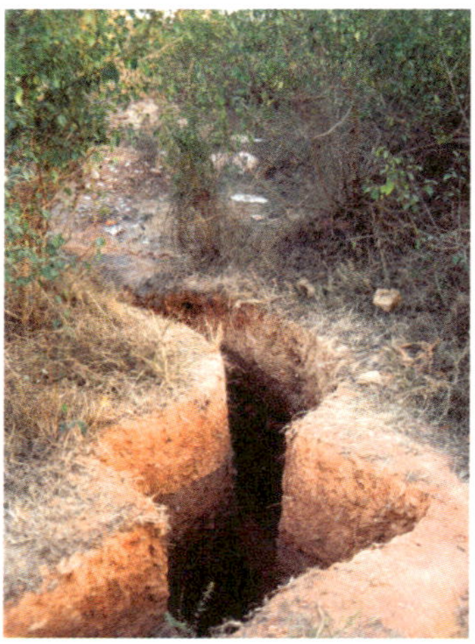
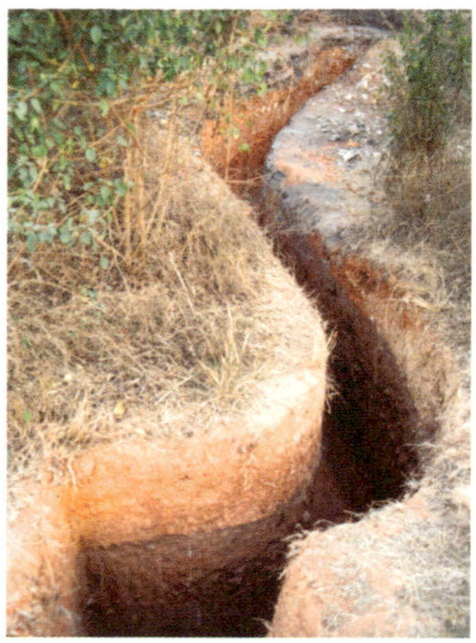
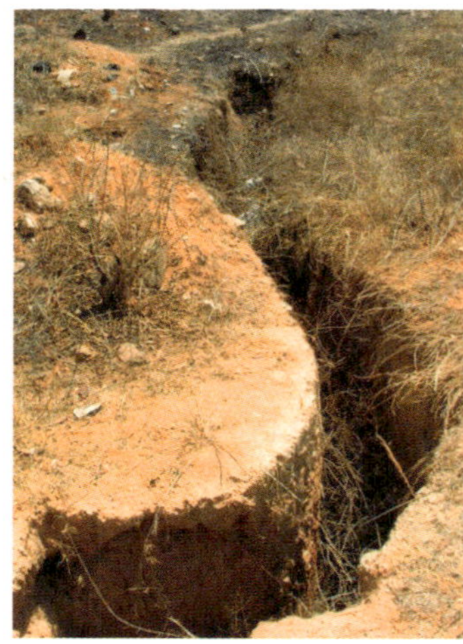
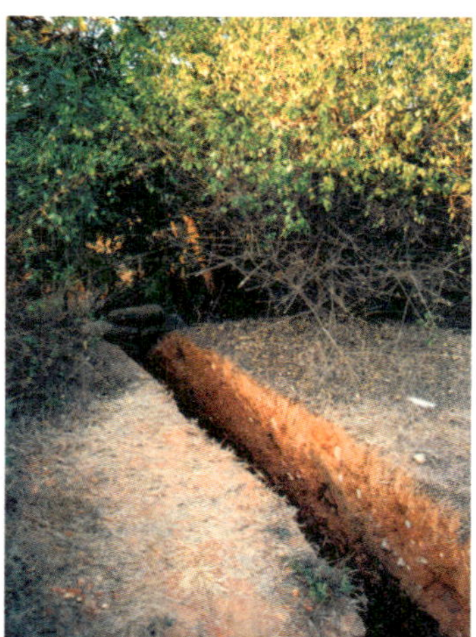
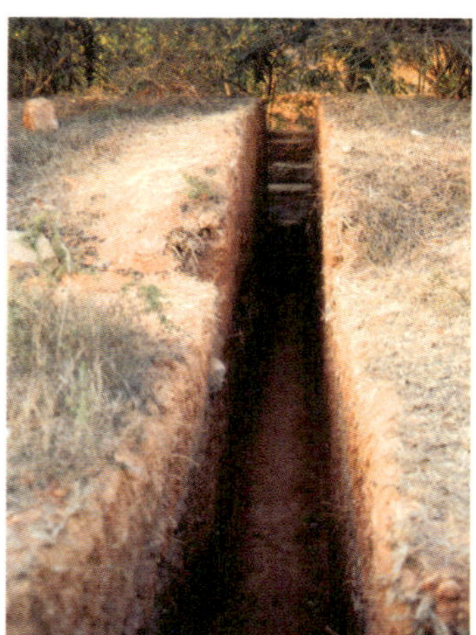
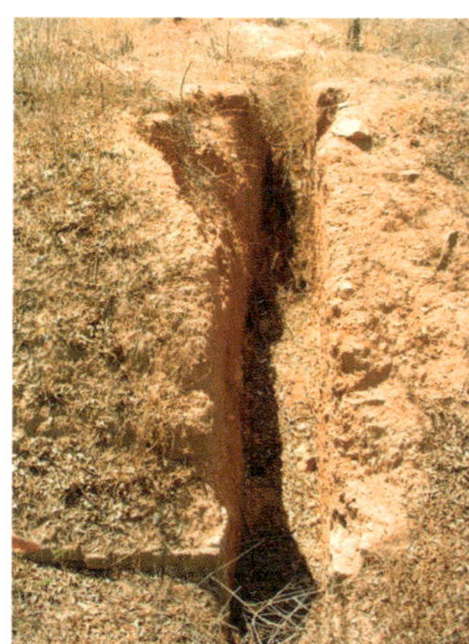

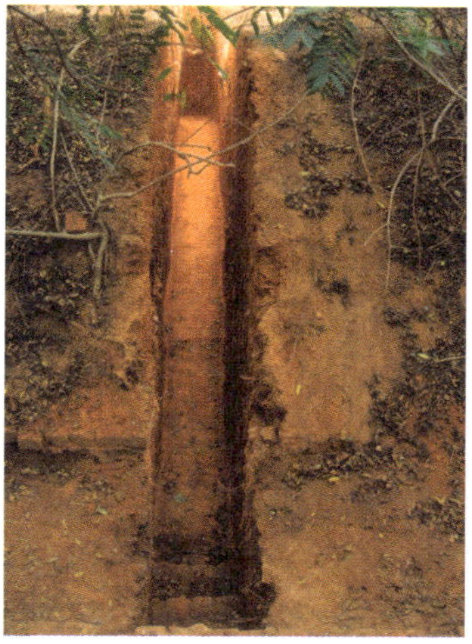

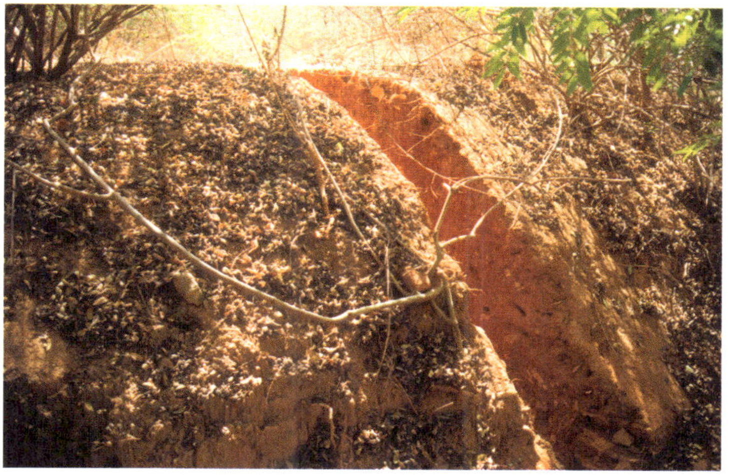

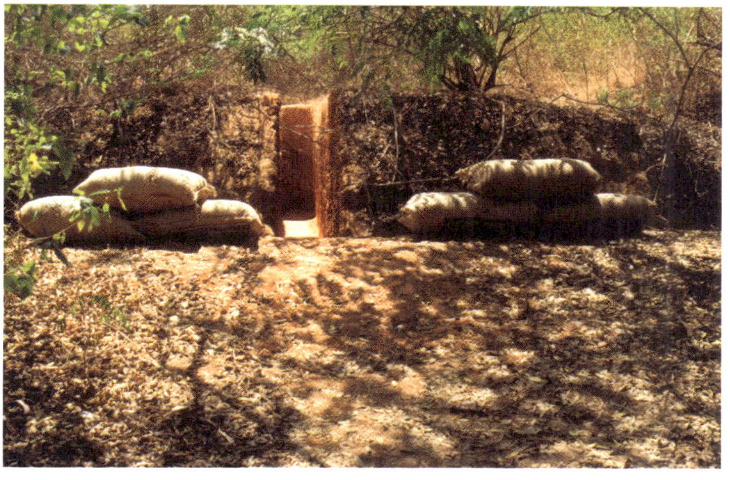

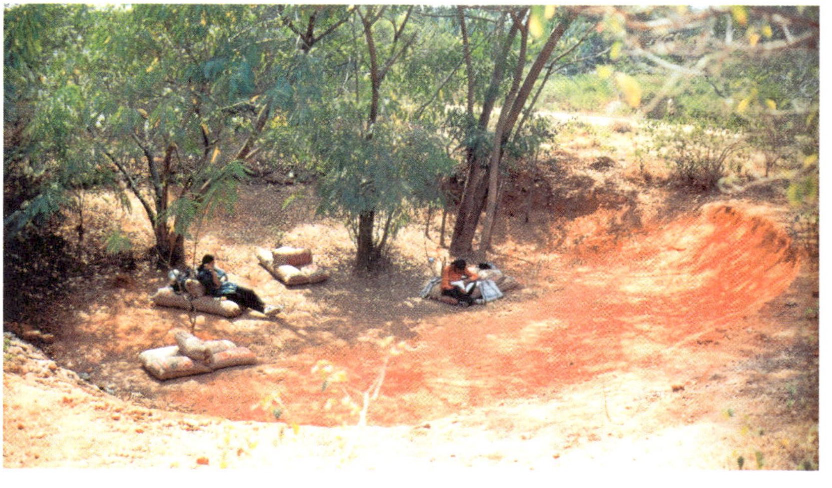

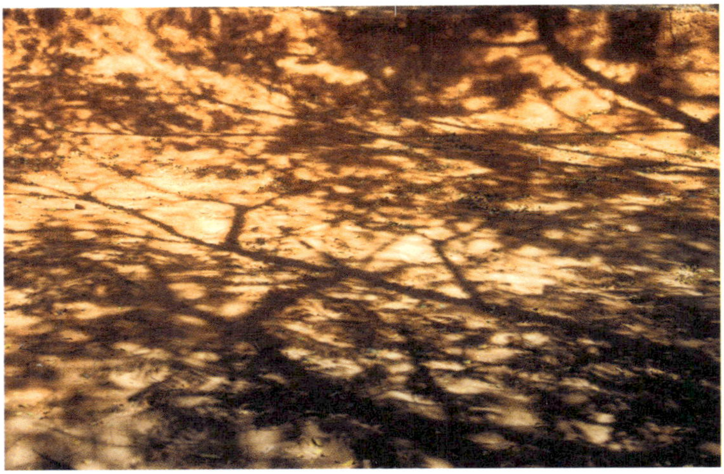

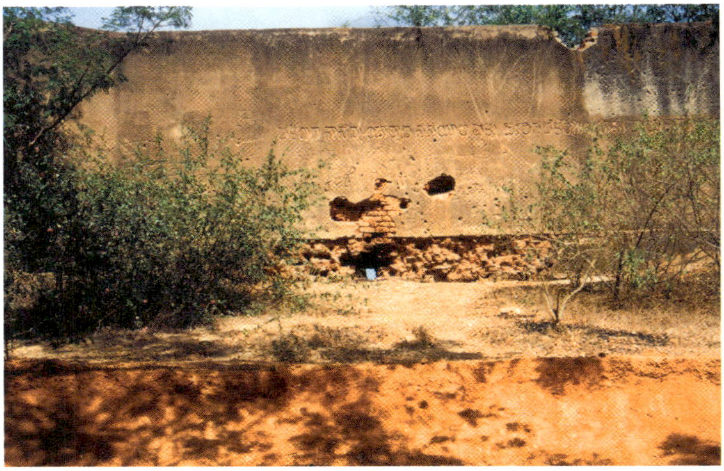

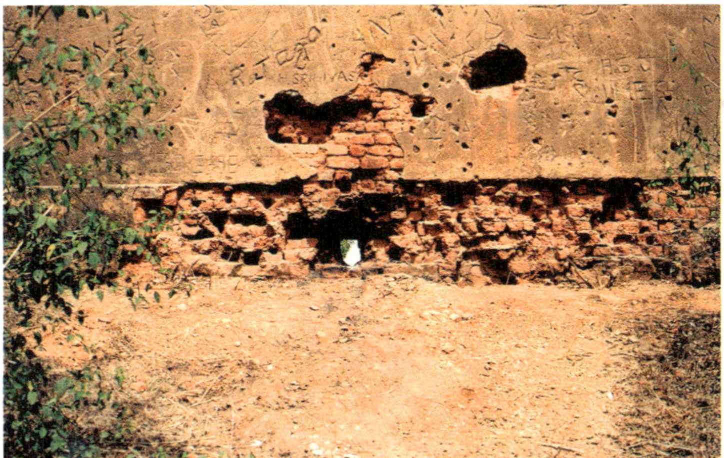

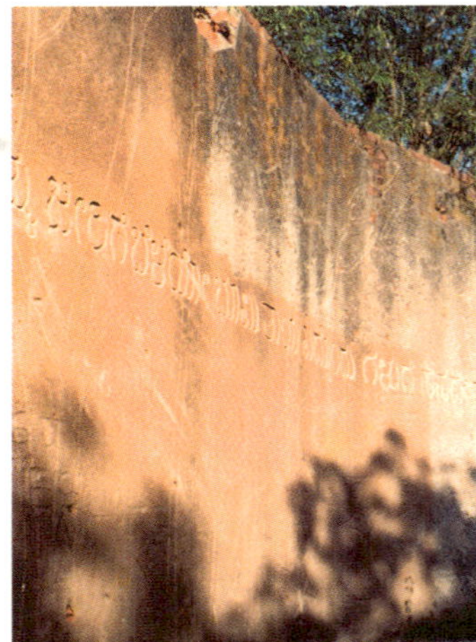

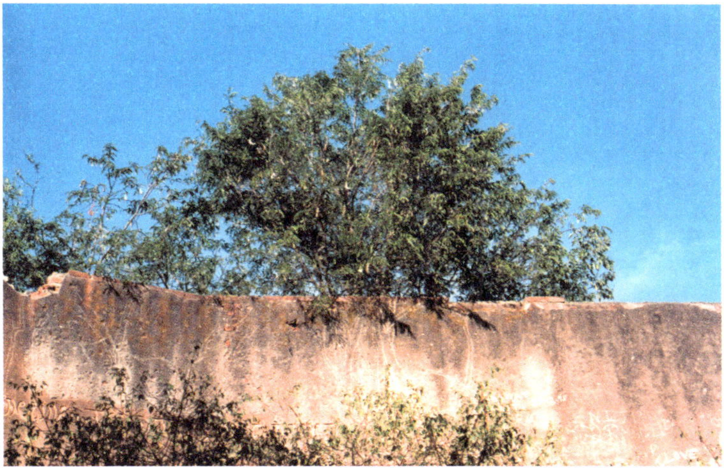

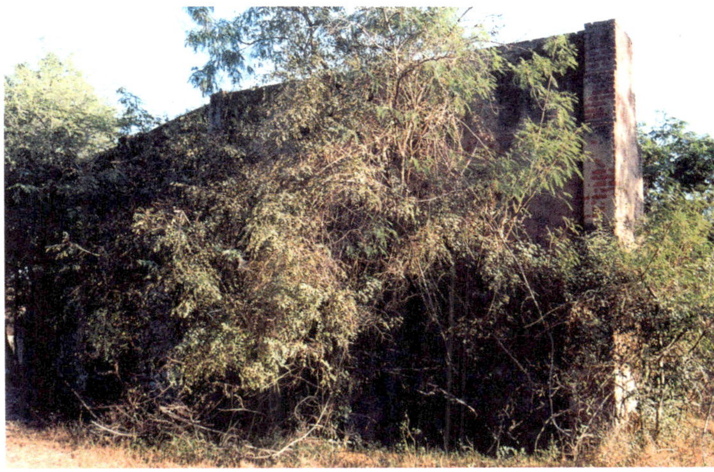

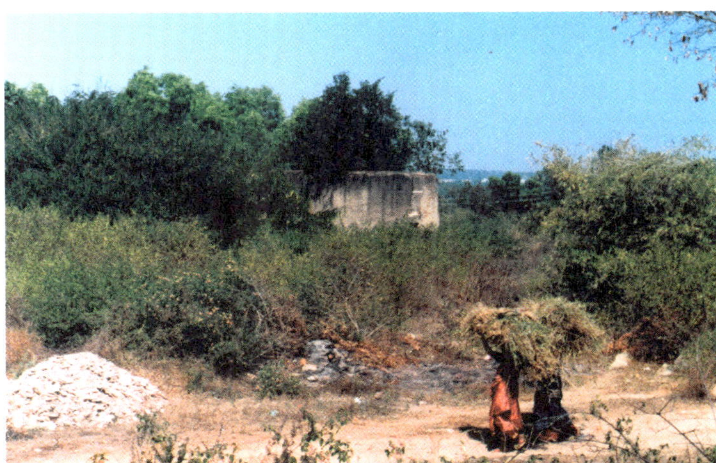

STEPHEN MORTON

THE SANTHAL FAMILY AND THE INVENTION OF A SUBALTERN COUNTERPUBLIC

In "Pterodactyl, Puran Sahay and Pirtha", a short story by the Bengali writer Mahasweta Devi, a tribal boy named Bikhia draws a pterodactyl on the wall of a cave in the fictional Indian village of Nagesia; this cave drawing subsequently takes on a life of its own in the consciousness of the tribal community as that community starts to die from starvation, water pollution and poverty. For the protagonist, Puran Sahay, an educated, middle-class, left-wing journalist who visits the village to write a report on the oppression of the aboriginal community in India, the plight of the tribal community is caused by state corruption, caste oppression, dispossession and famine. Yet, as Puran gradually realizes through a non-verbal exchange with Bikhia about the pterodactyl cave drawing, "[t]here are no words in [the tribals'] language to explain the daily experience of the tribal in India."[1] This non-verbal exchange involves a face-to-face encounter between Puran and Bikhia in which Puran tries to interpret Bikhia's eyes: "What do the eyes want to tell Puran? [...] There is no communication between eyes. Only a dusky waiting without end."[2] Despite Puran's attempts to decipher Bikhia's non-verbal message and the meaning of the pterodactyl, he ultimately realises that he cannot do this. For Bikhia's drawing of the pterodactyl stands as an uncommunicable sign of the way in which the tribal community understands its own history, its relationship to the land and its precarious future. And since this subaltern knowledge is encrypted in the cave drawing of the pterodactyl it cannot be translated in the secular terms of India's post-colonial narrative. In this sense, Bikhia stands as an example of what the postcolonial theorist Gayatri Spivak has called a guardian of the margin who protects the meaning of his culture by withholding it: "Having drawn that stone tablet Bikhia is the guardian of the new *myth*. He will protect it."[3]

Bikhia's protection of the pterodactyl's significance illustrates the crisis of representation that is often associated with the category of subalternity: a crisis of representation which is also staged in Ramkinkar Baij's 1938 public sculpture *Santhal Family*. Baij's sculpture raises crucial questions about existing structures of public representation in the subaltern sphere, before and after India's independence. The crisis of representation associated with the category of subalternity has sometimes been described in terms of the conflation of the aesthetic and political connotations of *representation*,[4] in which a political representative or proxy steps into the shoes of the subaltern and presents his or her own political rhetoric as the voice of those who are effectively denied a voice in the very event of aesthetic/political representation. But this crisis in representation can also be understood in terms of a failure of communication, in which the cultural and political practices of the disenfranchised fail to be recognised as sovereign speech acts in the dominant public sphere. That is to say, the cultural and political practices of the subaltern do not carry the necessary illocutionary force and social authority to be recognised as speech acts in the dominant public sphere. This is not to suggest, however, that such cultural practices have no political or rhetorical significance. Indeed, the cave drawing of the pterodactyl in Mahasweta Devi's short story gestures towards a subaltern counterpublic, which questions and challenges the social and political grounds

---

1 Devi, M. 1995. 'Pterodactyl, Puran Sahay and Pirtha' in G.C. Spivak (trans.) *Imaginary Maps: Three Stories*. London and New York: Routledge, p. 118.

2 Ibid., p. 157.

3 Ibid., p. 193.

4 See Spivak, G.C. 1988. 'Can the Subaltern Speak?' in C. Nelson and L. Grossberg (eds.) *Marxism and the Interpretation of Culture*. Basingstoke: Macmillan Education, pp. 271-313.

upon which subaltern constituencies are defined as subaltern. In this reading, Bikhia's failure to communicate the meaning of the pterodactyl and the plight of the tribals to the journalist Puran Sahay is a sign that Bikhia is a native informant, who guards or protects a marginalised tribal culture against misrepresentation and proscription in the dominant public sphere, which the journalist Puran Sahay represents.

To many of the South Asian Subaltern Studies historians, such as Ranajit Guha and Dipesh Chakrabarty, the subaltern is a "name for the general attribute of subordination in South Asian society whether this is expressed in terms of class, caste, age, gender and office or in any other way."[5] Crucially, the Subaltern Studies historians sought to emphasise how the concept of the subaltern signified the social and demographic difference between the elite and the rest of the population in South Asia. As Ranajit Guha argues, what elite historiography ignores is "the politics of the people", or "the domain of Indian politics in which the principal actors were [...] the subaltern masses and groups constituting the mass of the labouring population and the intermediate strata in town and country – that is, the people."[6] This is not to suggest that the category of the subaltern is synonymous with the people. Gayatri Spivak has argued in "Scattered Speculations on the Subaltern and the Popular," that, "Subaltern in the early Guha was the name of a space of difference [...] Although Guha seems to be saying that the words 'people' and 'subaltern' are interchangeable, I think this is not a substantive point for him." "Subalternity," Spivak contends, is rather "a position without identity."[7]

Spivak has tried to clarify her widely misunderstood assertion that "the subaltern cannot speak" by distinguishing between different kinds of utterance. In an interview with Donna Landry and Gerald McLean, for instance, she argues that "'the subaltern cannot speak' [...] means that even when the subaltern makes an effort to the death to speak, she is not able to be heard, and speaking and hearing complete the speech act."[8] In this interview, Spivak refers specifically to the way in which the particular circumstances of the young, middle class, Indian woman, Bhubaneswari Bhaduri's death fail to register as a speech act. Yet in Spivak's reading of Bhubaneswari Bhaduri's death it is clear that Bhaduri codified her death as an embodied act of writing. Spivak explains how Bhubaneswari Bhaduri was "a member of the many groups involved in the armed struggle for Indian independence" and that she had been "entrusted with a political assassination."[9] In Spivak's account, it was because Bhubaneswari Bhaduri was "unable to confront the task" of political assassination that "she killed herself." Spivak interprets the circumstances of Bhubaneswari's death as an example of *sati*-suicide, in which Bhubaneswari "perhaps rewrote the social text of *sati*-suicide in an interventionist way."[10] By doing so, Spivak reads Bhubaneswari's death as a sacrificial act that is perhaps consistent with certain readings of ancient Hindu scriptures, which define widow self-immolation as an exceptional and exemplary act of wifely devotion to a widow's dead husband. In Spivak's argument, Bhubaneswari's interventionist rewriting of 'the social text of *sati*-suicide' cryptically inscribed her singular predicament as a woman who supported the nationalist cause yet could not carry out the assassin's mission that had been assigned to her. Since Bhubaneswari was menstruating at the time of her death, however, Spivak argues that her suicide was not simply a pre-emptive response to the familial shame associated with an illegitimate pregnancy, as had been suggested by the authorities and by Bhubaneswari's family at the time of her death. As a consequence, the singular circumstances of Bhubaneswari's death are not intelligible within the social codes of family honour and

5 Guha, R. 1982. 'Preface' in R. Guha (ed.) *Subaltern Studies No. 1 Writings on South Asian History and Society.* Delhi: Oxford University Press, p. vii.

6 Guha, R. 1982. 'Introduction' in R. Guha (ed.) *Subaltern Studies No. 1 Writings on South Asian History and Society.* Delhi: Oxford University Press, p. 4.

7 Spivak, G.C. 2005. 'Scattered Speculations on the Subaltern and the Popular' in *Postcolonial Studies: Culture, Politics, Economy,* 8(4), p. 476.

8 Spivak, G.C. 1996. *The Spivak Reader: Selected Works of Gayatri Chakravorty Spivak.* D. Landry and G. MacLean (eds.) London: Routledge, p. 287.

9 Spivak 1988, p. 307.

10 Ibid., p. 307.

patriarchal devotion. Instead, Spivak reads her suicide as *both* a sign of her commitment to the nationalist cause *and* a refusal to carry out an act of revolutionary terrorism. Yet it is precisely because this embodied act of rewriting cannot be understood as a speech act—or a sign of Bhubaneswari's agency—within the available public codes of female insurgency that Spivak argues that the gendered subaltern cannot speak.

Bhubaneswari Bhaduri's careful protection of her involvement with the armed independence struggle is significant because it articulates a knowledge and history, which she deliberately withheld from public discourse and representation. In this sense, Spivak's reading of Bhaduri's embodied act of writing which was illegible at the time, both to the state and to Bhaduri's family, prefigures the invention of a subaltern counterpublic. As Michael Warner and Nancy Fraser explain, a counterpublic is a subordinate social class or group that does not have the 'privilege' of 'public agency' afforded to the enfranchised, white European/North American citizens of the dominant, bourgeois public sphere. In both the dominant public sphere and counterpublic spheres, the public participate in private acts of reading in which they can "scrutinize, ask, reject, opine, decide, judge and so on."[11] But whereas these private acts of reading are recognised as forms of public agency in the dominant public sphere, the same is not true for counterpublics, whose voices are often foreclosed. For this reason, Nancy Fraser's description of 'counterpublics' as 'subaltern' seems appropriate if subaltern is understood as a discursive subject position from which a sovereign speech act is not recognised as a form of agency within the dominant public sphere of a particular nation-state.[12] This is not to suggest, however, that counterpublics are without agency because they are excluded from dominant structures of representation. As Fraser argues, "subaltern counterpublics have a dual character. On the one hand, they function as spaces of withdrawal and regroupment; on the other hand, they also function as bases and training grounds for agitational activities toward wider publics."[13] By engaging with these rhetorics of a counterpublic, one can begin to trace the articulation of histories, experiences and forms of agency, which are not recognised by dominant structures of political representation.

Ramkinkar Baij's focus on a dispossessed family from the Santhal tribe as the subject of one of his most pivotal sculptural works is significant because it challenges the visual language of public sculpture, which tends to commemorate significant figures in the *dominant* public sphere, such as politicians or nationalist leaders. This tendency of public sculpture to represent figures from the dominant public sphere, as well as the systematic exclusion of the Santhali people from the dominant public sphere in West Bengal are further explored in Mahasweta Devi's short story "Statue". In this story, Devi raises questions about the significance of a public sculpture that commemorates the forgotten freedom fighter Dindayal Thakur; about the reputation of Dindayal Thakur among the village population; and more specifically about which public the statue is intended to address. As the narrator asserts:

> The decision to raise a bronze statue of Dindayal Thakur, the Freedom Fighter, in Chhatim Village, and to dedicate-unveil it with enough pomp and circumstance and soon, was taken at Calcutta Secretariat, and the announcement appeared in every newspaper. Naturally, the people of Chhatim village didn't know this. The village is *far from the madding crowd*, situated on the outskirts of a state forest area. Soil type *laterite*. Low-yielding. So this soil can't rear and raise a large farming population. The population of Chhatim and seven similar villages is less than three thousand all told. Government-quota Scheduled Tribes—for example, Santhal-Munda-Bhumij—and similarly Scheduled Castes—for example Bhunya-Harhi-Muchi-Shunri-Bauri—this is the popula-

11 Warner, M. 2002. *Publics and Counterpublics*. New York: Zones Books, p.123.

12 *Fraser*, N. 1992. 'Rethinking the Public Sphere: A Contribution to the Critique of Actually Existing Democracy' in Craig Calhoun (ed.) *Habermas and the Public Sphere*. Cambridge, Mass.: MIT Press, pp.123-5.

13 Ibid., p. 124.

> tion. There are not thirty literate persons in the eight villages. The literate are as occupied with filling their bellies as the illiterate. Nobody takes or reads a paper. The nearest police station is eleven miles away. The district town is seven miles away.[14]

In this quoted passage, Devi's narrator clearly highlights the dichotomy between the dominant public sphere, represented by the Calcutta Secretariat and the newspapers on the one hand, and the largely illiterate population of Chhatim village on the other. The narrator's suggestion that the public ignorance of the largely illiterate village population about the Calcutta Secretariat's 'decision to raise a bronze statue of Dindayal Thakur [...] in Chhatim Village' is natural foregrounds the way in which the exclusion of the village population from participation in the dominant public sphere is both systematic and naturalised. In so doing, the voice of Devi's narrator offers a commentary on the social structure of village life in West Bengal, and the limitations of public political representation after national independence. Not only are the villagers completely oblivious of the government's plan to erect a statue to the Freedom Fighter Dindayal Thakur, they "have almost forgotten that Chhatim village ever had anything to do with Dindayal Thakur."[15] Instead, as the narrator explains, the villagers' everyday lives are marked by poverty, the monotony of manual agricultural labour and an absence of social infrastructure:

> Their days pass in the difficult struggle of share-cropping rice in *laterite* soil, in the casual labour of *felling* sal trees in forest areas, and as field hands now and then in the fields of Madan Khan's son Sadan Khan. In their gloomy and isolated destitute village there are no services. No *health centre* nearby, no well with water in the village, not even a market, a roadway. You wouldn't know to look at the village that there was an arrogant highway just seven miles away. Kharagpur railway station is forty miles away. Undulating land all around, low hills, forests of dwarf sal, unrelieved poverty. There's a market on Mondays and Fridays at four miles distance. A market of salt and pepper, rice and coarse cloth, village-weave towels, eczema ointment and toothache medicine, plastic toys, oil-fried samosas, and fried molasses candy.[16]

To the impoverished, illiterate and disenfranchised people of Chhatim village in Mahasweta Devi's "Statue", national independence—signified by the local government's decision to commission a statue of Dindayal Thakur—makes no difference. It does not address the harsh material reality of their everyday lives. By contrast, Ramkinkar Baij's sculpture would seem to highlight the emergence of what Walter Benjamin called the tradition of the oppressed in his 1940 essay "Thesis on the Concept of History". For if Baij's *Santhal Family* foreshadows India's emergent postcolonial modernity, its sculptural depiction of the Santhal family foregrounds the plight of subaltern groups who are excluded from the national body politic. At first glance, the sculpture could be seen to situate the Santhali family as a synecdoche for the emergent postcolonial Indian nation. In this reading, the sculpture and the family it depicts can be taken to represent the nation in a local vernacular style. Yet the very idea that works of art from the postcolonial world operate as forms of national allegory, as the American cultural critic Fredric Jameson once argued of Third World literary texts, has been challenged by the Indian Marxist critic Aijaz Ahmad on the grounds that it elides the complexity of postcolonial artworks by reducing the work of art to a mimetic expression of the political. Moreover, the systematic exclusion of tribal groups such as the Santhal from dominant public structures of political representation in colonial and postcolonial India raises important questions about the political significance of this public sculpture. Geeta Kapur has situated Ramkinkar Baij's *Santhal Family* in relation to a radical nationalist history that includes figures such as

14 Devi, M. 1998. *Old Women: Statue and The Fairy Tale of Mohanpur.* G. C. Spivak (trans.) Calcutta: Seagull, p. 1.
15 Ibid., p. 4.
16 Ibid., p. 4.

the *dalit* jurist, Ambedkar, and Gandhi's attempt to constitute and deconstruct "the 'national' via (among other symbols) the oppressed figure of the untouchable."[17] Kapur's claim that Baij's *Santhal Family* is a "daring form" that assumes a "tribal persona with a radical affect" attributes an important political significance to this representation of the Santhal. Certainly, as Kapur goes on to argue, the "postcubist expressionism" of the subaltern bodies in *Santhal Family* can be seen to foreshadow "a dialectics of the modern and primitive/subaltern" in the work of subsequent artists, such as the sculptor, K.P. Krishnakumar.[18] And this view of Ramkinkar as a rural artist who invented a sculptural idiom that was capable of registering the singularity of India's postcolonial modernity is echoed by Tapati Guha-Thakurta:

> [The] rustic image of Ramkinkar [...] was integral to his self-positioning in a markedly rural habitat, at one with the natural elements and the toiling world of peasants and tribals, even as his formal language opened itself to abstraction, cubism, and post-cubist expressionism. With Ramkinkar's work is seen to arrive the 'modern' history of sculpture in India: a late arrival, but one which finally broke the bounds of commissioned statutary and academic realism to explore a new modernist vocabulary and a new genre of elemental and enlarged form in cement and mortar. From a romantic, ethereal motif, the Santhal figure [...] erupted in Ramkinkar's sculptures as a restless, disquieting, primeval presence.[19]

Yet by framing the subaltern body within the emergent vocabulary of modernist sculptural forms in India, *Santhal Family* also raises questions about the position of the tribal in relation to the emergent postcolonial body politic. The problem with the 'radical affect' of Baij's sculpture is that it may eclipse the conflation of the aesthetic and political connotations of representation, and thereby efface the position of the artist as proxy who stands in for the subaltern group he represents.

It cannot be denied that Ramkinkar Baij's position both as an artist and as a low caste Hindu from rural West Bengal is distinct from that of the Santhal family he represents in this public sculpture. But in presenting a Santhal family as the subject of representation, the sculpture also draws attention to the singularity of the Santhali people's history and experience, which it withholds from public representation. Like the cave drawing in Mahasweta Devi's story "Pterodactyl, Puran Sahay and Pirtha", the sculpture registers a history that cannot be easily decoded. In so doing, *Santhal Family* foregrounds the way in which subaltern histories cannot be accounted for within a Eurocentric paradigm of modern art history including public sculpture.

The South Asian historian Dipesh Chakrabarty has considered how the secular categories of historical causality and political agency are unable to account for the significance of the non-secular in acts of subaltern insurgency. Citing the example of the 1855 rebellion against the British in Bengal and Bihar by the Santhal tribal community, Chakrabarty considers the incommensurability between the ways in which historians such as Ranajit Guha have attempted to confer rational political consciousness and agency onto the Santhal's rebellion and the tribe's public statement recorded in the official colonial records that it was the Santhal god Thakur that made them rebel against the British.[20] In Chakrabarty's account, the divine or the supernatural are not adequate historical explanations for understanding why the Santhal rebelled according to the secular protocols of modern history: "The Santhal leaders' own understanding of the rebellion does not directly serve the historical cause of democracy or citizenship or socialism. It needs to be reinterpreted. Historians will grant the

17 Kapur, G. 2000. *When was Modernism? Essays on Contemporary Cultural Practice in India*. New Delhi: Tulika Books, p. 343.
18 Kapur, 2000. pp. 302, 343.
19 Guha-Thakurta, T. 2005. 'Lineages of the Modern in Indian Art', in K. Ganesh and U. Thakkar (eds.) *Culture and the Making of Identity in Contemporary India*. New Delhi, London: SAGE Publications, p. 95.
20 Chakrabarty, D. 2000. *Provincializing Europe: Postcolonial Thought and Historical Difference*. Princeton: Princeton University Press, p. 103.

supernatural a place in somebody else's belief system or ritual practices, but to ascribe it any real agency in historical events will go against the rules of evidence that gives historical discourse procedures for settling disputes about the past."[21] The Santhal's non-secular way of knowing historical events is not merely an object of historical study and explanation for modern historians, argues Chakrabarty, but it is also the condition of possibility for modern definitions of historicity and subjectivity: "Subaltern pasts thus act as a supplement to the historians' pasts. They are supplementary in a Derridean sense—they enable history, the discipline, to be what it is, and yet at the same time help to show what its limits are."[22]

If the Santhal chiefs' non-secular explanation of the 1855 rebellion is an example of what Chakrabarty terms a subaltern past, which questions the cultural, epistemological and above all secular assumptions that frame the interpretation of historical events and their public representation, Ramkinkar Baij's sculpture raises questions about the place of the subaltern as a subject of representation in postcolonial art history. For by visualising the plight of a subaltern group who have been excluded from the social and political life of the emergent postcolonial nation state in a style that articulates the aesthetic conventions of tribal art and European primitivism, *Santhal Family* supplements the emancipatory claims of elite nationalism with the imagined historical perspective of the Santhal, which Baij tried to evoke in sculptural form through the important and constant exchanges he had with the Santhal at Santiniketan. In so doing Ramkinkar Baij's *Santhal Family* gestures towards a subaltern counterpublic that remains to be invented.

21 Ibid., p. 104.
22 Ibid., p. 112.

MAHASWETA DEVI

STATUE

I

The decision to raise a bronze statue of Dindayal Thakur, the Freedom Fighter, in Chhatim Village, and to dedicate-unveil it with enough pomp and circumstance and soon, was taken at Calcutta Secretariat, and the announcement appeared in every newspaper. Naturally, the people of Chhatim village didn't know this. The village is *far from the madding crowd*, situated on the outskirts of a state forest area. Soil type *laterite*. Low-yielding. So this soil can't rear and raise a large farming population. The population of Chhatim and seven similar villages is less than three thousand all told. Government-quota Scheduled Tribes – for example, Santhal-Munda-Bhumij – and similarly Scheduled Castes – for example Bhunya-Harhi-Muchi-Shunri-Bauri – this is the population. There are not thirty literate persons in the eight villages. The literate are as occupied with filling their bellies as the illiterate. Nobody takes or reads a paper. The nearest police station is eleven miles away. The district town is seven miles away. There you have the necessary *paraphernalia* such as a *Block Development Office*, a *post office*, *Forest Office*, a *social worker training office*, a *school*, the *office of the Sub-Inspector of Schools*, a *health centre*, a grain-storage or agricultural loan realization centre etc.

The movie theatre is seasonal. Madan Khan of this town (now residing in the firmament) was a fidgety busybody kind of man. He was two-generations rich in the shellac business. Malicious people say that Madan's dad Badan Khan had received a disproportionate amount of money from the British for helping them capture terrorist Dinu Thakur, and had invested it in shellac farming forthwith. That money doubled in Madan's hands. For unknown reasons the post-'47 government figured Madan for a patriot and deluged him with *license-permits* as a reward for his service to the nation: licenses and permits for everything from liquor to bus service. Being rewarded for service to a nation he hadn't served, Madan realized the fruits of having garlanded the picture of Phalahari Baba with wreaths of mangoes-apples-bananas threaded together with a cobbler's needle. Then for some reason he becomes desirous of making himself immortal and, driven by said desire, he starts doing many things that benefit the townspeople. Still alive, he constructs a Madan *Memorial Boys' School*, a Madan Memorial Girls' Learning Centre, a Madan Khan football field, a six-bed Madan Khan hospital, etc., and inaugurates them by garlanding his own pictures himself. Finally, the culturalist boys of the town yell 'great national leader' at him and ask him for a Tagore Institute. Madan Khan agrees tentatively. But when the Hall is half-finished he says, 'My name absent from a hall built from my own money? It will be Madan-Tagore Hall.'

At this stage others enter the fray and explain the unreasonableness of putting the name 'Madan Khan' ahead of the name of Rabindranath Tagore. Madan says, 'My word is firm. Okay, let it be Tagore-Madan Hall.'

As soon as the tin roof goes on the Hall his view changes and he makes his instant decision known. 'There is plenty in the name of Tagore,' he says. 'I've decided the Hall will be in my name after all. And you know what? I have ordered my statue to be built. I will inaugurate it myself on Baisakh 25th of 1961, Tagore's centenary.'

However remote, the place is in West Bengal. The town's inhabitants are utterly dumbfounded. When they try to explain how it will be if a Madan Khan Hall is inaugurated by the living Madan Khan's own hand on Tagore's centenary, they get yelled at in turn and Madan says, 'If you go on like this, I'll make the Hall a paddy warehouse.' This wish of his is not fulfilled, however. For suddenly he is *transferred* to the firmament by *meningitis*. The said *Hall* is Tagore *Hall*. It is also the seasonal movie theatre. For when at harvest the farmer has money in his pocket, films are shown. At other times all the committee meetings, all the cultural functions like folk theatre, are held in that *Hall*.

When this is the state of the town, to hope that any one in Chhatim village would read the newspapers or know the news was unreal. A vain hope, like seeing *motion* in a Bengali *motion picture*. So Chhatim dwellers don't get to know that a statue of Dindayal Thakur, of the vanished Thakur clan, is about to be established and inaugurated.

At the moment the Thakur compound in Chhatim village is government property. The reason is Dindayal. In 1924, Dindayal was caught, imprisoned, tortured, and finally killed on the gallows for the attempted robbery and looting of a train. Consequently, the police subjected his parents, brothers and sisters to unspeakable harassment and confiscated their home and land. The people of Chhatim have no idea that the father-in-law of that very sister of Dindayal who was two years old at the time of his death is getting a monthly allowance from the state as his only living relative.

In fact, Chhatimites have almost forgotten that Chhatim village ever had anything to do with Dindayal Thakur. Their days pass in the difficult struggle of sharecropping rice in *laterite* soil, in the casual labour of *felling* sal trees in forest areas, and as field hands now and then in the fields of Madan Khan's son Sadan Khan. In their gloomy and isolated destitute village there are no services. No *health centre* nearby, no well with water in the village, not even a market, a roadway. You wouldn't know to look at the village that there was an arrogant highway just seven miles away. Kharagpur railway station is forty miles away. Undulating land all around, low hills, forests of dwarf sal, unrelieved poverty. There's a market Mondays and Fridays at four miles distance. A market of salt and pepper, rice and coarse cloth, village-weave towels, eczema ointment and toothache medicine, plastic toys, oil-fried samosas, and fried molasses candy.

If an old man has cataracts in a village like Chhatim, or if a man in late middle age gets short-sighted, they come to the market. Tufan Mollah, with nickel-framed wire-rims of his own manufacture on his nose, makes them for others for four rupees. Suren Hati removes cataracts with lotus thorns or hedgehog spines. Sometimes government functionaries come to market and shout out speeches about family planning on the megaphone and distribute free and official *literature* on the aforementioned topic in Bengali, in Hindi, in English. The illiterate marketeers rush for the books and the papers. Sell the stuff off to the grocer. If they find a picture they stick it on the wall of their home. Their idea is that the picture of the official happy family with father-mother-son-and-daughter is actually a picture of the former prime minister of India, her husband, and children. This shows how much in the dark they are. They don't even know that lady's *family-structure*, so ignorant.

Not everyone in Chhatim village knows that Dindayal Thakur was actually a freedom fighter. Yes, the Thakur family seat is here. There's a well in the grounds, with water in March and April. But noone takes that water. Impenetrable jungle all around. There's a python there. It's eaten a few goats. No one kills the snake. Why? The Thakurs told the snake to guard their property when they left.

In fact, the people of Chhatim village have forgotten they were always poor. In many of their ever-dark souls the reason for the eternal darkness in their village has come to be the disaster in the Thakur household. The Thakurs departed and Dindayal hanged in 1924. But this event of fifty-four years ago lives in their mind as part of the other folk tales, as myth. There are different *versions*, of course.

There's the *version* of the old Santhal aboriginal boatman Dashu Soren: 'Many moons ago the Karnabati River flowed here. There was a Bhunya king here. The king had neither son nor daughter. And beggars did not take alms because the king was barren. So the king was sad. He said to his queen, come let's drown and die in the waters of the Karnabati. Husband and wife leave their kingdom and walk to die by drowning, but the road doesn't end. The queen says, Look. This must be a divine illusion. I see the river from the rooftop every day, bathe in the river on feast days and fast days, it doesn't seem so far! The king is also surprised. Suddenly they see an amazing goddess. Snake-ornaments on her body, snake-crown on her head, standing in air above ground. The king and queen immediately bow down. The goddess says, I am the snake-goddess Manosha. Don't kill yourselves, go back home. You'll have a son. Build a shrine to me here. Let everyone leave a dedicated pitcher for me on the last day of the month of Sraban, let all families worship me. And you must offer me a service everyday, keeping a Brahmin priest. The king says, Ma, a forest kingdom, a wild king. Where shall I get a Brahmin? Manosha says, send a man to the north in the morning. If you walk due north for three hours, you'll see a poor Brahmin sleeping under a banyan tree with his wife and children. His fate was bad so far, now by my grace his lot will change. Let the Brahmin live well and find his feet. Then give him as much land as he can walk in a day in your kingdom. His situation will improve and yours will get better rather than worse. Pay your respects to the Brahmin, he's not just any old Brahmin, he's from the Holy City of

Varanasi. Dindayal Thakur was a son of that Brahmin family. The Bhunyas have lost their kingdom and become a farm family, and the Thakurs have left their village.'

This folk tale is not supposed to come from a non-Hindu Aboriginal. But it was indeed Dasu Soren who told the story. Almost everything in his story is supernatural. From it a reasonable explanation for the sudden attention of the Calcutta powers-that-be toward Dindayal Thakur's bronze statue cannot be deduced.

Barber Ratan Das's *version* is as follows: 'Karnabati is long mud-choked. There is a sword and a charter given by someone in the Bhunya house. We have always seen Sadananda Bhunya as a well-to-do farmer. But there's nothing after the land *ceiling* fixed by the government. Now they too buy paddy four months a year. Yes, the Thakurs were their priests. Their house worshipped Manosha. When they left the village Sadananda's father Mahananda asked them to take the image, and this too I've heard from my father, that he wanted to make a monthly allowance to keep up the service. But Thakur's father said, what did I get serving your goddess? I'll say excuse me and leave here. Then Mahananda Bhunya said, Not a three-a-penny goddess, this is Ma Manosha. Men must live with snakes, you a Brahmin will offend her? And Thakur said, I'm her priest, yet the police enters my life, my son hanged, evicted from my land, the police touch the body of my women. Worse than this? Let it be. Let mother goddess send a snake and end my line. I have nothing more to do with you. You know what this was? A fight between priest and helper. No, that tiff ended right off. When Dindayal died, this Sadananda was eight. Sadananda is sixty-plus, you can't tell. He's eaten well, lived well. His body has that well-fed shine. Sadananda is a feisty type. But his son, Nabin, a good kid. We'll send him to the Panchayat. Chhatim is a bad-luck village. The state forgets that there's a dump called Chhatim. Our Nabin is in *Class Eight.* He goes to the district *town*, gives in our applications and pleas. That's how we got our seed-loan this year. He's trying to pull the paved road from the village all the way to the bus route. For our seven cursed godforsaken villages there'll be a *health centre* in Chhatim. A rice-loan, farm-loan *centre*, right here. A lot of cash. Work worth fifty-sixty-seventy thousand rupees. Good boy, he runs, he runs. I know it won't be. Our village will remain like this. I didn't see, my father didn't, my grandpa didn't see when the village was nice. The village declined when Thakur and Bhunya differed at the hanging of Dindayal Thakur? No no no. A–lways decline, sir. I run a barbershop on market days, I even go to Kharagpur, see some more village places, how the village of Temukhi did change! *MLA's* village. Member of the Legislative Assembly! But that *MLA* is an asshole, he doesn't look after us. If anyone says the village was nice, and it fell because of Dinu Thakur, it'll be Sadananda Bhunya. Why they broke, I cannot say. How small we were then?!'

Even Ratan Das's telling doesn't solve the mystery of the administration's sudden focus on Dindayal Thakur.

Sadananda Bhunya's *version* is *twisted* and full of humbug. Just what happens if you've the name 'Palm Lake' but not enough water to dip a mug in. He points at four adobe rooms, two silos, three plough-steers and a super-strained budget and says, 'Once my forefathers owned as far as you can see. You might know Mansingh's name, in his time my forefather helped the Minister, and the Minister gave him the title of king. Much much more. The sword's there, we hear the handle was gold-plated, we didn't see that. There's a charter, illegible. Of course we're kings, but now we're in the ditch, no use talking. My boy loses his temper. Says, so we were kings, we were kings, that's why such punishment. King of six acres and a single harvest! He's hot-blooded. A twisted mind. He ploughs with sharecroppers, my boy. Hasn't married yet. Says, no income, I'll increase expenses? The next one is normal. Doesn't work with his hands, has a wife and two children. Work? What work will he do, with a *Class V* education? Now he has our household goddess worshipped monthly, after the priests went we offer the daily milk-banana-oil lamp-flower ourselves, that youngest boy gets the monthly rites done by a priest he fetches from Patke village on his bicycle. The eldest son has no taste for this side of things. He is most pigheaded. He'll carry a low-caste corpse to the pyre. How does the younger son support himself? Why? Don't we have the Manosha fair? We get a cut on all the geese and goats sacrificed that day, the fair lasts a fortnight, there are earnings there too. Why are we so badly off today, although we were kings? Because of Dinu Thakur. We lived in style. The Thakurs were our priests, yes. But they, too, were given twenty acres of land. Now the Thakur house is dense jungle.

I have seen with my own eyes a lo–ng two-storey, four-roomed adobe house. The soil here turns to pumice when it dries with sun in it. It lasts and lasts. Drawn verandah, a row of rooms. Barns on the other side of the courtyard. Kitchen quarters, open tank, now all dry as dust. Huge paved well. Cowshed, and a fence all around the house. Flowergarden, a guava-papaya-custard apple orchard at the back, their own established god Radhagobinda, how their shrine-house did glow! Everything was to our credit. Did they keep that dignity? Everyone knows after all – there's even a book printed, price 12 annas, I myself sell it – everyone knows, Mother Manosha told my forefathers and had them brought to Chhatim. They were poor beggars. Did they pay mind? My pa said, Please my lord, I beg you my lord, and still they didn't take the god? Did they take their own Radhagobinda? Does a priest ever leave his god?' (When the story gets to here Sadananda is extremely troubled and wipes the back of his neck repeatedly.) 'Then Father went to Patke. New arrangements were made after penance with new priests, and begging Mother's forgiveness. In the goddess-clan Mother Manosha takes ferocious form. By her curse the Thakur family went to rack and ruin, and our farmhand also died of snake bite. And then look in the village – how the police harassed us. Harassment in every house, set heavy taxes per head, all but the Bhunyas hid in the forest in the end. Knowing that no cronies of Dinu Thakur were hanging around here, they brought elephants from the landowner of Patke and leveled their home. The state repossessed the land. The Thakurs told a python – Mother's familiar, of course – to guard the house. It's still there. Sometimes it leaves the grounds, catches a goat or hen, huge in size. A feud between my father and Dinu Thakur's? Not a thing. Not a thing, just bad talk from bad people. Did Dinu Thakur live in the village, that anyone would have any connections with him? Feud? Oh no. That hanging sentence of Thakur's son, the police brutality, that's why bad suspishes entered Dinu Thakur's father's mind. That his son was caught through Badan Khan from town and my father. If this was true, then my dad would have got as much cash as Badan Khan! All lies. Grown up son, why didn't you control him? Why should I speak of others? My eldest son Nobne also believes these words.'

Sadananda Bhunya's *version* gives us some information about Dindayal Thakur. Not everything.

Nabin Bhunya's version is very brief. 'Yes, Dindayal Thakur's a freedom martyr, I know, I've heard he was hanged trying to loot a train in Kharagpur in 1924. Perhaps it's written in some book somewhere. I don't know. We need a road. Now. Then the village is connected to the outside world. I foam at the mouth talking about this road. I've said that we don't need *labour*. The people of our seven villages will build the road at a quarter of the *labour charge*. The Santhal tribals go *often* to do piece *labour*. Dasu Soren's bunch know all about *road labour*. They'll give *labour*. The road is needed. Then we can take everything from the village outside, at speed. We also want a *health centre*. Even now a snakebite is Mother Manosha, cholera is Goddess Badam, and water-magic a fever remedy. The *health centre* is seven miles away. There are more villages behind our village. They also benefit if we get a *health centre* here. Not much, you know, just seventy thousand rupees will build a seven mile road, a *health centre*, I'll give the rooms. We can get a *primary school*. With government support we can dredge the tank cut by my forefathers in the thin stream of the Karnabati and make its water usable. Dindayal Thakur? Feud with our family? Of course. There was reason. But I can't say why what happened. No. Don't ask. Snake? In their lot? Hey, you can find cheetahs in winter, and no snakes? Told it to watch their place? Who knows? The ones who say it must've got it from the python. Our palace? Didn't you see? Huge palace, the king repairs spades, the prince thrashes kids. In our village, d'ye hear me, we first need a road. *School*. Studying. The boys can't even get to Patke because there' s incredible mud in the rainy season. Ev–erything will follow if there's a road.'

One understands from Nabin Bhunya's words that his enthusiasm is not for the past but for the present. He has little enthusiasm for the freedom martyr from the village and he is unwilling to open his mouth about the feud between his family and the Thakur family. His chief concern is how to make the government spend seventy thousand rupees, lift dead Chhatim village from archaic and twentieth-century hearsay and half-truths and join modern times by way of a road. *Health centre*, *school*, road–buses, bicycles, and open minivans will run. Nabin doesn't care for the past.

Nabin cares about one person from the past. This person is a decrepit old woman. The old woman sits in a single-room hut past the courtyard of the Bhunya-house. She looks like the Manosha-crone of myth. White hair, torn clothes, emaciated body. Only the eyes have something that tugs at your mind. Her room is quite large. There is a broad dais in it. Nabin comes to this room. For about ten years now. Before that he too threw stones at the old woman, called her witch and ran.

Then he found out that the old lady is not a witch. His aunt, his pishi. His father's sister. In some distant past this aunt *generated* unthinkable events as a result of looking at a bridegroom in her widow's white clothes from under a distant rain-tree. So she was marked as misfortune in the Bhunya household. Rather than kill her physically they kept her in a room raised on the yard's far side. For the wives of Pishi's two brothers, Nabin's father's two elder brothers' wives, said that their children would die by the breath of this inauspicious misfortune, this sister-in-law.

Pishi earns her keep. Even at seventy-eight years of age she binds kindling in creepers, drags it and puts it at the other edge of the yard. Nabin's mother or sister gives Pishi some rice-salt-oil-lentil at month's end, two saris yearly. At least that's what Nabin knows. It's Nabin who brings her a bit of hair oil or a loose-weave washcloth from the household provision. He looks out for her in his busy day. The family is fiercely angry at him. Nabin's mother says, behind her son's back, the witch poured ashes on the family and is now making my son a stranger.

These days they're getting an opportunity to show their rage. Because of his constant conflict with his father, Nabin moves about outside the house, and sleeps at the residence of another part-owner of the property. So the amount of rice and lentils decreases and becomes irregular now. Pishi makes no protest. Long ago, a long time back, she forgot to protest against others' behaviour towards herself. She has accepted hunger pangs as *chronic* and inalterable reality. She died, possibly, long ago. From earliest consciousness she remembers that she was at once unwanted and indispensable in the household. Her mother had children yearly, their family was enormous. The Sadananda who carries on the silent torture with his wife and younger son, was, how strange, raised in her arms from birth. Her mother had childbed fever. It seems unreal to think all this now. Does she belong to this house? If close kin, then why outcast? If not kin, then why is she in the house? If the decision is not to feed her, then why give? If one feels like feeding, why give such a small amount of rice? These are most complicated questions. She often weaves a net in her mind with the questions, is herself caught in the net and gives up.

Sometimes she seems very busy. *Necessity* is supposed to be the mother of *invention*. Pushed by that necessity she does a lot of work. In a corner of the room the floor is dug up to make a hearth. There she keeps a fire going. Burns wood and makes charcoal. She lights the charcoal and keeps the fire going. Two reasons. First reason is that a box of matches is for her a luxury beyond reach. She never gets money, so the idea of buying matches does not arise. If Nabin thinks of it he gives her matches or hair oil. But he thinks of it only sometimes. Doesn't think of it *regularly* and even then doesn't remember. She has understood, therefore, that it is more intelligent to keep the box of matches in a jar and keep the fire going. The second reason was that with her belly always empty or three-quarters empty, there is nothing left in her body. She likes the fire's warmth and for lack of blood feels chilled all the time. She sits by the fire even in Boishakh and Joishtho, the high summer months.

Nabin asks, 'Are you crazy?'

'Why? What have I done?'

'Such heat, so hot, and you're sitting by the fire?'

'Warmth?'

The word 'warmth' blossoms and falls like a distressed flower. Her eyes become the sinless stars of dawn and she looks very lovely for an escaping moment. Nabin feels an amazing empathy and attraction. 'A lot of warmth Pishi,' he says, 'you feel such cold because you have nothing in your body.'

Sometimes she can be seen wandering in the dense impenetrable jungle of the Thakur homestead. She can be seen means the python sees her. Yesterday's orchard is today's jungle. She brings a ripe nona-fruit, an olive, a myrobalan out of this dense overgrowth, driven by the impossible urge to continue living. Nabin knows that Pishi eats whatever she gets. Knowing this, various emotions arise in his breast. When I start earning I'll screw my Dad and take Pishi to *town*. I make no money, but will I never? I still eat my Father's food, I won't forever. Pishi has survived so desperately for so long, anyone else would have died. Won't she last a few years longer?

Sometimes she is seen wandering near the Manosha shrine. She solves her life's problems in various ways. Sometimes people leave milk and water in clay pots as thank offerings at the shrine. She collects the pots. For one reason alone. Once when she was driven out she was given a pot to cook in, a frying bowl. That pot and bowl vanished long ago. She solves her utensil problems by collecting pots this way. The pots are Manosha's, her own clan-goddess's. She never thinks of it. Nabin has promised to buy her pots and bowls when he gets a job.

Sometimes you see her, in the hot month of Choitra, in early evening, far from the village, plucking ripe branches of lentils at speed from someone else's field. For one reason alone, to solve the food problem.

She looks unearthly then. Thin frame, the winds of Choitra in her white hair, a rapt look in her eyes. That rapt look is seen often and Nabin worries. Pishi has borne injustice all her life, perhaps she is thinking of that, he thinks. In fact she doesn't think of the past. She, too, believes in the present, as does Nabin. She thinks with dream-rapt eyes, when she lies down at night with the lentil seeded and wrapped in her cloth, how slowly she'll eat them in the dark. In fact, all her thoughts are bellycentred. When she dreams, she dreams crude dreams. In her dream she wears a whole cloth and eats a full serving of rice in a bell-metal plate. Every day. Only rice. No lentils, no vegetables. Only rice.

She is the source of Dindayal's martyrdom in 1924, of the forced departure of the Thakur family, their feud with the Bhunya family, the arousal of new interest on the subject of Dindayal in 1978, all. She doesn't recall this. Just as she doesn't recall that her name was Brajadulali and once she was as diffident and blooming as a fully flowering fragrant and white kamini tree.

No one wanted information from her, but she alone can recount the unwritten account behind Dindayal's martyrdom.

Once in a great while she leaves behind the clamour of the Manosha-fair and goes to the abandoned riverbed, on the last day of the rainy month of Sraban, when the sky casts a kohl-blue shadow, and in the gaps of the white bonshiuli herb, on the surface of the river bed, one sees cheerful clusters of the yellow kadamba. She can't say why she goes. She sits on a flat stone. Then she doesn't look human. She doesn't remember the stories she heard from her father in her childhood. 'Once a—ll this was ours. Year round there was deep water in the Karnabati then.' The pollen of the kadam falls on her thin body. She thinks and thinks. Then she forgets the past glory of the Bhunya family and thinks, 'Ripe kadam tastes good. I'll crush some and take it. I'll put some salt in the tart kadam and eat it with rice.'

She hasn't known, no one told her at first, that a statue of Dindayal Thakur was about to be established in Chhatim village.

II

The main motive force behind the renewed attention of the Administration to the martyred Dindayal Thakur fifty-four years after his hanging was a bunch of mice and a light-hearted young jail clerk with too much time on his hands; and researchers' interest in preparing a summary of armed revolutionary struggles against the British in the twentieth century. The object was to win a doctorate.

A researcher went to write a doctoral thesis on the neglected events of the history of the armed struggles in Midnapore district. And he pored over jail records at the same time. His cousin, a jail clerk, discovered that mice were gnawing through a lot of 1920-24 records. At his cousin's request he copied whatever he could rescue from those files.

And so he discovered that the martyr Dindayal Thakur was the inhabitant of Chhatim village in Midnapore. He even discovered a long letter written by Dindayal just before his hanging. All the expected stuff such as giving blood to the Motherland—quotations from Nazrul's poems—was to be found in the letter. But the most surprising thing was that, halfway to the end, nation, terrorism, and lines from the *Gita* disappear. After a page and a half of this stuff, the remaining six-and-a-half pages are an avowal of love to the 'Dulali' to whom this letter was written. For example—'If I'd known, if I could have found the courage, I would have gone away with you. You were too afraid, Dulali. You denied everything. Today I'm on my way to respond to the call of the other shore, if only I could take you along.

'Who says life ends at widowhood? Who says there can be no marriage between a Bhunya and a Thakur? Dulali, Dulali, I would have regretted nothing if I could have seen you once, I have not appealed and will not appeal my impending sentence of death by hanging. But at the other end I will wait for you, until we meet again.'

Then it is written, 'You and I wanted nothing more than each other. Even that this heartless society will not allow. I call you, Dulali! Dulali! Can you hear me?

'One day, sitting on a stone on the Karnabati river bed, you had said, Dinuda, let's take poison. But we hadn't the courage. We didn't do it because both families would have been shamed. Today I ask, why didn't we? Will they give you this letter? Who knows? Dulali ... now it seems to me that I always loved you, was it because I didn't know my own heart that I gave or received so much pain?'

Two things are obvious from the letter. Loving 'Dulali', Dindayal Thakur had faced some ferocious opposition from rural society, and he loved this woman. It seems as if unrequited love and participation in revolutionary activities were interdependent.

The researcher becomes highly interested. He looks at official reports on the subject of Dindayal.

The defendant is twenty-four, height five foot eleven, skin light, hair coppery and cut short. Brahman, wears the sacred thread. Knows some English, Bengali well. Exceedingly reticent, and it hadn't been possible to make him speak at the police precinct, in the lockup, and at the Central Police Station in Lalbazar, Calcutta.

In December 1924, at seven in the evening, Dindayal Thakur, Ramani Santra, and Sardeb Panda stopped the No. 313 'up' train not too far from Kharagpur (the train was carrying postal money) and entered the guard's room saying Bande Mataram. Dindayal said, 'We're taking money for Mother India's work. Money that a foreign government has taken from us by exploitation, don't stop us.'

As a result of this brief announcement (1) the train-robbers could be *categorized* as *terrorists*; (2) some time passes; (3) the armed guards get time to cock their rifles; (4) consequently the armed guards and the train guard are wounded by Dindayal's bullets. And now disaster strikes. Four white officers of a Calcutta merchant company were travelling on this very train. They had guns, for they were going for a shoot in Orissa. They entered the stage armed and helped *arrest* the three revolutionaries. The most significant thing to happen was that all three resisted tooth and nail and, before anyone knew what's what, Dindayal attempted to shoot himself in the temple with his revolver. One of the white men hit his arm and the bullet lodged in his ribs. He was taken wounded to Kharagpur hospital, the other two to Midnapore Jail. Finally, Dindayal had to be taken to Calcutta. First his bullet wound healed there. Then three officers with a reputation for extracting confessions from revolutionaries failed to get a word out of Dindayal. But the other two were younger, information was pressed out of them with the usual physical pokes, needle pricks, trampling with hobnailed boots, etc. Dindayal Thakur was not always a revolutionary. He was recruited in August 1924. Between August and December 3rd he had looted two Post Offices in the area and snatched the gun of a treasury guard. He's the son of apolitical Chhatim village. There follows a brief trial. There was evidence of the *terrorist* movement in Bengal through Gopinath Shaha's assassination attempt on a white man, mistakenly taking him for Charles Tegart, Commissioner of Calcutta Police. Tegart now forbade spreading news of the Dindayal event too widely. He said one event would *trigger* another. *Try and hang him as an ordinary criminal*. Since there was an order to *'hang'* before 'trying', the Judge had it easy. Dindayal was captured on the 9th and hanged on the 30th. He is highly relieved to hear a death sentence and is hanged in the usual fearless way of the terrorists. *Funeral by police*. After Dindayal is hanged, the police come to Chhatim village in mid-January.

The researcher is delighted. The state is looking for freedom fighters everywhere, here's a freedom fighter. He creates interest in the Administration. Consequently an old guy in his seventies receives an allowance from that state as Dindayal's only living relative. The researcher publishes his book, and he, too, is given a D.Phil. among others at the *convocation* of the University in the style in which fried *puris* are thrown carelessly at rows of wedding guests waiting to be fed. Since his book doesn't sell, he himself distributes it everywhere. He had published it at his own expense, so there's no problem. The book reaches a certain Minister's office and the Minister's Personal Assistant is *electrified* upon perusing it. A freedom fighter, a *genuine* martyr, a martyr from Midnapore, the proper cradle of revolution, yet nothing has been done with him! He is able to explain the need for erecting a statue of Dindayal to his Minister. Since the statue of a dead man is much more important than other living problems, there is no difference of opinion about the decision to erect a statue.

Sadan Khan enters at this *stage*. His grandfather was a passenger on the No. 313 'up' on the 9th in 1924. Badan Khan had identified Dindayal at the time of capture and, travelling to Calcutta, had helped the police at a *later stage*. His star was on a climb since then and it is for this reason that his son Madan Khan was marked as a patriot after Independence. Now Sadan Khan comes forth in some way and shows interest in the matter of the statue.

There is slight friction about the material of the statue. Not stone. Even the lion cub of Birsingha Village was not able to keep its head intact because the statue was of stone.

If not stone, clay?

'If you don't cover it, a clay statue will melt in water, if you do it'll be a nest of termites,' Sadan says.

'Bronze?'

At this stage someone jokes, 'Bronze is good. There's money in it if you break it and sell it in bits.'

This pains Sadan Khan greatly. 'Hey? What did you say? Such a good son of our country, who will break his statue and sell? We may be from a country town but we're not inhuman!'

Thus the decision is to build in bronze. Sadan's efforts unearth a 1918 school magazine of Surajmohini Boys' School. There you get a photo of Dindayal Thakur who got a First Division from the school in the college entrance exams. The sculptor is shown the photo and told, 'This is an eighteen-year old, raise the age of the statue by six years.' Hearing this the sculptor is blown away. But he says nothing, if he loses the *contract*, the loss is his. He says, '*Yes sir*' and leaves.

Sadan Khan returns to town and gives Nabin the good news. Says, 'I heard they've printed a letter written to Aunt Duli in the book. The reporters might ask.'

'What will they ask?'

'Think about it. With parents alive, why did Dinu Thakur write to your Pishi?'

When Nabin came back to the village and imparted this piece of news his dad was exceedingly enraged and Nabin too got heated.

'Why get angry?'

'No, I'll dance for joy.'

'Why're you angry?'

'All you do at home is eat. Home gossip gets out and I won't be mad?'

'Baba, times have changed.'

'Nothing has changed in the villages.'

'No, there won't be any trouble.'

'No problem?'

When Sadananda went to town Sadan Khan also said, 'What an idea! Reporters will ask questions. You tell them we don't know to whom he wrote a letter. Keep Aunt Duli away. Don't let her appear in front of anyone. Then all will be quiet.'

'Treason begins at home: my dear Nabin?'

'I'll explain to him.

Nabin was truly angry now. He said, 'I'll cover up nothing. Then it was a scandal, now no one will think of that. You can't just give orders from *town*. I will keep pace with them. Without a paved road, seven villages remain in darkness. Will that work get done if we put our shoulders together to the task? You get things done these days if you write in the newspaper.'

The topic of all this discussion was looking for ripe myrobalan in the dead bed of the Karnabati. She was pulling her creeper-tied bundle of twigs from site to site. Nabin found her right there as he cycled searching.

'Pishi!' he cried out.

'Who's that? Nabin?'

'What're you doing in this dense jungle?'

'Hey, it's ripe myrobalans, have one?'

Pishi came up pulling her bundle of twigs behind her.

Nabin says, 'Sit down here.'

'Why?'

'I must talk.'

'With me?'

'Who else do I talk to at home? Are they human?'

'Why? Does your dad scold you?'

'Forget them. Sit.'

Nabin takes Pishi's hand and sits her down. 'I'm trying so hard,' he says, 'won't I get a job, Pishi? Whatever I get I'll blow my horn in your brother's face and take you away.'

'Always the same thing, Nabin!'

'What'd you think I've brought for you?'

'Hair oil?'

'I forgot. Sorry.'

'That's all right.'

Nabin wrapped a cloth around her. Bought for seven rupees at the *town* market. A thin piece of cloth, hardly any thread count. But Pishi is dressed in rags, and Nabin's purse doesn't run to much. Pishi was in bliss.

'Oh Nabin, for me? What a lovely colour, how warm, smell its new smell?'

'I know. Take this.'

'What's in the box?'

'Gout ointment. There were hawkers on the

bus. You groan all the time with knee pain and lower back pain?'

'Where'd you get the money? Your dad?'

'Of course not! I don't go to *town* for nothing. Muraribabu from Patke has a printing press. I'm learning that work a bit.'

'Because your dad gives you nothing?'

'No. What's there to give?'

'Yet all the land is temple land. Your share is as much as Sada's, as your brother's.'

'No, Pishi, I don't want anything from them.' Nabin sat for a while with Pishi's hand in his hand. Three o'clock on a winter afternoon. Sand blows over the dry riverbed. You can hear the distant water-buffalo bells ringing. Dasu Soren's group is sowing the spring harvest on the riverbed. All around are the wave upon wave of the *laterite zone*; the murmur of the fall of leaves in the dwarf-sal forests. Desolate, melancholy-making afternoon. Nabin wants to bind this silent indifference in a paved road and take it into the lap of the present.

Pishi's white hair, soft and sad loneliness in her thin face, lined skin. In Dindayal's letter you read of her standing with her lean hip cocked, of her astonishing beauty—Nabin has read it in town. Now what he has to say to Pishi is most cruel. But the era that Nabin wants to bring to Chhatim village is heartless and unforgiving. The reporters won't leave Pishi alone.

'Pishi, one word—'

'Tell me.'

'Do you remember Dinu Thakur?'

Pishi is speechless. She places her helpless eyes on Nabin's and he notices amazed for the first time that, although Pishi is seventy-eight, her eyes are still alive.

'Do you remember, Pishi?'

'Yes.'

'Dinu Thakur's name is in a book, Pishi.'

'Where?'

'I don't have it.'

'Then?'

'Your name, too.'

'My name!'

'Dinu Thakur wrote you a letter before being hanged. That letter is printed in a book.'

'What'll happen, Nabin?'

'What'll happen to what?'

'Where'll I go if your dad sends me away?'

'No one's going to send you away. Listen.'

'Tell me.'

'There'll be a statue of Dinu Thakur in the village.'

'Where?'

'Their place will be cleared. There.'

'When?'

'I hear in three months. Then people will come, they might ask you some things.'

'What shall I say?'

'Whatever comes to mind.'

'Your dad …'

'I, too, have rights, Pishi, you said yourself. Who's going to blame you? If they do, you and I will go to town, we'll starve and see if we live or die.'

'Nabin …'

'What?'

'Your uncle, younger than me, now he's dead, he beat me a lot then. All the trouble, all my suffering, started then … but everyone had forgotten that stuff, again …'

'Pishi! Don't think of what happened then.'

'How many years ago?'

'Fifty-four.'

'Fifty-four? So long ago?'

'Yes, Pishi.'

'Your dad knew nothing. He was a tiny boy then. He too is grown up now … your ma … I'm thrown in a corner with less power than field-cattle.'

'I know.' 'Today, after such a long time …'

'Don't think of it. No one will say a thing. I'm on the Panchayat. There must be some respect for my word in the village? No one will object. Come, let's go home.'

'Let's go.'

'Hey, I keep forgetting. Here.'

'What, dear?'

'Five hundred gram ground chickpea and treacle.'

'Long life my love, bless you my love. A king's ransom for you.'

'Kings and queens! They don't even give you a handful of rice. And you wish a king's ransom for me?'

'All right, don't be king.'

'Pishi, the police evicted the entire Thakur family?'

'They did. And …'

'Yes?'

'Big brother, angry with me …'

'Let it go. Don't cry.'

'Tell your dad, Nabin, not to torture me any more. I'm ready to live in a shack upon this riverbed in the woods.'

'Always the same. Stop it.'

III

She had thought to have remembered nothing. But at night, pulling the straw door to and lying down on the platform, she remembered everything. How? She was not supposed to remember. All the disasters in her life are from that event. Is that why she hasn't forgotten? So many days, so many years, everything was buried somewhere. Nabin came as the North wind and blew away all the leaves today.

How long, how long ago?

Both were born with the century. Of the same age, of the twentieth century. But the twentieth century did not accept them as friends. It left them in the Middle Ages and went on ahead.

Suddenly she realized that she could not reach the mind, the love, of those days, of the two she was thinking of, any more. At seventy-eight the body becomes such that today's unappeased hunger appears much more real than the unrequited love of the past. It's impossible to become the Brajadulali of that time (in the mind) and to go back into the past. Possible rather to look back at the Brajadulali and Dindayal of that time as another girl, another boy, from a distance.

She thought of this because of Nabin. Nabin speaks to her, she sees the present through Nabin's eyes. Another reason is the peculiarity of her mode of existence in this family. She always wanders in wood and wilderness. She sees, and once in a long while speaks to, Dasu Soren's group, and the Bauri caste, and Ratan the barber. She knows they will not report these conversations to Nabin's father and brother. For many reasons they think of the Bhunyas as enemy, and of Nabin as friend. She herself also thinks that they want what Nabin wants. Paved road, health centre, market place—that's good. She finds no connection between their good and any good-happenings for herself. In fact, she thinks of herself as dead. At this age, undone by ceaseless worry about food, she cannot think of anything more good than today's chickpea powder, tomorrow's crushed parched rice. Dasu Soren often gives her a custard apple, a jujube or two and says, 'Your problem is that you're a king's daughter. Nothing to eat, yet you can't beg, most dangerous.' Dasu Soren often says that belonging to a royal family has been her bane.

At that time Dasu's father Kanu Soren sharecropped the Bhunya's land. The Thakur's land as well. Thinking of Brajadulali he could in no way remember her wedding. Vain effort. At four the wedding in the Bhunya house in Patke, at six a widow. As far as memory goes, Brajadulali is wearing widow's white. Brajadulali never wore shellac bangles, saris with borders, silver fish-pins in her hair, anklets on her legs— the Bhunyas behaved like the priestly Brahmin Thakurs. They were respected in the village for this.

Dulali never addressed Dinu with a show of respect. There was no cause to. From the age of ten Dulali would go to Dinu's mother. A widowed daughter, a lovely daughter, Dulali's mother made her do many rituals all year. At the end of these, instead of saying

May I be wife forever
With a bright-shiny home of husband and son
May I die with my hair-part vermilion

Dulali would say:

Father's house full to bursting
Brother's house bright and shining
As long may they live
As the hairs on my head.

The two met all the time. Every day. Dulali was the landowner's daughter. Although the king was now just a farming householder, the village people still gave respect. A village daughter, Dulali wandered everywhere at ease. Because Dinu's mother was always busy, because Dinu's two sisters were tiny heaps, it was Dulali who mended the clothes of Dinu's father, Dinu himself, and Dinu's brothers. It was she who put covers on Dinu's books. No one knew how to make ink from ink tablets then. Dinu's father would say, 'No one knows how to make ink from inkstone like Dulali.' Both of them said, 'Such grace in her limbs. Why was such a beautiful, wonderful girl born in that house, and why such evil fate, who knows?'

Uncle used to talk, and Dulali would hear vaguely. Uncle would say that if Dulali had been married two months later, she would not have been widowed. Dulali, oh dear how shameful.
At twelve she went to the wedding of a special friend. Kusum's aunt turned her out with, 'Out, out!' Fearing the Bhunyas, Kusum's mother said to her, 'Duli! You're not to see a wedding, dear, you're not to join in the wife-rites. Come and see when Kusi goes to her groom's house in the palki.'

Dulali came home and said to her mother with angry tears, 'Why did you have my wedding, then? I wouldn't be a widow if you'd done it later. I couldn't see Kusi's wedding.'

Four years later, it was another wedding day, the day Kusi's younger sister Malati was getting married. Everyone went from her house, Dulali stood alone behind the house, standing on her toes, holding the champak tree branch, listening to the wedding music. She hadn't realized that Dinu had come up and was standing beside her. She was startled when he spoke, with a sudden start of fear.

'What are you listening to?'

'Ohh! It's you!'

'What're you listening to?'

'Wedding music. Did you go?'

'No.'

'Why? Don't you want to see the groom? They've sat the groom in the other uncle's house, haven't they?'

'I don't know.'

'What do you need?'

'I've been looking at you.'

'At me? Why, all of a sudden?'

'Why sudden? I look at you all the time.'

'That you do, yes, but …'

What happened next was most unexpected. Dinu put his finger on her face, drew it down and said, 'You look like Saraswati, the goddess of learning.'

'What is this?'

'Look, I love you, so I want to touch you a bit.'

Dulali is very afraid. Her face gets hot, her body trembles. Then she says, 'You go to school in Patke, is this what you're learning?'

'Do they teach this in school?'

'Go, go away now.'

Dulali herself ran away. She went into her room and shut the door. She lay on her front, put her face in her pillow, trembled and trembled, and then fell quiet. Then she got up, and very carefully looked at her face in the glass. Clear light skin, a lovely face, this she has known forever. Mother says, 'Don't look in the mirror, dear.' So Dulali doesn't look in the mirror, doesn't braid her hair, just winds it on her fingers and puts it up anyhow. She doesn't do the widow's fast on the eleventh day of the moon's phase, just eats chickpea powder with milk and banana. At night she eats puffed rice, milk and bananas.

'I love you!' What a terrible sentence, how full of unease. From childhood Dulali has learnt to fear the word 'love'.

Charan Bauri's wife from the Bauri quarter had love with her husband's younger cousin. There was bloodshed in the Bauri quarter. The Panchayat had said that there couldn't be violence in the village because of this. A godfearing village. Brahmins live there. Charan must get rid of his cousin. Why has he kept him, seeing as he is a homeless orphan?

Charan's wife came to their house to get paddy. Quite disoriented, disaster was written all over her face. Everyone in the house looked at her with great curiosity, Dulali as well. Charan's wife looked at everyone with a piercing glance. Then she took her paddy and left. She went home, boiled the paddy, carefully tended the earth floor of the yard, then went off to bathe in the riverbed. The rainy month of Sraban, there was water in the riverbed. She did not return home. She and her husband's cousin ate the poisonous seed of the trumpet flower and died together. In the depth of the woods. There was a lot of talk about this in village life. Fear entered Dulali's heart. What is love like? Love means violence in the community, death?

There is fear in the word 'love'. Dulali's first cousin loved his wife, so his mother treated her daughter-in-law with incredible cruelty. Dulali's father used to say, 'What's the use of so much love and friendship? You've come to work in this world, do it. Marrying, having children is also the world's work. There is no good in loving.' This daughter-in-law lost her mind later. Her aunt sent her back to her father and arranged another marriage for Dulali's cousin.

Dinu loves her? How? Does anyone love someone whom he's seen all his life? Love starts when a new bride returns to her husband from her first ritual visit home after the wedding. When you see someone for the first time. Dulali decides she hasn't caught Dinu's meaning. He loves her as he has seen her forever, like a sister. She's a widow so she can't see a wedding, pained by her pain he had come to her.

It was the month of Sraban. Dulali puts some milk at the shrine every day. That day, too, she had put the milk down, touched her head to the ground, and was returning fast. It started raining on the way, she was wet through. She ran and stood under a tree. Then she saw Dinu coming home with an umbrella over his head.

'O Dinu! Stop a bit.'

'Dulali? You?'

'I was at the shrine.'

'Come, come under my umbrella.'

'Stop a bit, it's raining too hard.'

'Let's stop, then.'

The two of them under an umbrella. The sky dark with clouds. Who'll say it's afternoon, looks like night. Dulali was most uncomfortable.

Dinu said suddenly, 'Dulali!'

'What?'

'What have you done to me, Dulali! I can't think of anything but you.'

'Don't say it, be quiet.'

'Why did you come to be Mahananda Bhunya's daughter? Why were you widowed?'

Dulali, distraught with terror, said, 'Aren't you Priest-uncle's son? Aren't you Brahmin? You are not to say such things to me!'

Dulali ran off that day. But now she can't even explain anything to herself. She says, enraged, to her mother, 'You know I'm going to the shrine. Milk in one hand, bananas in the other. Couldn't you have sent someone with me with an umbrella?'

She is in a bad fix. She goes to the Thakur house a number of times every day. With fruit, with milk, to get dishes cooked by Thakur-aunt. How can she say, I won't go? People will suspect something. Gossip will grow with word of mouth. Thinking of all this she forgets to dry her hair. She has fever in the morning.

She had very high fever. What people call pneumonia fever. It was Dinu who brought a doctor from Patke. Mother put poultices on her chest and wept. Father would say, 'Get well my darling. You light up our house. My Dulali, I can forget everything when I see your face.'

She got well but she didn't get her strength back for a long time. At last, on the last day of Bhadra, the next month, she took her brother Sadananda on her hip and went to pick thankuni herb by the pond. Dinu came by. He said nothing, she neither. Dulali's heart was pounding. She picked her thankuni somehow and came away. Dinu appeared in the evening. He sat in a cane chair in the yard and said, 'Aunt, look at your girl's conduct. Here she was sick, I brought a doctor from Patke. She got well, she didn't say a word? Mother sent this water. She gave God some tulsi water in her name.'

Dulali came out at her mother's shout. She touched his feet at her mother's behest. Dinu said, 'Now come, my lady. Mother's waiting on your Highness' pleasure with some food from our home shrine.'

'Go Dulali. Shameful, she's waiting! Go quickly.'

Dulali had to go. Dinu said, 'So? See I made you well?'

'You made me well?'

'Didn't I call the Lord every day?'

'Dinu.'

'What?'

'Don't talk like that.'

'Why?'

'I hurt.'

'I hurt, too.'

'What can I do about that? Please be calm. I am of low caste, and then a widow. You are getting education; the eldest son of the house, you will be married.'

'We'll see.'

'You are uncle's strength and hope.'

'We'll see.'

'Tell me you'll calm down.'

'Will you be pleased if I calm down?'

'I'll be at peace.'

'You'll be at peace, Dulali? At peace? Good. Then I'll calm w—ay down. I won't bother you any more. Dulali, stand here, let me look at you. Duli, Dulali, Dulali, I love you so much, I never got the chance to say it.'

Running, almost running, Dinu went away. From there, from the village. Told his father, 'I won't be a priest like you. I'll go to school. It's hard for me to travel back and forth from the village. I'll live in Patke at my brother-in-law's house.'

Dinu didn't come to the village for a long, long time. He left, giving Dulali peace and a great deal of pain. He returns after eight months. On the day of the Manosha fair. Hundreds of people in Chhatim village that day, the village is agog since dawn with people, water buffalo-carts, and pouring rain. Dulali went to the fair. Dinu called her to the Karnabati river bed. 'What's happening to me, Dulali?' he said. 'I can't forget you, no way, what's this?'

'I, too, haven't forgotten.'

Dulali had spoken. In 1917 Dinu and Dulali, both seventeen, were no longer minors. They knew the responsibility of all adult emotions. Knowing the consequences, Dulali had said, 'I, too, haven't forgotten.'

The time was ineffable. A time to say the whole truth. Twilit dusk, the sky dark, in the background the roaring music of the Manosha shrine. There will be a recital of The Tale of Manosha at night. In front the roar of the groundwater pouring down the incline of the sandbank of the dead riverbed. The fragrance of kadam on the wind. The world was slow with cloud, the wind was lightning-struck in some unknown anticipation.

'You haven't forgotten? Then come close.'

Dulali had gone to him. Then she had raised her face and said, 'First listen to me, Dinu.'

With a most stern face, and slowly, Dulali had said, 'I love you but what's the good?'

'What's to lose?'

'What's the use Dinu? You will not be able to say this to people. I won't either.'

'No.'

'All you'll get is pain.'

'Yes.'

'Then what's the good?'

'I don't know.'

'Dinu.'

'Hmm?'

'We could both die.'

'Hush.'

'Then tell me you'll forget me?'

'But I can't forget.'

'What can I say, then?'

'There's nothing to say, nothing.'

They stood quiet for a long time. Then Dinu said, 'Let's see. This Chhatim is not the universe. You go back. We won't go together. People will talk.'

Dinu goes to Patke again. He sits for his school-leaving exams next year. He goes to Kharagpur before the *results* are out. Dinu's father knew that Dinu was in Kharagpur. But Dinu went to Calcutta with the Bengali teacher of Patke School. This teacher must have had a great effect on Dinu. For the Dinu who came back to the village after the exam results were out was a different Dinu. Spare of speech, stern and serious. At this time he went around in the fisher folks' neighbourhoods, the Bauri quarter, in the cholera season. He worked in rural relief. When cholera was contained, the *Health Inspector* came from Kharagpur, praised Dinu and said at the local police station before he returned, 'Start with village relief, end with *terrorism*, I've seen a lot.' The Police Inspector gave no importance to this and said, 'Poison-root breeds poison trees, can the son of a godfearing Brahmin priest turn out bad?'

Dinu makes no attempt to see Dulali. As if he'll get no peace if he doesn't spend himself completely, he now starts work with malaria prevention. Dulali also shrinks into herself. This is good, this is very good. She doesn't go to learn any rituals anymore. She keeps herself immersed in household chores. But when everyone is at the temple for the worship of the harvest Kali, he calls her into the garden of their house. He says, 'Dulali, I now know everything.'

'What?'

'I'll marry you.'

'Marry? Me?'

'I'll marry you.'

'Aren't you afraid of sinning?'

'What sin? Widows can remarry, by law. What fear? We'll go to Calcutta. A hundred thousand people and more, a huge city, who will find us? I'm telling you, Dulali, marry me, hold me, otherwise I'll float away.'

'Then let me die, Dinu.'

'Die—die—can't you say "I'll live"?'

'How'll I say that? If I go with you it'll be scandal, the blacklist, my father will be fallen.'

'He'll do a penance and reclaim caste.'

'I'll not forget, I'll burn out.'

'You won't be able to?'

'No.'

'Do you love me?'

'Yes.'

'Still …'

'I don't have that courage.'

'What can I tell you then?'

'There is nothing to say. Our castes don't match, I'm a widow, everyone in the village … respected line … shame …'

'Then go.'

'Go?'

'Go. Never come in front of me, never.'

Dulali wanted to die that day. Dulali didn't know what strong attraction pulled him, Dinu couldn't hold himself firm.

Dinu became a schoolteacher in Patke. 'I will not sit in the village and be the Bhunya's priest, father. Tell him whatever you like.'

It was a great blow to Thakur-uncle. Is it right to say, 'I won't do' my clan-work, caste-duty?

'Get married and go.'

'I won't marry.'

In 1919, no nineteen-year old village boy could say this to his father's face. Mother had said, 'You hurt your dad?'

'He has another son.'

'Why have you changed so?'

'I won't tell you.'

Dinu left. But fate did not allow them to be still. A fate self-created by them. Dinu fell ill in Patke, high delirium. He couldn't be brought back to the village. His mother went there to nurse him. Came back a few days later in a water buffalo-cart. She said to Dulali's mother, eyes swollen with tears,

'Kadu! What I say is for my son's sake. My Dinu won't last long. He calls Duli all, all the time. Sister, don't think of your modesty or mine, he calls in delirium. He calls you, he calls my Bhunya brother-in-law, there seems to be something he wants to say.'

Dulali's father says, 'Let's go, sister-in-law.' And to Dulali's mother, 'You come too. If you don't and Dinu doesn't last, we will be touched by a Brahmin's curse. If he doesn't go, then there will be words, why didn't they go to see him?'

They are more distressed at the possibility of Dinu's death. Dulali's mother is a simple soul. She says, 'You won't call Duli? The same midwife delivered them, is this a loose tie?'

Dulali enters with her parents and Dinu's mother. Dinu looks with bloodshot eyes and says, 'Sit there. Get up when I die.' A room full of relatives and in-laws. The curiosity in their glance undresses Dulali. Dulali, distraught with shame, fear and pain, sits there like a stone.

Dinu's fever goes in two days. Dulali returned with her family. Dinu's family returns a month later. Then one day Dinu's father calls Dulali's father to his place. 'A full grown girl,' he says, 'And then a widow, you have to be very careful, Mahananda.'

'Why?'

Dinu's father's eyes are not normal. Somehow the centre of his life has been destabilized. He says, 'Dinu says widow-remarriage is possible both by scripture and civil law. He will marry Dulali.'

Both of them turn to stone by the massive blow of these words.

Then Dulali's father says, 'You arrange a marriage for your boy, sir. I will discipline my girl. But what have you just said, Thakur-brother? Is this to be credited? Did the fever addle Dinu's brain?'

'Don't tell your daughter. What does she know. Maybe the fault is all Dinu's. The word will spread if you tell her.'

'What will you do to your son?'

The question contained the sorrow of a father's broken heart, but also a challenge. My daughter is not guilty, can't be. My darling never wore a bit of colour since childhood, she's never even raised her voice.

'It's Dinu's fault doubtless. But Mahananda, a man's guilt can be washed off, not a woman's.'

'Arrange a marriage for your boy, sir.'

Mahananda returns home afflicted by question and doubt. He tells all to his wife. Then Father calls Dulali and says, 'Don't go to the garden from the house, Dulali, I'm warning you.'

'I don't go, baba.'

'Then why did Thakur-brother say such things? Why did he say Dinu … with you …?'

'I don't know, baba.'

Dulali was getting courage somewhere in her inmost heart. Somewhere she knew she was not guilty. Loving Dinu was not a crime. Explaining this to Father and Mother was also impossible.

'You haven't done anything wrong, have you, little mother?'

'No, baba. Nothing wrong.'

'I knew, I knew.'

'Then I won't go to the shrine?'

Emboldened by his filial love Mahananda is extraordinarily bold. 'You will. You'll go as you went. My mind tells me you'll do nothing wrong.'

'Tell Thakur-uncle to take his son from the village, to arrange a marriage. I don't want to hear anything on his account. I'll kill myself if anyone says anything to you.'

She is very angry with Dinu for endangering her existence with incredibly immodest proposals even when she has not sinned by loving, when she has accepted the fact that her love will remain unfulfilled. At the same time an unbearable pain in her chest. Of joy. Dinu has said in public he'll marry her.

Dinu stood in front of her on her way back from the shrine. 'Let me go, Dinu.'

'What did you tell Uncle?'

'To get you married.'

'Whom shall I marry, loving you?'

'Dinu! If you don't marry I'll kill myself. A marriage between you and me is not to be, Dinu. As long as I live, I'll have to depend on my father or my brother, in this village. Do you want to grab my shelter?'

'Say once you love me.'

'I love you. You know that too.'

'Say it again.'

With her head held high, Dulali said, regally at ease, 'I love you, will love you as long as I live. But nothing will come of this love of ours in this life. Get married. Loving you, Dinu … I can lie in the dust for you, Dinu … if you walk on me my limbs don't hurt … if loving you, Dinu, I can ask you to get married, then loving me, can you not have your marriage arranged?'

'Let me see if I can, Dulali. Let me see.'

'Let me go.'

'Go, watch where you go. It's dark.'

Dulali comes home. Then one day it was heard that Dinu was going to be married. In that Patke village. With his sister's sister-in-law. His sister's father-in-law had just died. It was heard that Dinu was going to Calcutta. There he would be apprenticed at a printing press. His brother-in-law had fixed it.

Dulali couldn't bear it that day. By the riverbed she climbed on a hillock and clung to a tree. The bullock-cart passed by, Dinu's eye was turned to the village. Dinu didn't see her. She saw him full, filling her two eyes. Face thin with recent illness, light skin, close-cropped hair, a strange smile limned on his lips. A heart-rending smile.

It wasn't easy to fix the wedding day. Finally the wedding was fixed for November of 1924. There was music. A new thatched hut was raised to keep the marriage supplies. It was discovered that the moment for the groom's departure was in the morning. Before midday the groom will start from the house. He will sit beneath an awning under a tree. The groom will start at three in the afternoon.

In winter the sun goes quickly. Mahananda will give all the fish for the wedding feast, all the yoghurt, all the sweets, Mughal gold coins for the bride's trousseau.

Dinu lit up the tree under which he sat. Dulali didn't go, she didn't go all day. She didn't leave her room. She couldn't talk to anyone, yet her heart was breaking. Finally, winding her dry unwashed hair in her hand, pulling the end of her white borderless cloth around her body, Dulali came out step by step. Far away but still you can see him. White silk dhoti, ecru silk shirt, a big shawl around his shoulders, the sandalwood mark of worship on his forehead, flat gold circlets on his ears, this last a lineage custom. Dinu lifts his eyes from there, and sees her. He sees, he gazes, and then he stands up. Then he tears off the wreath from around his neck, throws his shawl down, wipes the mark off his forehead.

Dinu shouts in a terrible voice toward those from the bride's party who'd come to get the groom, 'Go back home, please. I won't marry.' These terrible and terrific words burst and rent the village sky, inaugurated an apocalypse.

Lying on this bamboo platform she can remember everything even after these fifty-four years. The pictures were arranged in her mind. In her adolescence painters would come to show pictures, unroll the picture slowly, show it, and then sing the narrative of the theme of the picture. Who were those painters, where have they gone, they are lost somewhere like her adolescence and youth.

What painter is sitting in her mind today and showing picture after picture, explaining everything? What a pain in her chest. What weight does memory have, why does it hurt? A great destruction had come down on the village. Even now the pictures are trembling, moving, breaking.

Thakur-uncle had said, 'You're not my son. Leave right now.'

'I will, I'll do just that.'

Dinu leapt into this house. Screamed and said, 'Come, Dulali. If we remain in the village after this they will cut you up alive.'

Dulali loses consciousness.

Dinu leaves the village. In rage, insult, and shame Thakur-uncle throws his wooden sandal at him. His forehead breaks open. The scar helped Badan Khan identify him later.

The village is filled with an unnatural calm. They are all the Bhunyas' tenant farmers. They say nothing. The kings are embattled. Thakur-uncle places a curse on Mahananda. The two families blame each other. Dulali lies forgotten in a corner. There is a search on for Dinu.

Then comes that morning of horror. The noise of Aunt's lamentation from the Thakur house. 'Dinu has robbed a train, he's been caught, he'll be hanged. O my Dinu-uu-uu!'

Then the news of the hanging. Thakur-uncle standing in the courtyard and saying, 'I return the sacred pitcher, I return the idol. You fed my son to that daughter of yours. I won't perform worship for the god of your house, I won't live on your land. I curse you, may your line die, die, die.'

Then police in the village. Elephants came from Patke, and a multitude of policemen. They kicked Thakur-uncle, Aunt and the children out of the house. The rider goaded the elephant, and the elephant demolished the house. Thakur-uncle tells Father, 'Do nothing. Let everything go.' Then he kneels in front of the Police Inspector and says, 'My son is gone, my house is gone, now please ask your elephant to walk over me, I beg you.'

The Inspector screams, 'What're you doing, please stop, I am only a Kayastha by caste.'

'What am I?' Thakur-uncle lifts up his arms as if to address the created universe, 'What am I?'

'You're a Brahmin.'

'I'm a Brahmin? Is that why an untouchable hanged my son, and an untouchable burnt him? Your constables drag my wife by the hand? I'm still a Brahmin?' Everyone is uncomfortable at his clamorous grieving, the Inspector too, he goes home without further discussion.

Father clasped Thakur-uncle's feet. Thakur-uncle had said, 'Your daughter is alive, Mahananda. You have not felt filial bereavement. And still you're thinking of what disaster may come to you. Why should I take your household god? The image? I wish you misfortune, yes. If this brings you tremendous misfortune, perhaps I'll get a bit of peace. You brought me such immense misfortune through your daughter?'

Thakur-uncle and his family left, are leaving, the Bauri untouchables and the fishers are moving them, the Bauris and fishers had come to love them. It's said that they spent the nights under trees, the fishers kept watch around them. They moved forty-two miles in four days and reached Kharagpur. Some people from the railway colony came under cover and gave them money, bought them tickets. They went to Puri, the seat of the god Jagannath. Then who went where? How do human beings get lost, like Dulali's cursed youth?

At the Bhunya house Mahananda had said, 'I'll axe Dulali.' He, too, is adrift. Loving his daughter, Dinu was banished, seditious, killed on the gallows. Dinu's father is a guileless man, his house has been levelled. The Manosha whose worship is his family duty has been deserted by her priest. The village is under divine rage, royal rage, Brahmin rage. All due to Dulali. Dulali's mother put a machete in her husband's hands and said, 'You can't just cut her down, cut me down too. Then, you are a man, have another family.'

'Everything will be as you say? There's no community?'

'Has the community asked for her death?'

'Asked that she be discarded.'

'Throw her away. I'll go, too. Mother and daughter will live as beggars.'

'Everything was destroyed because of her, and you still won't let her go?'

'Who is the community in Chhatim? You are the community. Whatever you say happens. You're giving me community?!'

An easy solution was to kill Dulali. But Dulali's mother stops them from inside. An obstacle comes unexpectedly from outside. Dasu Majhi's father Bulan Soren says, 'Dinu Thakur told us when he left, she's your sister, watch over her. You can't kill her. Then we'll burn everything. We'll find Dinu Thakur's pals and tell them everything.'

Mahananda is a householder. He became brutal at a time of a terrible disaster, and came to his senses when obstructed. But he was the head of village society. It is his job to outwit the sins of the home. It is by way of his daughter that the village fell into divine ire.

Dulali is made an outsider at home. This room is raised. She is not allowed to enter the household. There is an arrangement for her upkeep—rice, lentils, oil, salt, wood, paraffin, sari, washcloth. Then the shrine room is raised again after penance. This life since then. As long as Mother was alive, she'd come and sit outside. Mother would weep. Dulali didn't have the strength to weep. Day and night she thought, why didn't I listen to him, why didn't I leave, he had said there is a huge world outside Chhatim. She'd think why, for whose pride and respect, did I say 'no' to him? Dinu was gone, would never come again, for a long time it was piercingly painful to accept this. Then day by day that feeling of pain lessened. Sadananda was then eight.

Today Sadananda is an old man of sixty-two. The head of the house. Where is anyone, where was the Thakur-house, where and when did someone, seeing her from a distance, get up saying 'I won't marry,' what distant tales. Everything became a lie. The aching belly remained, and the tedium of passing each day.

Her sorrow will end when Nabin gets a job.

She fell asleep. Before she slept she tried to bring to mind the sharp burning passion of that past Dindayal, that past Dulali. No, it's not there. The light is dim in the winter sky, a slight cloud cover, breeze, the smell of ripe aman paddy on the wind, the horn playing, a huge fig tree outside the Thakur-house. Under it a shoddy awning. The groom is sitting on a high bench. Fiery complexion, aquiline nose, reddish-black hair, the tilak mark burning on his forehead, ornaments in his ears, a chaplet of marigolds around his neck. A girl is gazing and gazing at him, leaning against a raintree. She is wearing the plain white cotton sari of a widow. Its end is wrapped around her because it's winter. Her dry hair is roughly wound in a bun. The young woman's eyebrows are arched and long, her nose is slightly short, full lips, her skin the colour of the linseed flower, eyes black, wide open, unblinking. The groom lifts his eyes speaking to someone, his words stop, his mouth opens, it shuts, the groom stands up. He tears the wreath from his neck, throws the shawl from his shoulders. Says, 'Go back home, please. I won't marry.'

Yes, it's a picture of some other Dulali, some other Dinu. The picture is recalled, the picture speaks, but it is no longer possible to be of one mind with them. Fifty-four years is too long a time. Living has happened for too many days, too many. Seventy-eight is too old to be. No one lives this long. Mother used to say, 'The body wasn't used, no child was made in your belly, I'll die, Duli, but I am afraid to think how long you'll live.'

No one is left in the village from those days. Where are the companions with whom she played hopscotch in childhood, singing

One foot in water
Under the kadam tree
Two feet in water
In hellhole you'll be—?

They are long dead and gone. Where Dinu stood and watched Dulali is now a thick undergrowth of cactus. She has lived too long, time has gone on, leaving her behind. Dinu will remain the same in memory, a handsome young man of twenty-four. And Dulali is now an old woman of seventy-eight. And so she walks around. She never kept company with a man in her life. So her body was not quite ruined. Sadananda's daughter broke caste, married a Kayastha, meeting him at her maternal uncle's house. Some cousin of Sadananda's has supposedly married an untouchable Kaot woman and settled in Durgapur. The woman is a *nurse*. No one has lost caste this way; there is no shame. What a waste, what useless living. Only Nabin, as forthcoming as Dinu, in the evening of her life, says to his pishi with the same self-confidence that he'll take her into a new life. Evening. Time to pick the flowers of the little gourd, time to listen to fairy tales. The little gourd blossoms in the evening. In Dulali's youth, when hundreds of gourd flowers bloomed on the lattice in the courtyard, Mother would say, 'Tear off a few, my love. All those flowers will pull at the tree's life, it won't bear fruit.'

After picking off the flowers of the little gourd Dulali would sit to prepare oil-lamp wicks. Andimani, an old maid servant, would then gently pat Dulali's younger brothers and sisters to sleep and tell fairy tales, 'Moonlight was silvery everywhere then. The moon shone on the king's daughter's face. And said right then, I want this daughter!'

In the evening of life, at the time of picking the flowers of the little gourd, at the time of listening to fairy tales, Nabin says he'll take her to a new life. Constructing a paved road he will drag a new time into the village by the ear. Make the government build a health centre.

Let them get good fortune, let them. What is Chhatim village guilty of, that it will remain in darkness for so long? Light here is paraffin, music the tin horn and bamboo-stick drum, the road is of dirt, the village quack for snakebite, Ratan Barber's magic for sickness, otherwise a doctor from Patke.

Let them see better days.

IV

A few days later Nabin called her. 'Tell me what you see,' he said.

'Let's look first.'

From the fisher quarter and Bauri quarter, every villager is clearing the growth from the Thakur house wilderness.

'What'll happen there?'

'Don't you know there's going to be a statue? I myself have applied from the Panchayat. Set the statue in those grounds. We'll clear the wilderness with village *labour*.'

'You'll cut the fig tree?'

'No, Pishi, can such a large tree be cut? So many trees in these grounds. These tamarind trees will be sold. Also the jackfruit tree. They don't bear fruit. The money will go for the work of the Panchayat.'

'There'll be a statue if you say so?'

'Nothing comes of just saying, Pishi. The lady will dance only if you burn a lot of midnight oil.'

The tree felling went on for a few days. Contractors came from town and bought all the mango, jackfruit, tamarind trees that didn't bear fruit. They all took a lot of kindling. They burned dried leaves to take the damp off the grounds.

Then a few days went in weeding, watering and levelling the ruined foundation of the house, and in general sprucing up. Dasu Soren told Nabin, '*Labour* given. Cleanup done. So look, we're forty-two people, worked hard for over a week.'

'If there's a road, you'll get back the cost of your *labour*. You'll get double what you didn't get now.'

'Will there be a road?'

'That's what they've said. PWD *sanction* has come.'

'Where will the statue sit?'

'There.'

'On what?'

'There will be a dais.'

'That's a job for construction workers.'

'Government will do it.'

'Government?'

'Let's see, let me go to *town*.'

Sadan was full of hot air. 'It's our country's pride Nabin, our country's glory. You poor villagers did so much, I'll have the dais built. Let me find out how big a dais, I'll send the workers.'

'Did you find out about the road? When will they start?'

'I don't know yet, have you heard?'

'I've only heard that the MLA said everything will be done.'

'Then all's well. It's Patke's gain, Kannati's gain, and Kandor's gain if there is a road in Chhatim.'

'That's what I'm saying. What's it to me if there's a road! You have a fertilizer farm in Patke, you have a small warehouse, you pull your goods by bull-cart, now there'll be trucks. I have no business, no trade. When the road's finished I'll have wheat and peanuts grown in the village.'

'Very good, very good. Peanuts are a *cash crop* and wheat will grow well there.'

'I'll reconstruct our ruined tank with village *labour*.'

'That's a very good idea. Really, Nabin, I say from my heart, even to see that you think of others, work for others, pleases me. And see what evil inclinations I have? My father did the work and left all this, and I'm making it more and more.'

Nabin goes to the house of the *MLA*. The *MLA* says—of course there will be a road.

He instantly becomes a campaign platform speaker and harangues Nabin, 'What do you mean there won't be? All the progress will be elsewhere? Chhatim, Dinu Thakur's village, will remain in darkness? There has to be a road. By that road the labouring masses of the village will travel to the outside world with the goods produced by their sweat, and come back smiling to the village with the wealth gained from their labour.'

Nabin realizes that sir is in full *flow* and it's not right to admit impediments in the way of the stream. Then, after the necessary pause, he says, 'I worked very hard for you before the election. I also worked before the Panchayat. I don't want anything for myself.'

'Then why are you a press apprentice? No peace at home?'

'Not at all sir, just learning the work. Look sir, we suffer a lot in emergencies—disease and accident—because there is no road here. If there is a road … the *fire department* goes to Temukhi village only because there is a road. The *ambulance* goes there from *town*.'

'True, but that village is close to *town*, after all?'

'Yes, we know Chhatim is far from any *town*. We don't hope that *fire* trucks and *ambulances* will go to Chhatim, that can't be. But if there's a road …'

'I know, I know. You don't have to explain the need for a road to me. But …'

'What?'

'If another village puts in a *claim* …?'

'What's this you're saying now? I've been coming and going non-stop for three years for this road. And some other village—?'

'Well … you know … our MP, our Member of Parliament …'

'He knows, too.'

'See how some MPs have transformed their constituencies with roads and transport.'

'Let's see what happens.'

Muraribabu at the press hears everything from Nabin. He's a born pessimist. He says, 'Since there's so much talk, there'll be no road.'

'No, no, there will. I've been trying so hard for so long and there'll be no road? Come on!'

'So you're trying, do you know if others are too? Even if they don't, then how many thousands will you pour on this area before you shell out for a road?'

'How many thousands for what?'

'Nabin, you talk like an idiot. How do you think the statue will come? By truck. Covered truck? How will all the functionaries and officers, the big fish and the small fish come? By road? Where's the road? You'll have to build a makeshift road for now. From the *highway* your village is through some green fields, some stony fields, some rice fields, and Karnabati's dead riverbed. So won't you need money to build that unpaved road?'

'If I give *free labour* for that road? We won't need much building material, after all.'

'Don't get into that. Listen, I wasn't born yesterday. I know ev—erything that goes on. It's a PWD hassle, let PWD do it. I tell you what—go and tell that MLA Bhushno, let the labour come from the village. Let the villagers get a bit of cash.'

'All right.'

This is a *town*, not a city. But Nabin is weary of these hundred twists and turns of the town's way of thinking. After all the necessary discussion he comes home.

Difference of opinion in the village as well. In his own family.

Sadananda says, 'Nabin, you're mad about this road, but have you thought of the consequences?'

'What consequences?'

'What's going to happen if there's a road?'

'You know it too, baba.'

'What progress will happen—tell me that. You go back and forth to the *town*, what progress do you see, tell me? Our village ways are still decent. The girls don't wear *nylon*. The kids don't walk about with *transistors* pressed to their ears. Every place now full of mischief, and so poverty rises.'

'Let that be, baba.'

'I know these words are poison to you, my son. But still I say, where do you see any good? It's all where's the next meal coming from, and pain and lamentation. What solution will getting the road be? Flood water will come in from outside. Will anything good happen?'

'Why not, let's see?'

'The only gain is that I won't get field hands, men to help with the thatch over our heads. Every mother's son will either leave, or say give us outside rates.'

'If you can you'll give, otherwise not. If you can't afford more than eight anna wages and a handful of rice, don't. So shouldn't they go elsewhere if they get a few pice more? They'll remain bonded to you?'

'You'll say that, sure. You have no feeling for the land.'

'True, I don't. Who benefited from this land of yours, this kingdom?'

'You're eating the rice grown on that land.'

Suddenly Nabin gives a hard smile. 'I have the same right as you,' he said. 'This is temple land.'

'I see! Who gave you this information?'

'She who can.'

'That witch?'

'She, too, has the same lifetime rights. That witch had an ounce and a half worth of gold as her bridewealth. That, too, has gone into your household.'

'Nabin, leave what you don't know ...'

'I don't need to know. You stay right here with your reckoning. It's people like you who keep the village in such shape, can such a frog in a well survive today? If you'd had a road, Baba, your third son wouldn't have died of pneumonia at six years. We would've taken him to the hospital right away.'

'We could've. If hospitals and doctor's medicine cured everything, the *towns*folk wouldn't ever have died. You, too, will die Nabin. You'll die trying to be better than others. Didn't Dinu Thakur die?'

'What names are you saying in the same breath, baba? He and I? You can compare?'

Sadananda suddenly loses his temper and says, 'If there's a sun and a moon I curse you, there will be no road, no road, no road. My son's a *leader* now! Such a saint outside, yet no respect for his father?'

'Keep up the food supplies to Pishi in right measure. I'll make a big problem otherwise. Don't forget! I'll stop your sowing and your reaping. I'll see who works on your land if I say "no"!'

Sadananda is now worried and says no more. His sister should say nothing about Dinu Thakur's statue. He wanted to tell Nabin this. He didn't. If Nabin's good he's good, if bad he's bad. What's more, all the villagers dislike Sadananda and his youngest son. Nabin is their own. He shouldn't bother him and do himself harm.

At night Nabin's mother said, 'Why should you tell Nabin? Go once on the quiet and visit the old woman, threaten her.'

'I'll go to her room?'

'What's the problem if you stand in the door frame? Look, the god has no god-muscle these days. It was through her that we lost our worship practice, the priest was displaced. Wasn't the Brahmin's son hanged? Yet she wanders in the wilderness and the goddess's familiar, the python, doesn't bite her? So many people die of snakebite, was she born with the gift of life forever? And she made my son a stranger.'

'You're quite right. I'll stand on the threshold and tell her everything. And what he said about her food supply ...'

'Don't I give her stuff? Does she live on nothing, or can she?'

'Nabin is so single-minded ...'

'He's got too stubborn.'

With or without reason a human being can sometimes be punch-drunk with the strangest bliss. If your head is constantly buzzing and dim due to eating too little for a long time, then such *euphoria* can easily attack you.

Such is her condition. Dinu's statue will stand in the village–the new look of the Thakur compound– the easiest conclusion from all this is that the village is graduating into modern times. Reaching the present from the past. Result–the dreamy drunkenness in her mind. Her head is in such a state from eating little, that it often seems to her that she's floating rather than walking. Now she often stands in front of the Thakur house. She fills her eyes with the shiny smooth broad plot of earth. A cactus fence all around. She looks and looks, and then returns.

She doesn't feel like cooking every day when she gets to her room. She eats a little chickpea powder and lies down. She strokes the piece of cloth that Nabin bought. She'll put it on the day Dinu returns to the compound. Nabin has said that it's the road rather than the statue that will be the true memorial to Dinu Thakur, that will show him respect in the proper way. Once he, too, had wanted to change his own times. The village has remained in the same shape from his time to this day. All will change if there's a road. That will be to show him real reverence. In Nabin's opinion, building a statue is secondary. The road is the real thing. Today these words are also her words. She doesn't know since when Nabin has become as necessary to her as Dinu, in another shape.

'The road will be called Shahid Dindayal Thakur Road,' Nabin has said. 'If there's a road little by little there will be a school, a *health centre*, all kinds of things in the village. The school will be called Dindayal Memorial School.'

She laughs a lot. Affectionately. In her toothless face, with her skeletal frame, pebble white hair, on her forehead and cheeks ringed with a million wrinkles, through her eyes of profound loving kindness, that smile is as exquisite as it is affecting. Nabin's heartstrings tear in pain. Pishi is like neglected soil. She looks cracked and dry like thirsty neglected soil. She still doesn't know how to complain. Just as thirsty soil, begging love, dresses itself in grass with just a bit of water, Pishi too wants to pour herself out with just a little love from Nabin. Always a smiling face, as if Pishi has acquired a king's ransom.

Daughter of a royal line after all! Dasu Soren, Ratan Barber, Sadan Khan, Muraribabu – they all say from their childhood memories of the Manosha fair, that Pishi had been very beautiful. She looked like the daughter of a divine house. How she walked about! No one ever could say a bad word. Whatever happened, happened by the turn of the wheel of fortune.

Nabin loves Pishi even more. Unlike Baba, Pishi never holds out her hand for the smell of the pure butter of yesteryear. It's Pishi who's correct. Pishi says, 'What there was in the old days, not even grandfather or great-grandfather ever saw, why me? Yes, I saw land, but many people had land like that then. Dinu's sister was married into the Misra family of Patke. The Misras had much more land.'

If Nabin is ever a wage-earner he'll make Pishi lie in a soft bed, wear whole cloth, eat food cooked by himself. He'll rub oil into her cracked hands, give her oil to put in her hair. He'll light a paraffin lantern in her room. For that long ago event, that caste-duty crossfire, they ruined Pishi's life. So many lives were torn apart. Why is the Thakur family extinct? Because a Brahmin boy loved a Bhunya girl? Such marriages happen all over the place these days. Does any one worry about this any more?

Nabin flares up with rage when he sees Pishi. Pishi complains about nothing. Pishi came only to endure. It's as if even the evil treatment she received at the hands of Nabin's father and brother was her due. How did it all fall due for Pishi? By whose judgement?

She's never known how many thoughts Nabin has on her behalf. Rapt in her own thoughts she returns home at evening. She has no clue how she looks. Like the village-goddess, the spirit of the village. As if she wanders asking and asking for a bit of attention, affection, compassion from the community. The village, too, is aging. Getting exhausted.

Her sparse hair flies in the wind.

When Sadananda first stood in front of her room, at first she couldn't believe it.

'Sister.'

'Who's there?'

'It's Sada.'

'Sada?'

'Sadananda. Nabin's father.'

'Is anything wrong with Nabin?'

'No. Come here for a minute.'

'You … you … whatever you have to say, say it from there. I can hear.'

'Dinu Thakur's statue is going up.'

'I know.'

'You should know first. There's Nabin! However. What I have to say is, fine, there's a statue. Whatever happens, happens. But you won't show yourself. Not a word to anyone.'

'What can I say?'

'Whatever happened, happened then. All the disaster came from you. Thakur-uncle threw away the house-worship, did not take the image even when Father begged on his hands and knees on bare earth. The line perished because of divine ire. We could no longer hold our head high. D'you remember all that?'

'Yes.'

'Don't you say any of that. Reporters might come. It's no use raking up old scandal. If you try to say anything, remember you'll have to get out.'

Sadananda left. She sat like a stone. Again those memories, talk about the past. She closed the door like an automaton. Poured herself some water to drink. Then she climbed the platform and lay down.

V

What happened in 1924 was a many-layered *tragedy*. Multiple destructions with one explosion. The explosion was caused by Dinu and his tempestuous unrequited love. And later that became important. For example, Dinu's hanging—police violence in the Thakur-house—after which violence the conflict between Mahananda and Dinu's father.

The priest returned the worshipped and-to-be worshipped image. Thus did the curse descend upon her life. The event was quite unthinkable for those days. Even killing the daughter through whom such disaster came would not have satisfied Mahananda.

Remembered, all is remembered.

After Dinu's departure Thakur-uncle's appearance is that of a lightning-struck coconut palm. He was enraged even by the Bhunya name. Yet he is the priest of the instated Manosha. He cannot say no. Apparently he asked the sculpted five-snake-headed Manosha on the brass pitcher constantly, 'Did I neglect any detail of your service? Any detail?'

Mahananda would say in private, 'This happened to him by the god's rage. He must have erred somewhere. This god is most ruthless. If there is error the consequence will be a curse.'

Then came that fearful, fearful day. The news of Dinu's hanging. The entire village is in the courtyard of the Thakur-house. Thakur-uncle enters the shrine-room, holds up the worship-scrolls and the brass image of the goddess, above his head. Then with tearless lamentations he tears the air and says, 'Mother, we worshipped you for a few generations, and you took my son as sacrifice? I will not serve you with these hands.'

The god belonged to the Bhunya family. At that time Mahananda's brother's wife had had a daughter, the household was in the uncleansed ritual period of a birthing. Manosha being an exceedingly short-tempered goddess, she had to be taken to the Thakur-house for any excuse at all.

Thakur-uncle says, 'I will not serve,' and runs toward the Bhunya-house holding the goddess on his head. He keeps shouting—'Mahananda! Mahananda!'

Mahananda runs out of the house. Sees that the priest is running to him with the goddess on his head. Up to now he, too, was stunned by the violence of the blow of Dinu's hanging. Now, seeing the priest enter the environs he forgets about Dinu and screams – 'Uncleansed! Uncleansed! Don't bring the god!' – and immediately realizes that if he is in the birth-uncleansed period, the priest has sinned greatly by touching the god when unclean by death in the family. Manosha can't be kept clean any more. The moment this springs to his mind, before it can end, Thakur-uncle enters. Dulali has turned to stone. She stands holding the lintel. She sees it all.

Thakur-uncle is throwing the scrolls out into the courtyard, throwing the image. 'I return the god,' he says, 'I return the shrine-room. You fed my son through that daughter of yours. I won't worship your god, I won't stay on your land. I curse you, let your line die, die, die.'

'You dropped the god of my line on the unclean yard?'

'Wasn't the eldest son of the line hanged by an untouchable?'

'You can't do this.'

'I just did it.'

'Don't make me a sinner, brother, don't become a sinner. Where will I go if you throw away the god?'

'Everything is so sunk in sin, Mahananda, you and I are not going to be saved by worshipping our god.'

'Brother!'

'No.'

Holding his sacred thread, he runs saying, 'No, no, no.' Mahananda falls to the ground and howls weeping. Holds up the Manosha pitcher and cries, 'Threw you away, Mother? Threw away?'

His eyes fall upon his daughter. 'Murderer!' he says and then swoons. The eldest son Shyamananda picks up the god, the pitcher, and the scrolls. The women of the Bhunya house also raise their voices in lament. These are the memories of a terrible, terrible disaster.

Mahananda keeps going to Thakur-uncle, keeps going. Thakur-uncle doesn't let him in.

Then one day the police come. The scene of the police coming across the Karnabati riverbed is seen first by the fisher folk of this village, they leave their huts, run into the forest. An elephant comes behind. The landowners of Patke use the elephant to demolish the houses and barns of the tenants.

The police and the elephant come directly toward the Thakur-house. Unverified *report*: Badan Khan points out the Thakur-house and hides in the woods on the low hills by the Karnabati stream and, when the police create great violence, he walks by the stream a bit, climbs up, and escapes to Patke. Apparently he had nagra shoes on his feet.

Then, amazing everyone, the Inspector drags out Dinu's unconscious mother, and the old female servant with his two-year old sister in her arms. He drags out and throws to the ground Dinu's younger brother, and Thakur-uncle. Uncle falls on his face and when he stands you can see blood coursing down his forehead. A bloody sacred thread down his fair form. Mahananda runs forward, pushing all the villagers aside, all others with them. Thakur-uncle raises his hand and says, 'Keep off. Don't touch. I'm impure.'

He lifts up his wife, his children, the old servants. 'Don't you weep, anyone. Anyone weeps, I'll behead them. It's a time to look, look on.'

The trained elephant demolishes the structures at the mahout's goad. Pots and pans, rope-strung clothes-racks, cowrie-strung wall-brackets, bed, low-table, image-idol, rice basket, lentil-urn.

Mahananda runs up to say something to the Inspector, but Thakur-uncle says, 'Say nothing. Let it all go, let it.'

Fire drops on thatch. Into the paddy stack. New straw and the autumn harvest burn merrily. The villagers can't bear it any more. 'Who is punished for whose guilt,' they cry and they mourn.

Then Thakur-uncle kneels in front of the Inspector, saying 'Son gone, house gone. Please, walk your elephant over me, I beg you.'

The Inspector is leaving with his group, he has left. The Inspector is turning around and saying, 'I am a servant of the Crown, I have to do shit-eating work, please forgive me.'

Thakur-uncle is motionless under the tree with his hand on his forehead. He just stands there. Mahananda lies prone on the ground holding his feet. Rubbing his forehead on the Brahmin's feet. Saying, 'Take the god back, brother. I will raise a new roof right away. I will give new land. Great harm will come to me, brother. It has never happened that a priest has thrown away the image.'

'Why? She can throw me away, and I can't? She can light a living pyre in my chest, and I can't throw her away?'

'Gods can curse humans without reason, when has a human thrown away a god?'

'I have shown the way. Am I still a Brahmin, that I'll conduct a worship service? An untouchable hanged my Dinu, an untouchable lit his corpse, where is the Brahmin in me? Constable-police manhandled my wife in front of you? They pulled me to the ground, the divine couple, Radhakrishna's little shrine throne swam in elephant piss. Does a Brahmin remain a Brahmin after that? Does he? Tell me yourself!'

'Great harm will come to me, brother. I hold your feet and eat dirt, I eat dirt, brother, take back the god, don't make a sinner of me.'

Thakur-uncle's eyes dance with a terrible joy. He understands that to refuse the god will be to give the greatest blow to Mahananda. He says in a stern, harsh, rough voice, 'Your daughter is alive, Mahananda, after all. You have not known the loss of a child, and so you wonder what disaster can come to you. Why should I take your god? I wish you harm. I do. If this brings you harm, it will bring me peace, however minute. You brought so much harm to me through your daughter?'

All is recalled. Will be recalled. Dulali is poison in the Thakur-house, for Dinu's death. In this family Dulali is poison, for the divine rage, Brahmin's rage. Sadananda came and reminded her of all this after such a long while.

VI

The dais was built, spacious, lofty. Engraved below:
Dindayal Thakur,
martyred freedom fighter
(1900–1924)
He who gives life to the last drop,
cannot, will not, perish.

Some confusion arises as to whether the passage should run 'he who gives' or 'who gives'. Since neither of the Tagore anthologies *Chayanika* or *Sanchaita* was immediately available, this could not be *checked*.

The dais was there. Then a most temporary unpaved road. Sadananda asked Nabin, 'Is this your Dindayal Road?'

'No. This is for jeeps and trucks.'

'The government will kiss goodbye with this road alone.'

'Let's see.'

'Then what about electricity?'

'Might come.'

'The village will go to hell because of you. Once it was your Pishi. Now it's you.'

'I'm letting you get away with it. If I had heard Pishi's name in your younger son's mouth, I would have crushed his face.'

'Why not crush your father's face?'

'Don't think I don't feel like it.'

Nabin says such things often these days. Sadananda provokes such words. The father feels a certain pleasure and the son a certain resentment at being fooled.

Sadananda can't remain quiet after this. 'Trucks will break down, Nabin,' he says. 'The statue will not reach the village.'

'That would please you, but it won't happen. The police are accompanying the statue, they will guard it, bring it carefully.'

'Police!'

'Of course. The Minister will unveil the statue.'

'Police! Minister! So much nonsense around a village priest's son, penniless Brahmin stock, who became an armed robber, and went to the gallows!'

'You're the one who needs the road, Baba. When the road's done I'll show you the world. You'll see that there's a world outside the kingdom of the Bhunyas.'

'Yes, yes, I know, how many people have the sword and charter of Man Singh at home?'

'There are factories, wheat growing on arable land, outcaste doms and chandals going to school and college, there are other things to see. Charter and sword? If you search this very Midnapore district you'll find a thousand such charters and swords.'

Nabin moves off to Pishi's room so his father notices. So his father hears, he shouts, 'Keep the red lentils, the potatoes, and the onion, Pishi. Boil up everything together. I'll eat with you today.'

Nabin's mother bows weeping before the sacred pitcher. Sadananda says, 'Dinu's father left you and insulted you so, have you lost your powers in this latter age, Mother? Dinu's statue will be set up in the village, and you can't do anything about it?'

The brass Manosha, with her wide-open indifferent brass pop-eyes, has been hearing the prayers of devotees for two hundred years. She hears them still.

Nothing happens with Sadananda's prayers. The statue inauguration day approaches. Finally one day the inhabitants of Chhatim and the other seven villages stand in line on both sides of the dirt road. Bronze-hard Dindayal Thakur returns home fifty-four years after his death, riding a Public Works Department (*Roadways*) *truck*. The long forgotten and suddenly rediscovered martyr is raised to the dais bound in rope much tougher than the hangman's. The square pedestal under his feet is placed in the basin of the dais and stabilized with poured concrete. The school magazine photo supplied by Sadan Khan was not very credible. As a result Dinu's hard energetic air, his astonishingly bright eyes, are transformed into a new Dinu with a calm serious detached gaze. Dinu's statue, with its neatly folded hair on both sides of a cut parting, a tunic on its body, a dhoti around its waist and legs, a cotton scarf on its shoulder, is relieved to see from on high that the village has remained as sunk in the darkness of ignorance, poverty and underdevelopment as he had left it. Then the statue is wrapped in *cellophane*.

The police light a portable gas lamp and guard the statue. They have strict orders, so they cook and eat the staples they've brought along and sleep in the *truck* in shifts.

The next morning droves of jeeps keep coming as soon as it's ten o'clock. Under the huge marquee put up by Nabin and his group, and paid for by the money of the Panchayat, are placed dhurries and chairs given by Sadan Khan. The students of Patke

School come to sing the national anthem. No fault can be found with the event—*reporter*, *mike*, garlands for statue and minister, tea and sweets for the guests.

Nabin says, 'Aren't you coming Pishi?'

She says, 'No Nabin, I beg of you.'

'Why not?'

'I'll take a look at it later.'

'Are you crying?'

'Won't I cry? That day they beat and chased him off like a mad dog … his forehead was cut … today you, with so much respect …'

Nabin leaves. Nabin must admit that his role had always been minor in the entire thing. Today's event, too, is externally arranged and controlled. Neither reporter nor government functionary pays any attention to him. *MLA* and Minister are talking to him. But that is in the interest of keeping up mass contact.

First there is a speech inside the marquee. Nabin greets the Minister, Sadan Khan, and invites them to their *chairs*. Other important guests take their seats.

The singers are on the dhurrie in front. The villagers overflow the dhurrie on all sides. Sadananda is noticeably absent. Ratan Barber's thin pot-bellied eight-year-old daughter Mira, wearing a cheap pink nylon dress and a ribbon around her hair glistening with oil, garlands the Minister, Sadan Khan, and the *MLA*. Consequently the *officer* from *PWD Roads* gets no garland.

Next the *Minister*, the *MLA*, and Sadan Khan give long speeches about Dinu Thakur. In closing Nabin is asked to say something. When, after thanking his audience, Nabin says, 'Now, thanks to their generosity we're getting a road, Martyr Dinu Thakur Road …' then suddenly the *MLA* pulls his *shirt*. He pulls Nabin down into a chair and says, 'I, too, am interested in building a road. But currently the government is moving through a variety of obstacles. Therefore the road cannot be brought within the purview of a particular scheme. It is necessary that this road be built and I'm submitting a request to our distinguished Minister to consider this road under some future plan.'

Forgetting protocol Nabin shouts, 'You've promised a road, a *school*, a weekly market, a *health centre*.'

'Don't put the cart before the horse, Nabin. Let the government be stable, everything will follow.'

Now it's proven that Nabin is a rural boy. He does not have the militancy and ready wit of the town. For his eyes fill with tears and he weeps loudly. He doesn't even think of asking the villagers to surround the Minister and extract a promise by chanting: 'What do we want? A road. When do we want it? Now.'

Muraribabu from *town* and Ratan Barber from the village hold his two hands and say, 'Nabin! Let's do the task at hand now. Can work be done so easily? Do they care? We'll see. If not today, tomorrow.'

Nabin frees his hands and says to the Minister, 'You know, when Dinu Thakur left the village, there was no *school*, no road, and we lit our lamps with mahuafruit oil. There still is nothing in the village, the difference being we light paraffin. Just a road. If that can't be arranged …'

'I'll keep it in mind.'

All rise and the Minister says to Sadan Khan, 'It's true about the road. But that you, too …'

'For us it's more important to have a statue of Dinu Thakur,' Sadan says. 'Otherwise Bhushan would not have asked for it.'

'Of course. The village martyr. The nation's pride. And the statue is impressive.'

The Minister climbs the dais and opens the covering. Cameras click. Then suddenly the Patke schoolchildren start the national anthem.

Nabin moves to the thin stream of the river. He can't stop his tears, the 'hail and triumph' of the refrain of the anthem, in raised childish voices, pursue him.

The whole day passes. Nabin lies clasping his pishi all day. And all day Pishi strokes his body, his head, and consoles him.

'I'll go away to town with you. Muraribabu says the Press will let us stay.'

'Your Panchayat?'

'I'll come here and do the work.'

'Do that.'

'You'll come, no?'

'Sure. I've nothing to worry about if I go with you.'

'Here you eat half a bellyful alone, there we'll both half-starve.'

'All right.'

'Muraribabu says he's old and can't keep everything under control. I'll look after the Press. A lot of work there. I, too, will work on *commission* basis.'

'All right. Your father?'

'I won't eat their food any more.'

Dusk falls. Then Nabin sees. Pishi is putting on a clean cloth, combing her hair, wrapping herself in the shawl Nabin had given her.

'What's up?'

'Get up.'

'Why?'

'Don't I get to have a look?'

'They didn't want to see you at all?'

'What did you expect?'

'They talked so much, did they know him?'

'Those are the ones that speak. Your father sees you as bad, calls you bad names, does he really know you?'

In all that day, Nabin was more deeply consoled by these few words than by the hundred assurances offered by Muraribabu. The villagers had told him, the thing didn't get done by your words, but we haven't lost faith in you. Still, Nabin hasn't been able to get over his shame. As their spokesman he could get nothing done. His mind says, if I'm Nabin Bhunya, I'll get a road made. Yet pain and sorrow–can one lose the pain of disappointment so easily?

Nabin took the flashlight. They stepped out of the room. Pishi stood before the statue. Slowly raised her face. Nabin shone his flashlight.

'So big! So high! You can see the sky behind him.'

Nabin now sees with Pishi's eyes. Very big, very high. In the dark, at night. Human pain and compassion in the bronze eyes.

'He is looking at us, look Nabin!'

'Yes.'

Pishi looks her fill. Goes forward. Passes her hands over the statue's feet. A strange, unknown feeling. Why can she not match this high, great statue with that Dinu? Has Dinu become a god? Like the open shrine of Manosha?

'Pishi, you'll catch a cold.'

'Yes, let's go.'

Suddenly Pishi surprised him and said in a voice of tearless dry pain, 'The flowers at his feet are already wilted, Nabin. Crows will shit on his head, dirt will cover him, haven't you seen the distress of the god at Manosha's open shrine all year round?'

Drawing Pishi close with great care, holding her hand, walking toward her room, Nabin says, 'They spent 74,851 rupees for the statue–the dirt road–the *function*. They could have gold-plated the village with that money Pishi, they would have got road, *health centre*, *school*, ev–erything. The living are dead and yet ...'

The statue behind them stands in the same glory. It's not Dinu, it's a statue. Setting up–establishing–inauguration–subsequent neglect–a statue has nothing to do with this. Yet for the sake of a statue a great disappointment can descend on the Nabins of this world, it has happened to this Nabin.

Nabin and Pishi keep walking in the dark.

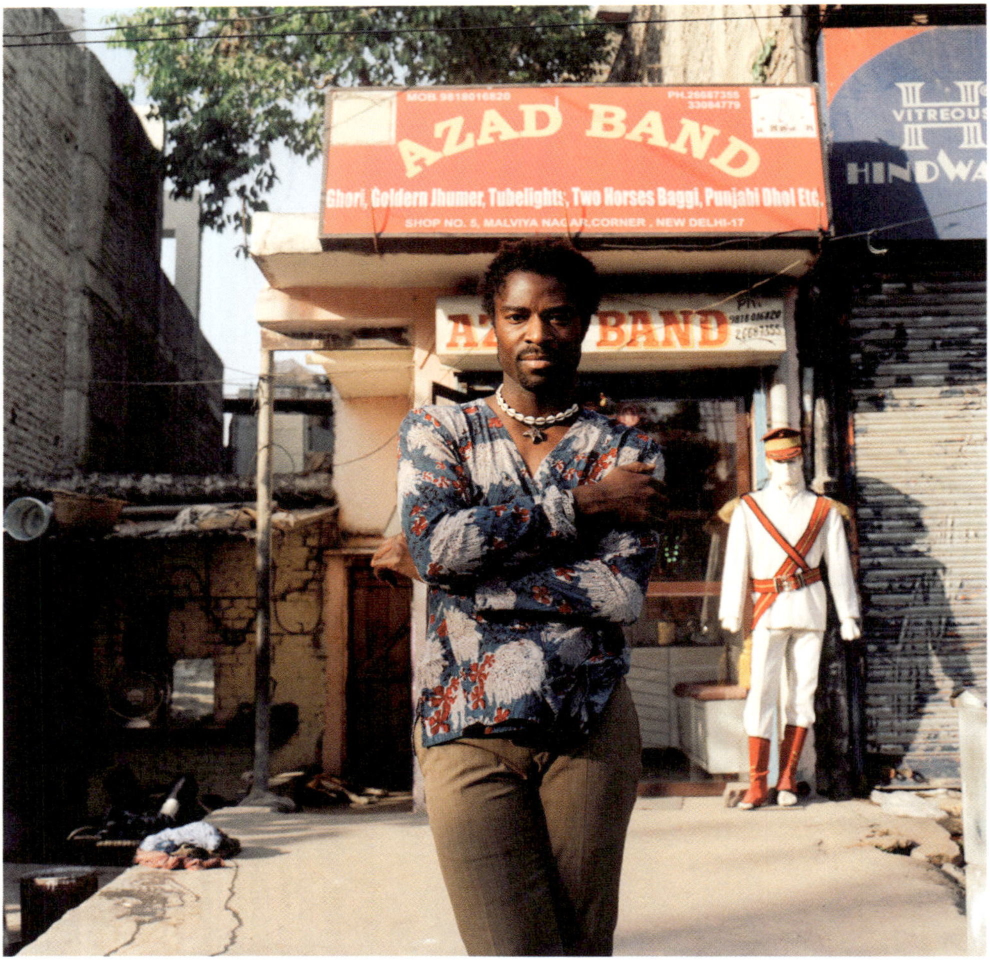

SUNIL GUPTA
Mr. Malhotra's Party

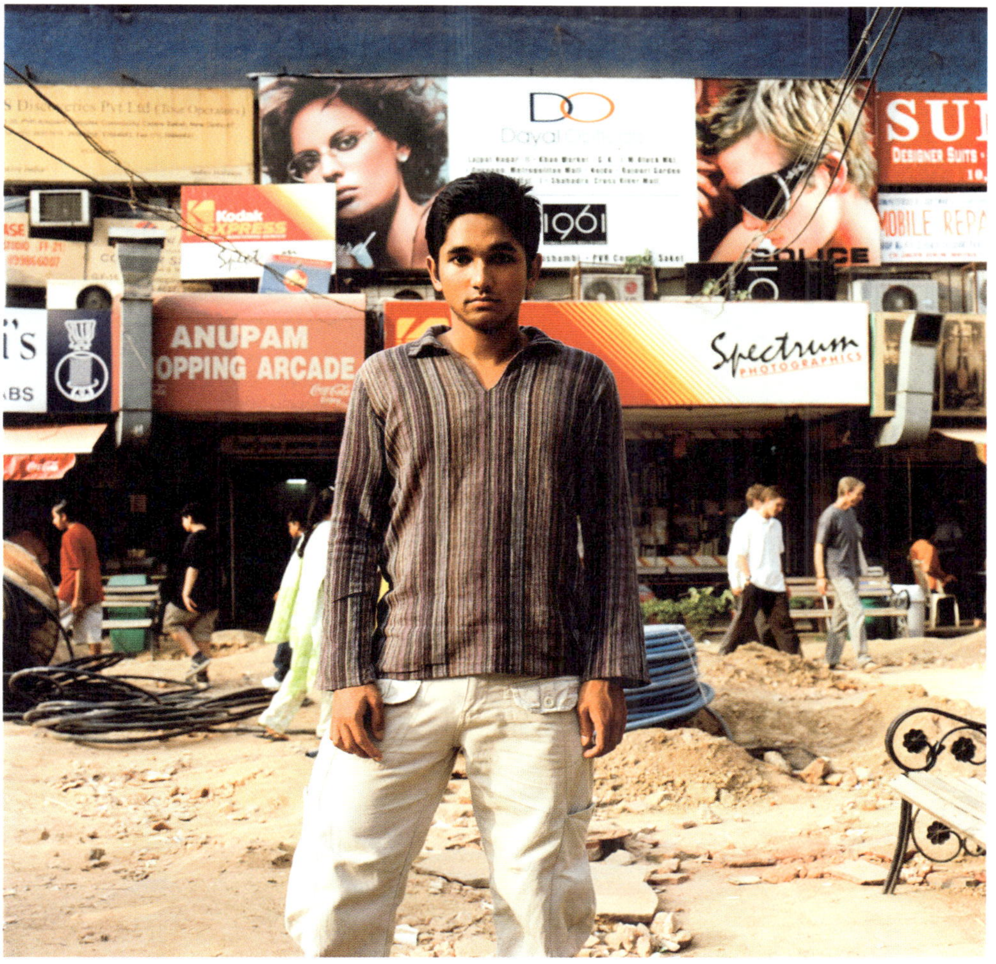
Kodak
EXPRESS
1961
ANUPAM
OPPING ARCADE
Spectrum
PHOTOGRAPHICS
DESIGNER SUITS

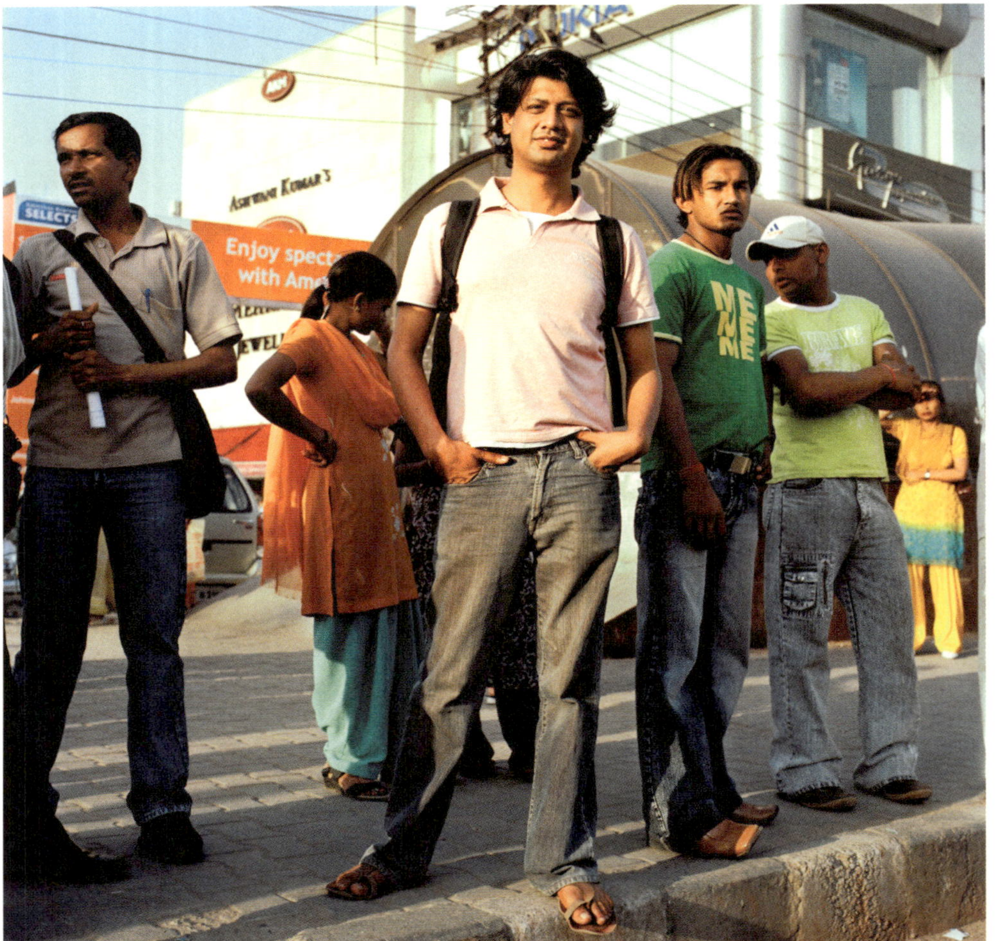

SUNIL GUPTA
Mr. Malhotra's Party

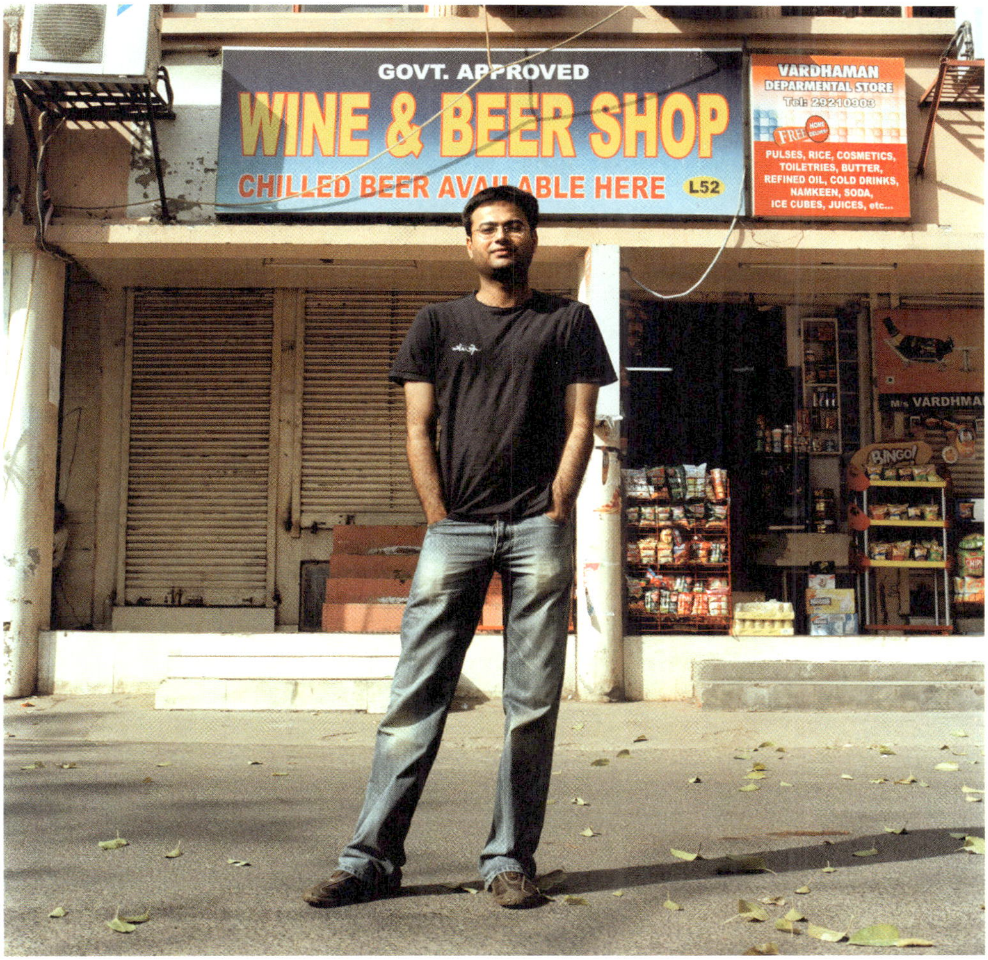

SUNIL GUPTA
Mr. Malhotra's Party

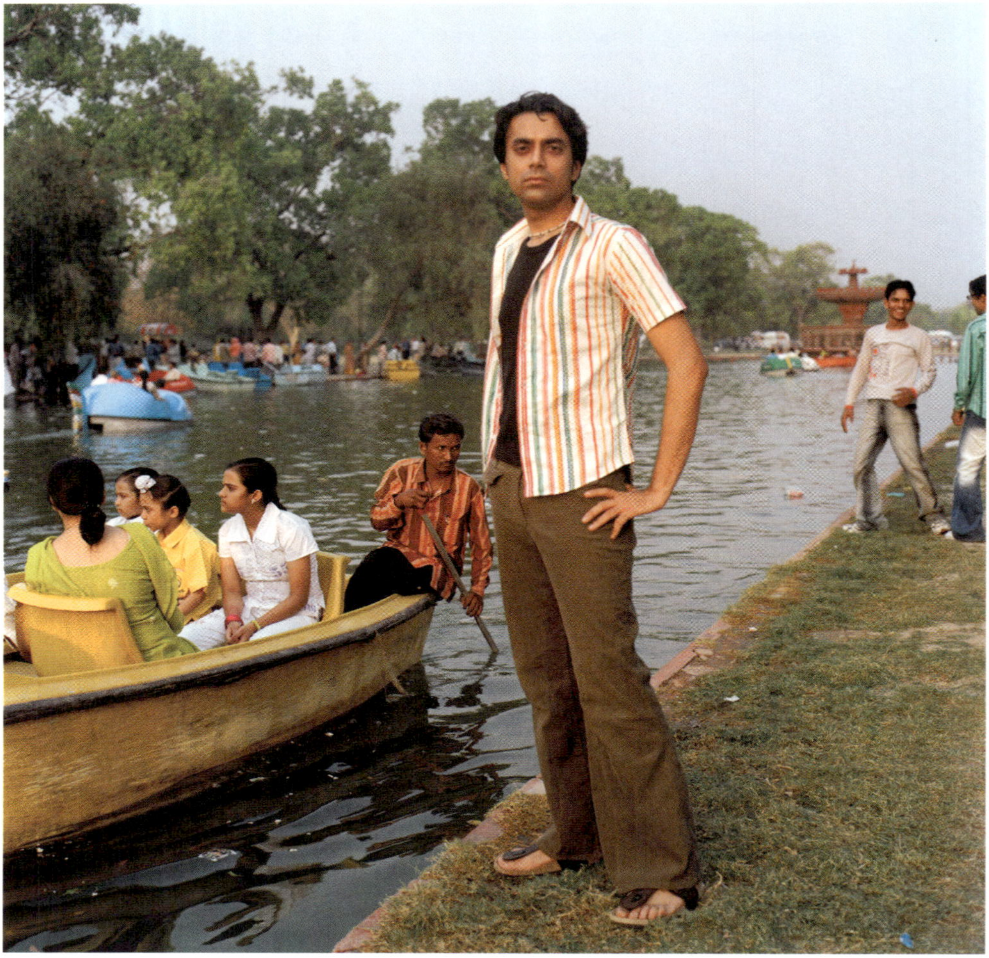

SUNIL GUPTA
Mr. Malhotra's Party

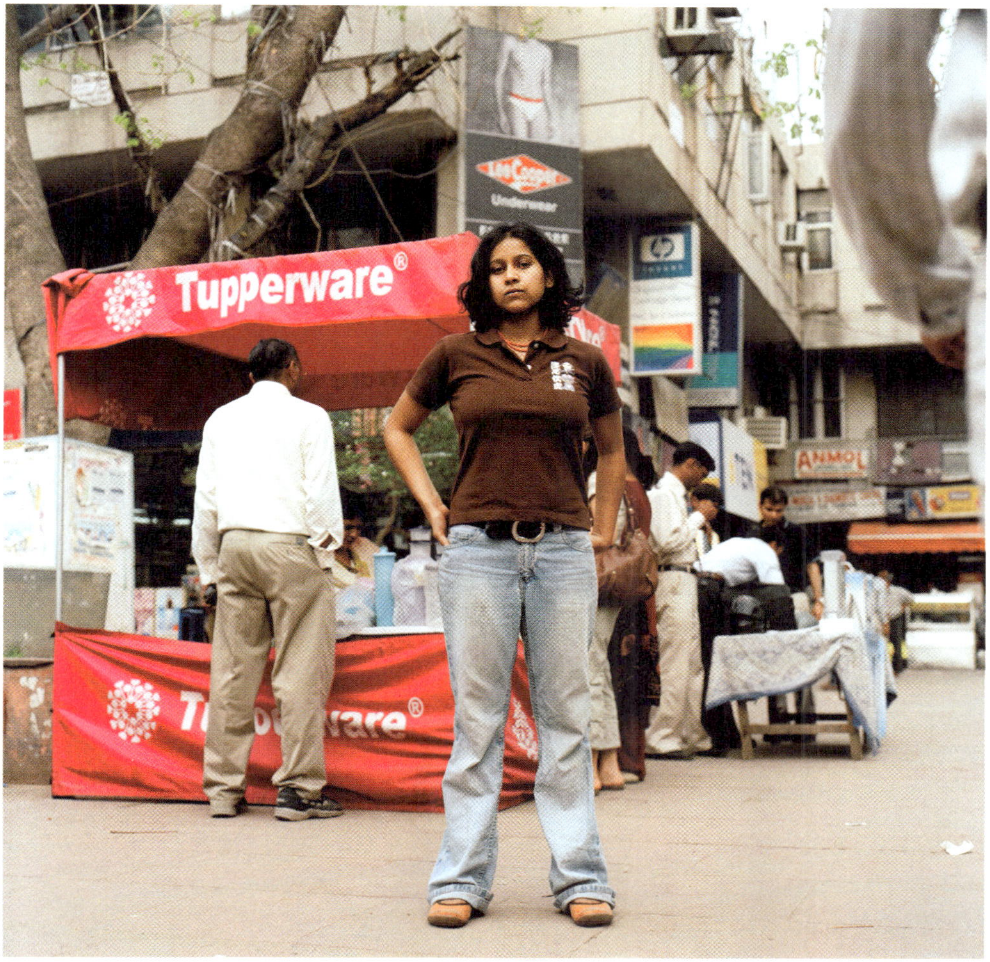

SUNIL GUPTA
Mr. Malhotra's Party

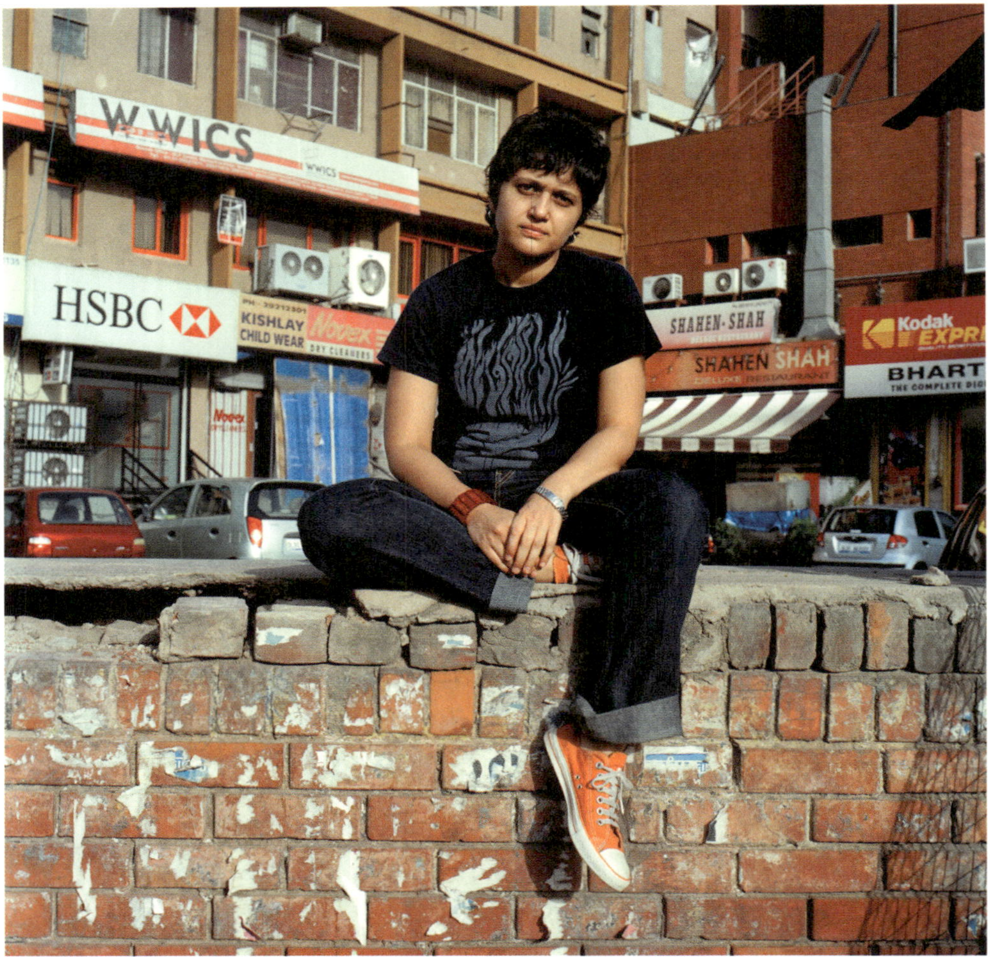

SUNIL GUPTA
Mr. Malhotra's Party

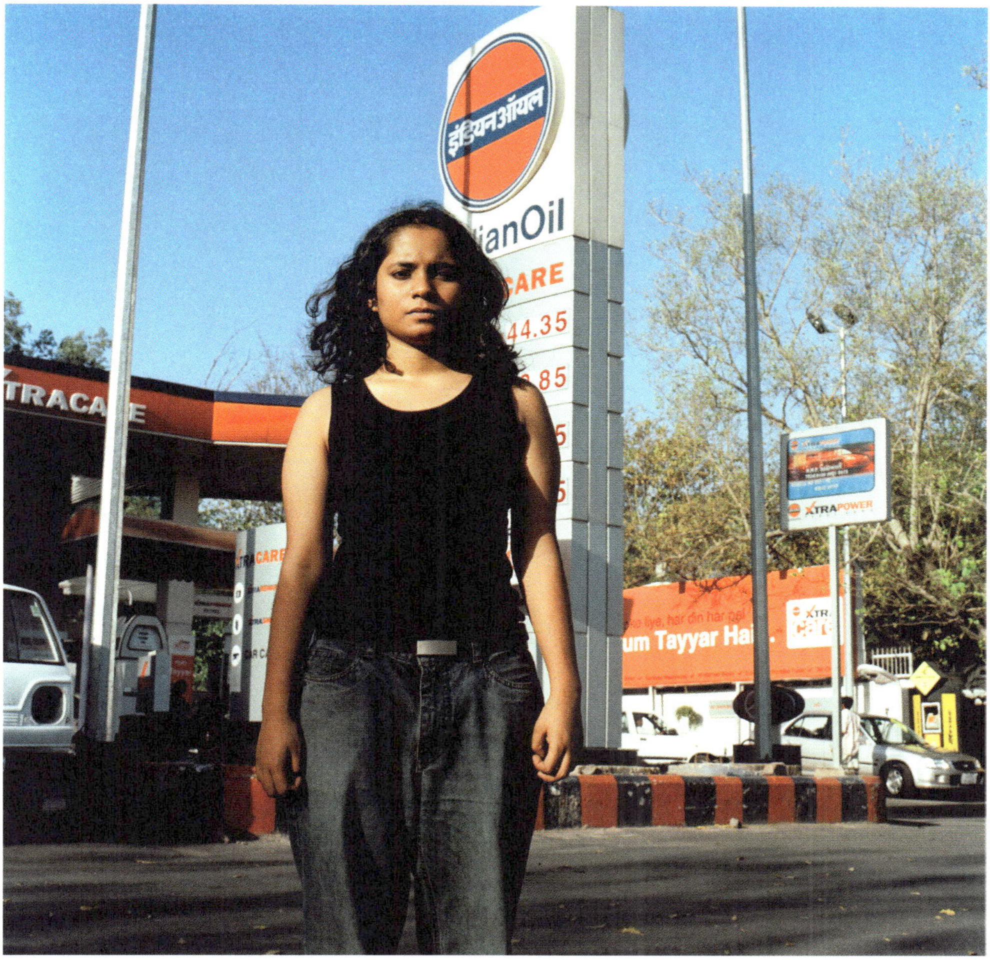

SUNIL GUPTA
Mr. Malhotra's Party

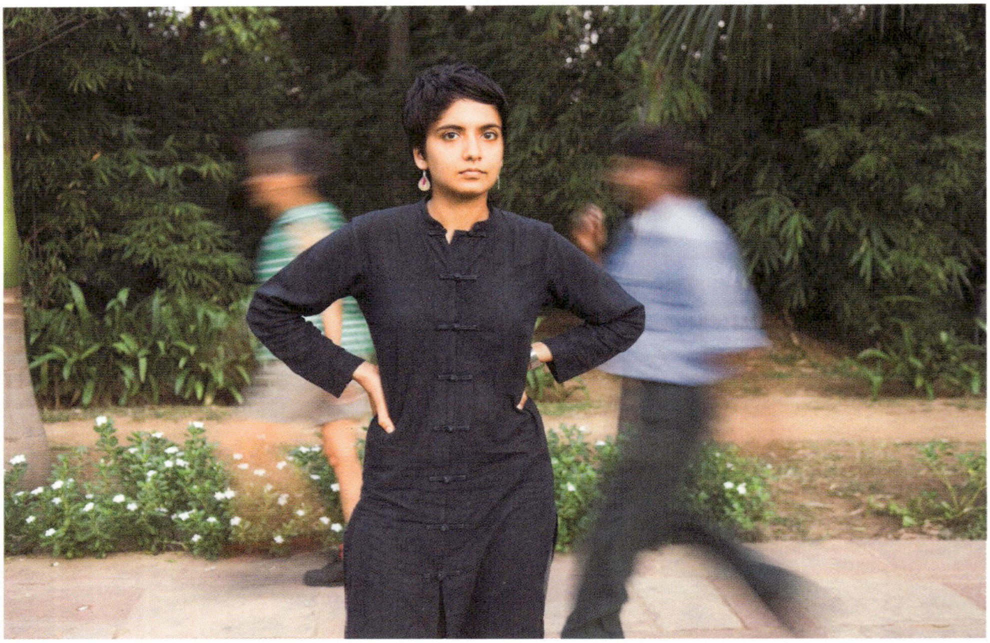

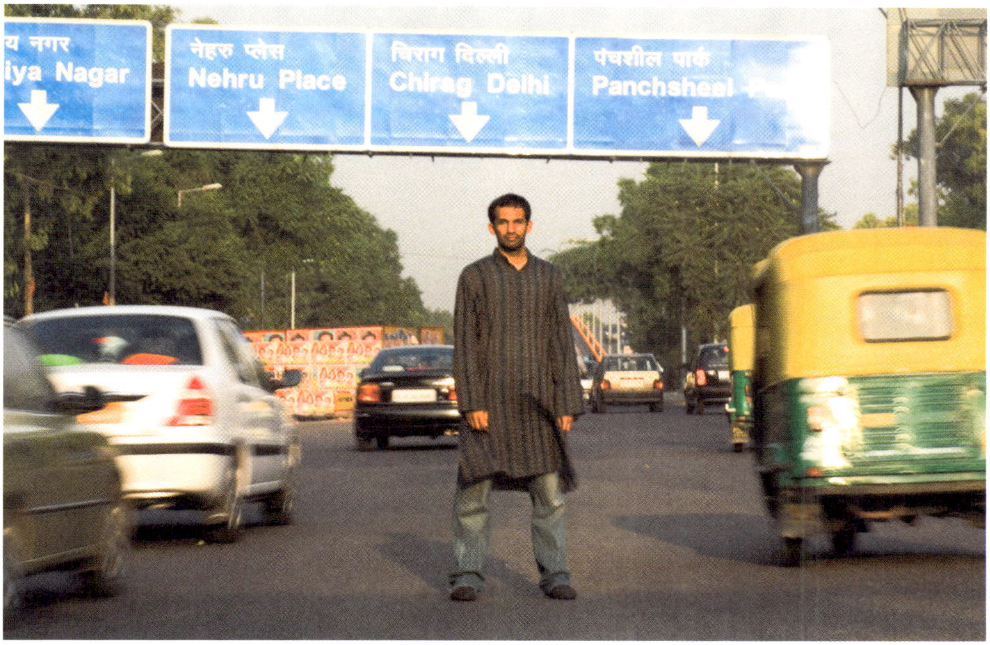
Nehru Place
नेहरु प्लेस
Chirag Delhi
चिराग दिल्ली
पंचशील पार्क

SUDEEP DASGUPTA

BETWEEN THE AESTHETICS OF MIGRATION AND MIGRATORY AESTHETICS

We are, so to speak, *of* the connections,
not outside and beyond them
EDWARD SAID [1]

He almost never succeeds in
corresponding with himself
ALBERT MEMMI [2]

Oh… there are so many attachments!
BHRIGU, IN *KOMAL GANDHAR* [3]

The relationship between aesthetics, as the making of art, and migration, as a particular experience of displacement, is not one of reflection (mirroring) or overlap (one folding into the other) where the two terms remain separate. The artwork need not be related to the experience it wishes to convey (migration) through the drawing of a straight line or the folding of a surface. Rather, the complex connection between an artwork (in this case, film) and the "theme" of migration may be considered as itself being a particular *mode* of displacement. By "mode", I mean the strategic deployment of the synchretic materiality of film whereby the film becomes the site of a construction of migration, whereby the spectator is continually displaced within this filmic experience. It is here that Art becomes an externalised *concretion* of the Idea or Spirit of migration. And as such, it assumes a somewhat contradictory character of the performative re-presentation. The term "performative re-presentation" functions here to grasp at an understanding both of the non-referentiality of art's productivity—its performativity as something that cuts against the grain of *re-presentation* or faithful and transparent reflection of real events—and of the inescapable fact that this performativity does not function *ex nihilo,* but operates within conditions of felicity and a "field of constraint".[4] The strategic deployment of displacement as the mode through which to approach migration is concretised in Ritwik Ghatak's *Komal Gandhar* (1961), which could most literally be translated as a "a flat note", but is in actuality translated as *Soft Note on a Sharp Scale* in English because the literal translation is insufficiently evocative of a particular melancholy mood. Ghatak's film is an apt point of reference because its cinematic construction of displacement may be seen to operate on three levels: in the film itself, through the disjunctive deployment of sound and image, and the latter's composition; between the film and its historical context; and lastly, within the complexly articulated migration between poem, song, theatre and film.

Articulating a philosophy of art in his *Aesthetics*, Hegel highlights displacement as a function of Art's (various, consecutive) failed attempts to concretise the Idea adequately.[5] For Hegel, (Romantic) poetry comes closest to synthesis (of artwork and Idea) at the end of a teleological narrative where this concretion of the Idea has already migrated from architec-

---

1 Said, E. 1994. *Culture and Imperialism*. London: Vintage, p. 65.
2 Memmi, A. 1965. *The Colonizer and the Colonized*. New York: Orion Press, p. 140.
3 Ghatak, R. 1961. *Komal Gandhar*. Production: Chitrakalpa, B/W, 134 minutes.
4 See Austin, J.L. 1975. *How to do things with words*. Harvard: Harvard University Press. The second is Judith Butler's response to the voluntarist readings of her theory of performative agency. See Butler, J. 2004, *Undoing Gender*. London and New York: Routledge, p. 1. Also see Derrida, J. *Limited Inc.*, Chicago: Northwestern University Press.
5 The dialectic as the movement of Reason in History *must* pass through Art as the place where the spiritual (not to be confused with religious) freedom of man is most clearly made manifest. See Hegel, G.W.F. 1975. *Hegel's Aesthetics: Lectures on Fine Art*. Oxford: Oxford University Press. This is the most obvious place to focus on, though Spirit's movement through Art also occupies a place (in relation to religion) in Hegel, G.W.F. 1977. *The Phenomenology of Spirit*. Oxford: Oxford University Press

ture (the Greek temple) through sculpture to music. Thus, in Hegel's narrative, the concretion of Idea or Spirit (for our purposes, the experience of migration) cannot be accomplished completely or adequately in an artwork, as it migrates from one art-form to the next, for each artwork only partly succeeds in erasing the troublesome materiality of its form, thus requiring the Idea's continued migration into yet another form. Hegel is perhaps unprecedented in his attention to the specific materiality of the work of art, but for him this is always an obstruction to the Idea. Something related, but distinct takes place in *Komal Gandhar*, a film that may be understood to move through different forms of art within a single artwork. Ghatak deploys the materiality of cinema to construct a process of displacement through which this migration between forms is approached. And this modality of displacement in the construction of the film in turn echoes displacement as the experience of migration.

The aesthetics of migration can be read as the forms of aesthetics produced from the perspective of the experience of migration. A migratory aesthetics occurs on the level of a migration of aesthetics itself across the (arbitrary) borders that separate music, architecture, theatre and film, say. Such conjunction between a migratory aesthetic and an aesthetic migration is palpable in the work of Ritwick Ghatak. Forced migration affects the content and the tonality of his work in literature, theatre and film, and in *Komal Gandhar* migration is figured through multiple displacements. The link between migratory aesthetics and aesthetic migration colours all his work, and finds its sharpest articulation in the conjunction (already evident in the title, *Komal Gandhar*) of a musical note that floats above the film's thematic and aesthetic production as a complimentary and undecidable "feeling tone".[6]

If we *are* "of connections" as Edward Said argues, our "being" is marked by the failure of a correspondence between them. This disjunctive conjunction shapes not just the film and the man (Ghatak's biography) but also speaks of an experience of non-correspondence that marks both migration and aesthetics. The Tunisian postcolonial theorist Albert Memmi's subtle narrative of the changing relationship between—and permutations of—coloniser and colonised is here translated in a postcolonial and post-imperial situation, producing non-correspondence as the "structure of feeling" of both human subjectivity and aesthetic practice.[7] The self-estrangement of human subjectivity and the (non) correspondence of art and reality are conjoined in Ghatak's film as one mode of thinking migratory aesthetics and aesthetic migrations *together*. And as Ghatak's own involvement in politics was structured by forced migration, it is worth attending to his biography in considering his film.

Rows and Rows of Fences

Ritwik Ghatak (1925-76) was born in Dhaka (then part of Bengal in British India), in a part of the country that was split into two in 1947 (with West Bengal becoming a part of India and East Bengal being assigned to Pakistan) and which after a war of independence became Bangladesh. The Bengal Famine of 1943-4, World War II and, finally, the Partition of 1947 forced Ghatak, along with millions of others to migrate to Calcutta where he became actively involved in the Indian People's Theatre Association (IPTA), the cultural front of the Communist Party of India (CPI). Ghatak's political and cultural activities were profoundly marked by the experience of forced migration resulting from the Partition, which is discernible in the title of his 1983 book on cinema, which alludes to people crossing over endless rows of fences that separate them from their homes. His cultural exposure from childhood was global in scope. Originating from the small, educated minority of an essentially feudal landed aristocracy, his access to language

---

6 Jameson, F. 1979. 'Reification and Utopia in Mass Culture', *Social Text* 1, p. 133. For Fredric Jameson, this "quasi-material 'feeling tone' which floats above the narrative which only intermittently realizes it" is apt for a literary consideration of the music and songs in the film, though as it will be argued below thus "realizing the theme" is also accompanied by a failure to adequately represent it in the materiality of sound.

7 Raymond Williams' term, the "structure of feeling" captured the dialectical holding together of objective conditions and subjective fluidity, as a precedent on another register of the complexity of the notion of performativity. See Williams, R. 1961. *The Long Revolution*, London: Chatto and Windus. See Memmi 1965, p. 48.

included Bengali, English, Persian, and Sanskrit. Both Hindustani and Western classical music were familiar to him, as well as the literary and philosophical writings of Europe including Freud and Marx. During his involvement with the IPTA, he acquired a familiarity with the writings of Carl G. Jung, Erich Neumann (particularly his *Great Mother*) and Joseph Campbell, as well as the language, music and cultural practices of tribal India.[8]

Formed in 1943, the IPTA was the first organised national theatre movement in India that developed and staged plays addressing class injustice and British imperialism. Ghatak's IPTA involvement began in Calcutta in 1948, and involved writing, directing and acting in his own and others' plays, including revivals of Dinabandhu Mitra's *Neeldarpan* ("Indigo Mirror," 1860), and Bengali-language adaptations of Nikolai Gogol's *The Government Inspector* or Maxim Gorky's *The Lower Depths*. In the same year, Ghatak became involved with other aspiring filmmakers, like Mrinal Sen, in discussing filmmaking as well as in unionising film workers and technicians. One of Ghatak's first intensive involvements with cinema was as an actor in Nemai Ghosh's ground-breaking 1950 film *Chinnamul* ("The Uprooted"), which charted the story of a group of farmers from East Bengal who are forced to migrate to Calcutta because of the Partition. Calcutta's Sealdah railway station was the location for the film and the actual place of disembarkment for the forced migrants who were played by actual refugees.

For Ghatak (and many others), the lived experience of forced migration translated into a political and cultural involvement, which moved across a number of simultaneous cultural migrations. At the first level, the involvement in/migration between theatre and film, reveals what one calls "cross-mediality" these days, where the specificities of each art form *and their inter-relations* become the mode through which the experience and consequences of migration are externalised. The film *Komal Gandhar* which literally refers to a musical note, is inspired by a poem of the same name by Rabindranath Tagore. In this case, music and film find their inspiration in poetry. The three cannot be separated in understanding the film. And thus the specificities of the material of each form in their displaced inter-relationship can be seen as contaminating the teleology of aesthetic migration that Hegel's *Aesthetics* constructs; the film underlines the impossibility of thinking poetry (Tagore) either in isolation or as the apotheosis of a synthetic drive. The materiality of the poem is displaced and externalised from one sound (recitation) to another (music in the film), and to film itself with its specific orchestration of different materials. Aesthetic migrations and migratory aesthetics continually overlap, disrupt and comment on each other. On the one hand, not just the experience of migration, but the migration of aesthetic forms were re-tooled by Gatak (not unlike Bertolt Brecht's notion of *Umfunktionierung*[9]) through a disjunctive conjunction between a variety of musical styles, mythological motifs and dramaturgical conventions specific to the Bengali region of India; and on the other hand, themes from "Western" artists (Gogol and Gorky) and their particular aesthetic styles (Stanislavski in theatre, and most importantly Brecht and Pudovkin in film) became important points of reference.

Between Theatre and Film

Why should I go?
Tell me... leaving my fertile land... the Padma river...
For food! This is your last chance to be a refugee
Refugee?
Landless refugee... named by media persons

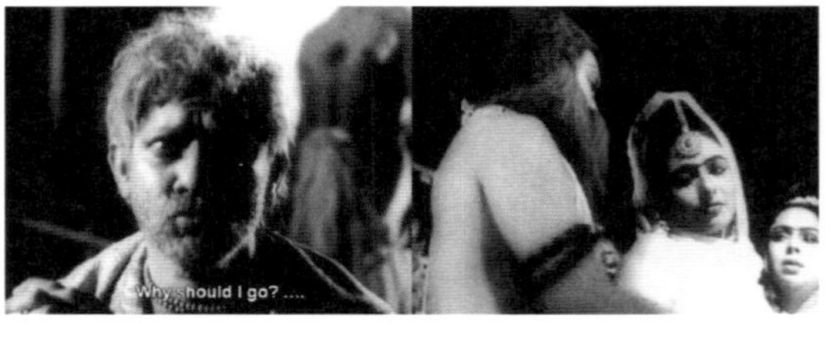

The personal experience of migration as forced displacement is produced in Ghatak's film, not through a simple representational strategy of directly linking sign and referent, but through a double-presentation of overlaps and disjunctures. The diegesis operates at two levels—at one level, the film tracks a theatrical troupe comprising East Bengali refugees as it prepares for and finally stages Kalidasa's *Shakuntala*. The actual staging of the play, which deals with forced migration operates on the second level. The film then, is not a representation of migration but approaches the topic through displacement—by making the process of staging a play about migration its focus. The film's two main protagonists are Bhrigu (Abanish Banerjee) who is the leader of the theatre troupe and Anasuya (Supriya Chowdhury) who plays the title role in the play, and who is known to have belonged to a rival troupe. The experience of migration is approached through a presentation of the difficulties experienced by migrants as they struggle to produce a play about leaving home. Ghatak chooses to displace a *re*presentation of migration, emphatically producing the phenomenon at one remove. Here, the difficulties of theatrically representing migration withhold the representation of migration as a reified condition.

Aesthetics and migration thus become dialectically linked—migration approachable only through the problem of aesthetic presentation, aesthetic practice becoming a function of the displacement of migrants (of Ghatak and the other refugees in the IPTA active in the making of the film, as well as the two theatre troupes which comprise refugees in the film). On the one hand, each phenomenon (aesthetic practice/migration) can only be approached through an externalisation or indirectly. On the other hand, an internalisation (or intrinsic quality) of migration in aesthetics and vice versa is evident in a relay that the film establishes between (the playwright) Kalidasa's written text, the stage action which this script is transformed into, and the production-of the film where both are imbedded. "The film examines", in Ghatak's words, the "agonizing saga of degeneration, alienation and rootlessness" which marks the "perpetual homelessness" of the "ravaged psyche" of Bengal after the Partition.[10] But this real-life saga is captured on celluloid, onto a film that opens in the midst of a play itself seen from the middle—the first scene shows the words "Act 2". The dislocated link between forced migration and aesthetic displacement finds an almost iconographic manifestation in the subsequent close-up of an old man asking "Why should I go?" to which he is told he has been *named* a "landless refugee"—a term the old man does not understand—by "media persons." It is thus doubly significant that Ghatak's aesthetic intervention documents the political involvement of those refugees who have chosen to externalise their experiences at a remove from the mass media which attempts to name them (using names they do not identify with). In their struggle, they choose theatre, a cultural form that is itself displaced from the dominant field of media.

The constitutive failure of a neat fit between migratory aesthetics and aesthetic migration at the diegetic level results in displacements which, at a second level, that of theoretical discourse, provides another vantage point from which the relationship between aesthetics and migration can be perceived. In numerous instances, the subject matter of the play performatively produces—*and* referentially displaces—the (diegetic) experiences of the theatre troupe. There is thus a two-way traffic between the content of the play being staged and the actions of those who are involved in its staging. Unexpected deployments of images structure this permeability of the migratory and the aesthetic. An example: Bhrigu and Anasuya are engaged in a conversation shown through a series of close-ups. Suddenly, this back and forth of close-up images is interrupted by a matching shot of an old woman with tears in her eyes. In traditional

---

8 The presence of these influences in his artistic work is discernible explicitly in Ghatak, R. 1987. *Rows and Rows of Fences*, Calcutta: Seagull. For an excellent critical assessment of Ghatak's film *oeuvre*, see Banerjee, H. 1985. *Ritwik Kumar Ghatak: A Monograph*. Pune: National Film Archive.

9 The term is critically deployed by Walter Benjamin. See Benjamin, W. 1978. 'The Author as Producer', in P. Demetz (ed) *Reflections: Essays, Aphorisms, Autobiographical Writings*. New York: Schocken Books, p. 228. Benjamin suggests that "the concept of technique provides the dialectical starting point from which the unfruitful antithesis of form and content can be surpassed." Ibid. p. 222. This twisting of Hegel's logic in the *Aesthetics* is significant. Technical experimentation that violates the propriety of specific art forms, which comprises Benjamin's understanding of "technique", relates directly to Ghatak's productive displacement of the resources of sound and image in film.

10 Ghatak, 1987 pp. 61-7.

film language, the use of such a similar shot would imply that the woman is part of this conversation. Soon though, we realise this shot is not closing the sequence between the two protagonists, or implying that the woman occupies the same space they do. Rather, it is a displacement. The shot is linked to a completely different space, that of an audience watching a play, in this case *Shakuntala* being staged in a theatre as part of the IPTA activities. Ghatak's close-up sequence displaces a scene without giving us any clues of this displacement; in conventional cinema a shift in space would be established via a long shot, then a medium shot. The sudden appearance of the woman's face, to whom we have not been introduced before, within a rally of close-ups, functions as something of a shock, and produces a question: "Who is she? Where is she?" Only *after* the close up of her face has given to a sequence of establishing shots, do we realize that we are now being displaced into another space—that of the theatre where the play is being staged.

Later, as the same old woman watches a crucial scene of the play where a mother mourns the loss of her son she asks: "They killed my son with their feet. Doesn't your blood get heated...? You young are sitting idle!" The extreme close-up of this old, low-caste woman records her watching the scene above her, but—as if to contradict her low placement vis-à-vis the stage—she too has been observed from below or above the camera (her framing reminiscent of Eisenstein's famous close-up of the mother in Battleship Potemkin).

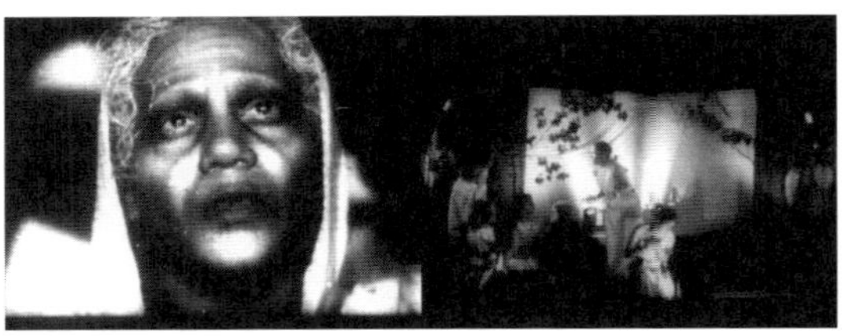

After the play ends, the woman approaches Bhrigu, the head of the troupe, and offers him a medal once awarded to her son, also a performer, who was killed in the upheavals during the Bengal Famine, so that this medal can be sold to find more funds for restaging the play. The on-stage theatrical plot is mirrored off-stage after the play. Here death, injustice and art coincide and are displaced. The coincidence takes place in the conjunction produced by the camera between the mother robbed of her son on stage and the old woman in the audience. The displacement works on two levels. On the one hand, the plot in the play (the murder of the son) is displaced off-stage (when the old woman reacts to the loss of *her own* son). Furthermore, the response to this double injustice is also a displacement—whereas in the play on stage, the response to the son's murder is revenge, off-stage, in the film, the old woman responds by offering the posthumously awarded medal to Bhrigu to fund subsequent stagings of *Shakuntala*. This double displacement is enacted by the filmic presentation of the play and its environs. The extract from *Shakuntala* is shot frontally, capturing the typical perspective of an audience member in front of the proscenium stage. The camera zooms out, revealing that the protagonists on the stage are being watched by the old woman whose extreme close-up shows her responding to their conversation. The sudden change of perspective displaces the shot-countershot movement of classical cinema through the extremity of the close-up, which evacuates any background. The initial puzzlement (who is this woman? What is she looking at? Bhrigu and Anasuya?) results from her not having been introduced through a medium- or long-shot, as one would expect within the conventions of cinema. The sequence displaces the theatrical mode of visuality—frontality—into that of a filmic close-up; albeit the latter is already displaced from conventional shot sequencing. At the level of form and content, as well as between the elements of migration and aesthetics, an overlap (of close-ups) is followed by a displacement (the sudden spatial shift from house/audience to theatre). Each level and each element is thereby reconfigured.

This displacement *within* the film and its diagetic relationship moves to another level of displacement in the reception of *Komal Gandhar* in Bengal. In the film, the play is sabotaged, partly by one of the sponsors, by Shanta (Anasuya's rich aunt) buying a large number of tickets she promises to sell for the premiere, but withholds from the public in a fit of egotistical rage. Rowdy audience members then disrupt the performance. This episode needs to be displaced to another space/time, that of the Bengali reception of Ghatak's film. Ghatak made the film after a rancorous split from the IPTA, in the midst of the growing political orthodoxy of the Communist Party of India, evident in the "cultural" line of its Soviet-inspired aesthetic policies. His experiences, not solely of migration, but of the stultifying hold of institutional Marxism on aesthetic experimentation, becomes the subject of his film: the opening sequence of *Komal Gandhar*, with the staging of a play, is punctuated by Shanta's derisive snort "Ha!! Drama..."; to which a member of her troupe responds wryly, "Do you know the name...? 'Experiment'?"—this derogatory dismissal brings to mind Brecht's own notion of theatre as an experiment in need of an educated public, which resulted in his *Lehrestüke*. The film was seen by party apparatchiks as a direct assault on them, and they responded by buying up tickets and disrupting the performances. After a very successful first week, the disruptions sabotaged further screenings and the film closed as a failure. Ironically, and predictably, it was only when Ghatak's œuvre was screened in Paris in 1983, and uproariously welcomed by the critics of *Cahiers du Cinema*, that interest in his work awakened in India. The fate of the play displaces the theatrical diegesis (killing of the son) to the filmic diegesis (the bereaved mother's response off-stage), while the fate of the film comes *post facto* to mirror that of the play within it. At all three levels (the diegesis of play, the diegesis of the film, and the extra-diegetic reception of *Komal Gandhar*), the conjunction of performative effectivity and representational failure secures the productivity of art as an intervention in the social space distorted by migration.

Between Sound and Image

The French embrace of Ghatak was predicated on his juxtaposition of sound and image, reminiscent (to the *Cahiers* critics, that is) of Robert Bresson, Jacques Tati and Jean-Marie Straub. This relationship between sound and image operates on at least two levels in Ghatak's entire corpus (theatrical, filmic etc.). At the intra-visual level, Ghatak was the first Indian director whose visual aesthetic caused much puzzlement in India since it broke with both the static frontality that had dominated early Indian film (a displacement from Parsi theatre) and the mode of his influential contemporary Satyajit Ray, whose cinema absorbed (though not exclusively) many innovations of Italian neo-realists like Vittorio de Sica. The divergence from *both* theatrical frontality and the static absent-presence of the camera-as-witness produced a dizzying displacement of the spectatorial position. Ghatak introduced a range of strategic choices: traditional medium-shot frontality was often skewed through angular camera-placement, while the frame-composition was frequently off-centre, partly excising objects that should be centralised.

Geeta Kapur rightly rejects the Indian critique of Ghatak's strategy as being simply melodramatic, suggesting that the effect of such camera use was a perpetually renewed displacement of any fixed spectatorial position. I would argue further that Ghatak's displacement at the level of content (the plight of refugees and political upheavals mark a majority of his films) is externalised via a mode of errant visuality. My claim here is not simply that the content determines the form, however, for this externalisation is also a *displacement of* the content—one motivated less by a naive mimetic desire than by a pedagogic one: Brecht's *Verfremdung-effekt* is amply exercised within Ghatak's visual strategies particularly in relation to the displaced dialectic between aesthetics and politics. Not surprisingly, the championing of Brecht within the circle of the British journal *Screen* made Ghatak's visuality crucial for the development of a critical context around what came to be know as Third Cinema. (Kapur's essay on Ghatak appeared in the first anthology on Third Cinema published for *Screen* by Paul Willemen.)[11] Here, shot/frame

11 Reprinted most recently in Kapur, G. 2000. *When was Modernism? Essays on Contemporary Cultural Practice in India*. New Delhi: Tulika Books, pp. 181-200.

analysis demonstrates the visual linking of sharply divergent perspectives on a given action, which is augmented by the use of multiple cameras—some hand held, others digital—to produce varied visual textures. Further, Ghatak is understood to displace the rule of cinematic narrative development through logical spatial sequencing of shots (long-medium-close-up shot). All these become tenets of Third Cinema.

Ghatak's visual strategies of disorienting spectator positions and undermining narrative through non-sequential montage overlap with, and displace, the thematic concerns of forced migration—linking an aesthetics of migration to a migratory aesthetics. Moreover, as both Indian and French critics remarked, this visual dialectic extends to the audio track that accompanies the image, or vice versa. The connections are again multiple, involving overlapping and estrangement. For example, in a pivotal scene where Bhrigu and Anasuya are standing at the end of the railway line that runs along the bank of the Padma River, which separates East from West Bengal, there is a moment when they hear a song sung by a group of fishermen. The song reminds Anasuya of her mother, who brought her up on the other side of the river, and impels her, for the first time, to recount to Bhrigu her past across the river, and her mother's death during the bloody Noakhali riots now made famous by Gandhi's visit. The song brings back memories of a past located on one side of a once united region (Bengal – in Bengali "Bangladesh", the land ["desh"] of Bengal, *not* the name of the *state* of Bangladesh, which comes into existence two decades after the time of this conversation). It invokes a temporal and spatial displacement in Anasuya, to which Bhrigu responds by bringing up another music—the Komal Gandhar. This *raga* metaphorises Bengal to him, feminised as a sweet yet melancholy girl, which he explicitly relates to Rabindranath Tagore's original poem "Komal Gandhar" and the celebrated modern poet Bishnu Dey's 1951 version of it. Anasuya's memory of her mother's killing and her own childhood becomes Bhrigu's remembrance of his own mother and a metaphorical one (Bengal as a girl).

Spatial displacement (the pair's position on the wrong bank of a now dividing river that connected two parts of one land) evokes musical connections that work contrapuntally—bringing up audio-visually the kind of connections that, in Said's terms, act as the very being of human subjectivity. Importantly, this connective "being" is one of *non*-correspondence, precisely because displacement is both the condition of possibility for the connections and for their failure to correspond to each other. The contrapuntal simultaneity of sound and image captures the non-correspondence of the connections, which as it were "make the man".[12] Interestingly, Bhrigu's feminisation of Bengal as a young girl is followed by Anasuya's reversal of her mother's desperate observation that, instead of men, it is now up to young women to save Bengal. She reverts her mother's gender-specific words by saying that *men like Bhrigu* are the hope that her mother had for saving Bengal. Bhrigu's feminisation of Bengal as a sweet, melancholy girl (via Komal Gandhar) is reciprocated by his own feminisation in the (unconventionally feminine) position of avenger. Here too, we find a clear invocation of the double modality of Durga/Kali, as avenging/nurturing goddess of Bengal. (Anasuya's striking eye make-up, when compared to other women in the film, also brings up associations with Kali's most common visual representation.) The chain of displacements triggered by Komal Gandhar move through nation and gender, switching the meaning of both (Bengal as woman, Bhrigu as woman, Anusuya as Kali). Any fixed relation of realist sound to iconic image to referential meaning becomes impossible. Geeta Kapur puts the point succinctly, when she argues that "mythologies, as also travesties of the divine, are so structurally embedded in social practices that it needs a *many-pronged* narrative to loosen their hold. Short of that realism can become a reformist procedure for sifting the accumulated bad conscience of society."[13] Further, the vast array of audio accompaniments in *Komal Gandhar*, which turns music into a protagonist in its own right (rather than an overlay or companion to the image) defied any then-existing typology—merging IPTA group songs, *Baul* songs associated with that region of Bengal, tribal marriage songs and the pivotal refrain *Dohai Ali* ("Mercy, Ali!") which also closes the film.

In the case of the making of *Komal Gandhar*, serial displacements construct a particular modality in art capable of approaching the question of migration. Movement and migration are not just the content of the film which can be represented "realistically"; rather, the mode of presenting the experience of migration operates through a series of displacements—between the play and the film, between sound and image, and the film and its reception.

The Concrete Idea of Migration

For sound, the last external material
which poetry keeps, is in poetry
no longer the feeling of sonority itself, but...
a *sign* of the Idea which has become
concrete in itself.
G.W.F. HEGEL [14]

In his *Aesthetics*, Hegel's search for the most perfect embodiment of the Idea forces him to construct a narrative. In a sense, it is a narrative of the migration of the Idea (*Geist*) since its concrete embodiment moves through the different arts (architecture, sculpture, music) and ends in poetry. Poetry then, for Hegel, transcends "the last external material" which is sound, since sound becomes a sign of the Idea itself. In *Komal Gandhar*, we have seen the poem not as the end point or the culmination of the Idea of migration without any material remainder. Rather, the poem itself becomes the *starting point* for a series of multiple displacements or migrations. Tagore's poem, transformed into Bishnu Dey's verse, re-appears through sound and image, as the soundtrack in the episode by the river, and also as the occasion for divergent memories of loss and displacement. Here, sound (as musical soundtrack and songs) and its relation to image, concretises not some unified idea of migration but instead a network of specific, multiple and individual experiences of migration. Sound and image in the film preclude the perfect synthesis of Idea and art-form (migration and its filmic representation). In Hegel's philosophy, Life's continued alienation from Spirit is developed through a narrative of restless aesthetic migration. But what if a poem *about* alienation multiplies and displaces the contradictions between Idea and Art that Hegel wants to reconcile? Poetry's concretisation of the idea of migration (Tagore's melancholy metaphorics of the loss of the homeland in "Komal Gandhar") is only graspable when it migrates into the materiality of film.

Appendix
Komal Gandhar

I have named her *Komal Gandhar*
in my mind.
She would sit stunned if she learnt about it,
would ask smilingly, "What does it mean?"
That the meaning is unfathomable is its most
certain meaning.
The world is about work and vocation,
It's about good and bad—
Things with which she has made acquaintances
with others.
I watch, sitting by her side
how she has infused her surroundings with a
peculiar melody.
She knows not her own self.
At the spot where her Beloved's altar is placed
an agony-incense burns by His feet.
From there, a shadow of smoke engulfs the eyes,
like clouds masking the moon—
Covering the smile a little.
Her voice carries a fading strain of melancholy.
She is unaware that is the strain which
binds the strings of her life's *tanpura*.
The notes of *Bhairavi* permeate all her
words and actions.
I cannot conclude why.
That's the reason I call her *Komal Gandhar*—
It is hard to comprehend why
teardrops glide into the heart
when she lifts her eyes.

Rabindranath Tagore, circa 1893-1900.
My thanks to Bishwati Ghosh for her translation.

---

12 For an explanation of contrapuntal analysis see Said, 1994 p.59. Said convincingly argues that C.L.R. James' *The Black Jacobins:Toussaint L'Ouverture and the San Domingo Revolution* (1938) orchestrates a contrapuntal reading between Toussaint L'Ouverture and Napoleon. He then orchestrates such a musical relationship between James and Toussaint, on the one hand, and Ranajit Guha and S.H. Alatas on the other. See especially pages 297-316. In my argument, Ghatak's film orchestrates such a contrapuntal orchestration between and within sound and image.
13 Kapur, 2000 p. 260. Italic emphasis has been added.
14 Hegel, G.W.F. 1975. *Hegel's Aesthetics: Lectures on Fine Arts*. Oxford: Oxford University Press, p. 90.

MELVIN MOTTI

FAST ASLEEP

Walking through Calcutta, I had the awkward experience of receiving memories of places I have never seen or been to before. These memories were triggered by the button on my camera: the moment I am about to push it, I recall having seen the untaken picture before. After a while, my collection of untaken photographs grows out of proportion, and the memory of places I have never been to before confuses my whereabouts. So I set aside my camera altogether and replace it with my pen, in order to portray that which is impossible to reveal visually, the city's streets.

As I sit here, writing this down, on one of the few places on this street where one presumes to be left unnoticed, a man (looking like an Indian desperado; unshaven, shirtless, the voice of a villain) comes up.

"What are you doing?"
"I'm observing", I reply.
"Do you have permission?"
"...Well, do you have permission to observe me?"

He turns around and walks away, disregarding our short conversation and clearly not interested in a discussion about public and private domains. As a matter of fact, there is little of what may be called the private domain on the streets of Calcutta. In this densely populated part of an otherwise already densely populated country, one senses this most acutely when standing in a queue—which has never been my favourite place on earth. Something about the constant feeling of somebody's genitals pressing compactly against your ass makes me want to assume a parallel position. But once dislocated and disconnected, you're both invisible and more visible; you become vulnerable as an individual, in the private realm.

One of the biggest advantages I feel during my stay, is that I could remain dislocated and disconnected, yet stay relatively invisible due to my appearance. Apart from my closely cropped hair, which is associated with rituals of death and birth, and not commonly worn in-between, I look sort of 'like them'—short,

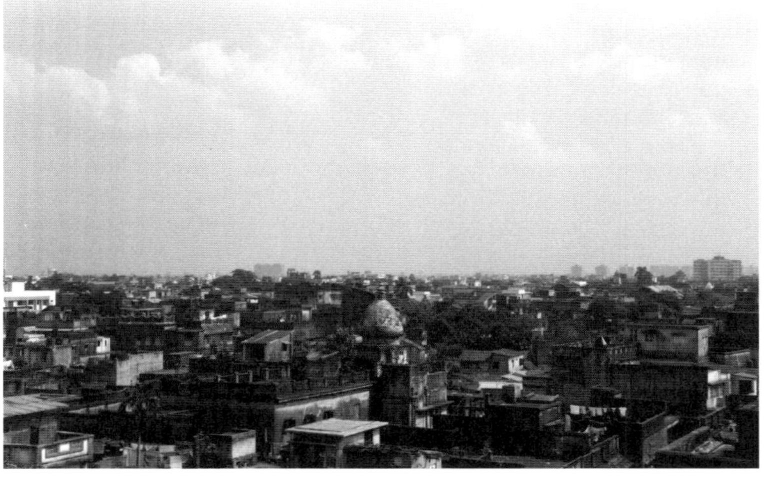

skinny and brown. Like a spy, masterly trained never to raise suspicion while investigating, I cross all corners of the city (formerly known as Calcutta), always on duty (this city never sleeps either) and always on air (which is so thick, you can almost write your name in the sky).

I just returned from the Marble Palace, a baroque sibling of the monumental and classic citadel that Catherine the Great had build in St. Petersburg. The colours to be found in the palace do not epitomise the colours of the city; the pallette is generally brighter and shinier then the earth-colours one tends to encounter on the streets. The contrast is formed by the two colours on the outer scope of the chromatic range: black and white. These tones, hardly represented in the streets of Calcutta, do unexpectedly animate four sculptures, representing four continents. The one representing Africa shows a woman with black features, carved in white marble, wearing a Greek dress. Opposite her is America, represented by a marble native Indian, which is off course historically correct but politically sensitive. Where you would have expected a colour, one faces whiteness. The palace, however, has not been totally spared from the process of fading. This is mostly due to the dust, which turns into heavy and thick dirt, diminishing objects under a coat of blackness. Since there are enough objects to choose from, a hierarchy now sets in; the dirty mostly smaller objects are pushed towards the walls, and the vivid ones are presented to the public without interference.
The palace becomes a jam-packed amalgam of neo-classical, baroque and rococo artworks, joined by carpets (mostly rolled up), all kinds of domestic goods with a royal panache, taxidermied animals (exotic ones, like monkeys and alligators) and countless small objects one cannot focus on in the mayhem of display.
The pushing and shoving of objects gives one the idea of being in an antique store, but at the same time, reminds one of the pushing and shoving that continually fills the streets (the queue). Jam-packed-ness is readily associated with Calcutta, but no humans are packed together so closely as the books one can find on College Street, just two blocks away from the Marble Palace. This is the place to be when in need of any out of print publication. Thousands and thousands of books are piled on top of each other, without much semblance of organisation (there is a faint thematic order, however—ask a man who is supposed to sell computer books for a book about economy, for example, and you have a fair chance that he

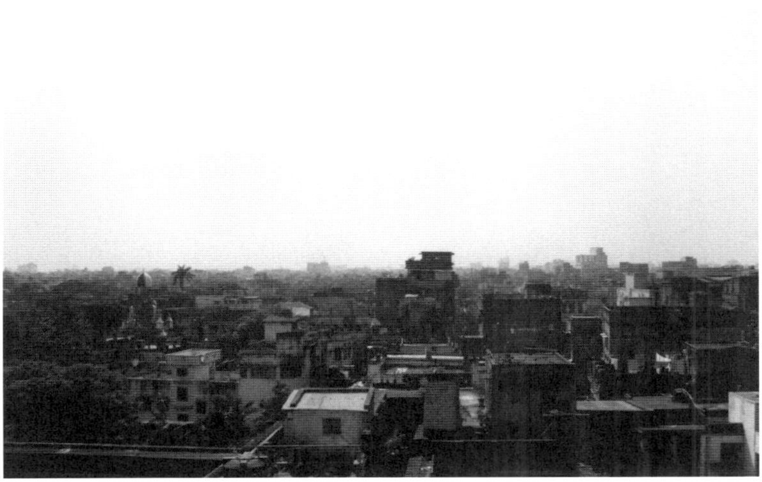

can dig one up from under the table). Because of the scatter, the layering of objects and subjects, the disorganised, unfiltered and often-impenetrable conditions, both the city and the palace feel like a big marketplace.

The first thing I smelled after descending from the plane was rotten fruit. The same smell I remember from when I descended the plane on the airport of Surinam (which comes close to a royal entrance; because there is no tunnel, the plane stops on the landing strip from where the travellers walk to the terminal, waving at their family who are gathered on the balcony of the building). Surinam is about one thousand miles closer to the equator and has a more tropical climate, but apparently produces a similar aroma. The second smell I noticed in Calcutta was the soapy odour of incense, wrapping up the whole city in second hand blossom. A very promising and encouraging smell (the smell is always in front of you, you walk towards it), it is sweet, but becomes especially pleasant when mixed with the smell of fresh sweat it becomes a pleasant reality.

I'm looking at a crow that is picking out his lunch from a carriage, giving me a chance to observe it. It's a fresh element amidst the street sights, jumping, wiggling, seemingly unharmed by direct sunlight. As the sunlight collides with its feathers, it is deflected towards the sides, creating a ray of rainbow colours on the shiny feathers. Actually, this crow is one of the few performers in this society that remains glistening, which is remarkable for a creature which is pitch black (blackness has the capacity to make even dust appear more visible). I guess this is because, when these dark birds fly, they kick up all the dust, contributing to that smoky atmosphere, eventually to be absorbed by somebody or some entity from the mortal world. Their elegance and composure is a welcoming, calming factor in the city; you can follow their movements and notice that they are completely unruffled by the alarms of the city and gracefully ignore the anxiety all around. I imagine that this is what a bird's-eye-view does to you: flying over the rooftops, looking over the rusted and soot-covered houses, one can form a different narrative of the city—one which is not given purely to deconstructing social layers on the streets, one which is not given to differences in dialects, clothing, age or size, but one which could be revealing, even in black and white, of a view onto a formal shape of steel plates placed in a loosely repeated pattern by individuals who remain unseen.

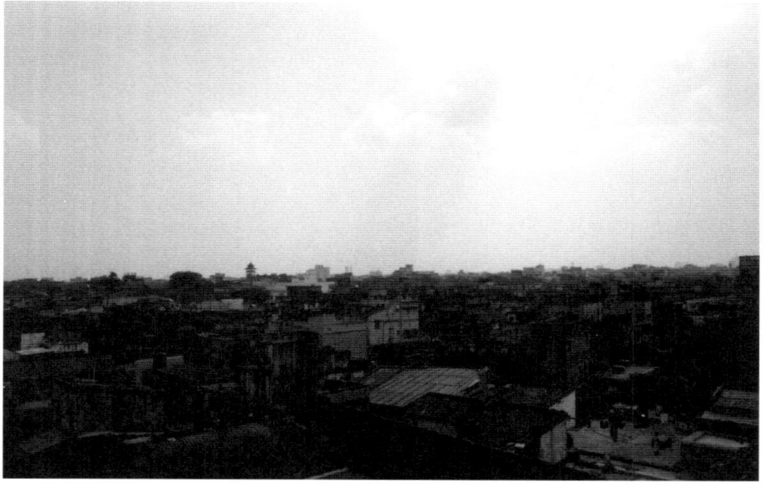

It was this very crow, whom I am observing still, that guided me from the Marble Palace to the place I am sitting now. I followed it from the garden of the Palace, along College Street, down south a few blocks until I lost it and I decided to sit down on the pavement, and there it turned up again—actually I am not sure if it is the same one, they all look so similar. On the way from College Street, it humped on the head of a George Washington bust whose hair is blown towards the air and then towards the side, like a lion's mane. Behind George there was a poster of a roaming lion, who seemed to be aiming for his head, but could not quite reach it. I wonder how long this cruel scene has been frozen, in the very climax, a second before disaster. Without ever making eye contact, the crow makes clear that it is about to guide me to the next place. With a piece of tasteless wood pressed between its spout, it flies up, accelerates briefly, then gently holds the pace for me to follow. I am looking slightly upwards while walking, by no means a comfortable angle as any eye pointed away from traffic is life-threateningly dangerous.

It takes about three hours before I arrive at my prearranged destination, during which time I am hardly walking of my own volition, but remain almost solely carried by the masses going in the same direction. On the way I buy one portion of Pakoras, but realizing this is way too little for something tasting so good, I buy another one at the following corner. The crow takes me right to the entrance of the Indian Museum, where I enter another queue, to buy a cheap ticket only meant for Indians and proceed to the courtyard. I am guided to the first stairs in view and upon entering one of the upper rooms, I find myself amongst about three hundred dead animals, enclosed in glass, hung on the wall. The only bird amongst them is the only living creature here and it just escaped through the window. I'm on my own now. The animals around me have been caught in their most vivacious position, then stuffed for eternity and grouped neatly according to species. They are like mummies, messengers from an ancient world, only able to transmit and not to respond. I walk through the impressive yet decaying showcases of rare—and not so rare—inhabitants of the animal world, and look up at the hundreds of curling antlers, clustered according to size and form. The light and dark brown colours of the antlers stand out against the bright blue wall on which they hang. They almost float above the head of the visitors, swirling like the forty-five propellers

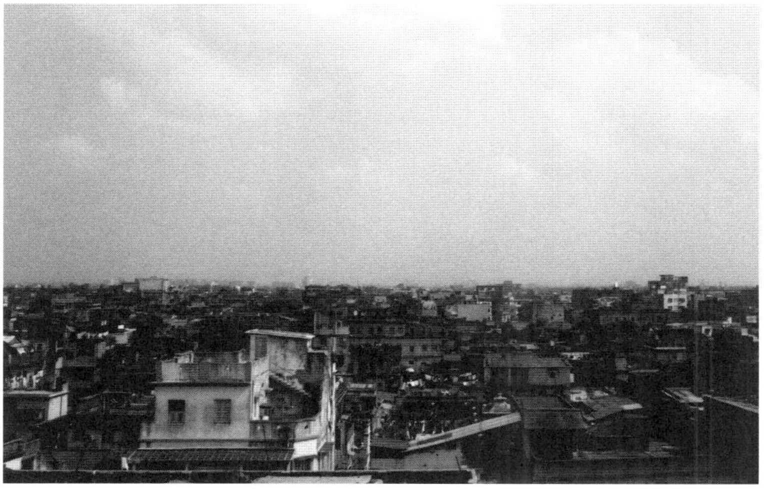

on the ceiling, blowing the air from one side to the other. On the way to the assembly hall, I see the first and cutest tiger cub and it is as cuddly as I would have imagined. The next hall is unoccupied by animals; here there are about five thousand cabinets filled with some one million items, all stones of all colours and sizes. Again, there are about forty-five propellers constantly spinning above my head and in the distance. It's almost impossible to concentrate on any cabinet or any part of this space individually, as one is easily distracted by the totally-controlled madness one witnesses. In this hall, which is supposed to be about 'archaeology', history is covered by history, then covered by more history, until the history exposed is too coated to penetrate. The stones are mostly labelled, yet the labels only display the scientific names of the objects, words that an average visitor, not being a qualified archaeologist, is unable to decipher. The stones thus remain stones, with an ostensible historic value, but look suspiciously similar to the stones found in any backyard. As I move closer to one cabinet, and actually try seeing what is inside, more wonders descend upon me. First of all, the cabinets are not lit from the inside, making them almost impossible to look into. Stones, stones and more stones—some are minerals, some have been coloured and some are just old stones. There is an empty pedestal with an old mark of a stone that previously occupied it. Then there is a perfectly square box, about forty inches on each side, wrapped up in a newspaper, held together by a green ribbon. It is a secret present, perhaps containing century-old air, but kept locked and keeping the viewer in suspense. I wonder what historic value this present has, apart from the primeval promise it seems to keep. And I wonder why one would put an empty pedestal in the midst of archaeological artefacts. History and reality appear to us as such, crossing (or standing in) our path without any categorisation or filter. No curator has divided these prehistoric artefacts in a thematic narrative or tried to relocate them chronologically. Looking at the display of objects, it seems to me that I have entered a storage area; one where the wrapping and platform of the historic objects are valued equally to the museum exhibits.

Against the bottom exterior of the cabinet, there is a stack of stones, placed nonchalantly on top of each other. Again the question lingers: am I looking at some fossil from another millenium or are these leftovers from a recent renovation? The complete indifference with which objects—whether artefacts or not—are placed beside one another makes this hall in the Indian Museum feel utterly erratic; beware visitors, history is always on the lookout and is ready to jump on you at any time, unannounced and unexpected. The animals might be stuffed and still, but history is on the loose. This feeling of suspicion with which the Indian Museum should be entered has transgressed into the streets of Calcutta. Do I see a white marble bust of Indira Gandhi, suddenly arising from the muddled scene of an overcrowded street market? Confined and cornered in a little niche, somebody has tried to spit in her eye, painting it red, though over time this mark turned a light brown… her original skin colour. The motionless portrait is in stark contrast with the smell of publicly packed red onions spreading all over the area and the hurriedness of street-market-economies in action. Maybe that is why her eyes are on the verge of popping out, turned as they are towards the upper corner of her eyeballs, in soap operatic code for madness. This is Indira Gandhi on acid, jumping at me from the most unexpected angle, in the most unanticipated moment of my walk.

Wariness is elemental when operating on the streets; I've been asked to secure permission when photographing, writing or even before thinking. But to be wary also means to anticipate and to stay alert, which is the best active mode one can be in, both in the museums and throughout the city of Calcutta. How often have cyclists jumped in front of me as soon as I turned a corner in an unsuspecting moment? Although I react by leaping back, I know well that it is too late for any reflex. Yet, unbelievably I remain undamaged. So, did the cyclist or did I suddenly turn into a ghost, when he ran straight through me? One must remain prepared at all times when operating in this city; it prevents you from falling asleep (suspicious soldiers sleep with one eye open, I've been told). To see the city moving and sleeping at the same time, reminds me of a somnambulist. It walks ever so slowly, android-like and in reverse, chasing lost times, with the almost suffocating cultural and economic wealth of the pre-colonial and pre-war period in the back of the mind. I once heard somebody say that Calcutta has no dreams for sale. But, as with any sleepwalker, there is always an undeviating connection between waking-life and sleep. So why buy a dream when dreaming is all you do, all day long, whilst walking?

To prevent the city from being totally paralysed and slipping into an everlasting sleep, the inhabitants have agreed to produce as many alarms as possible. People shouting, cars honking, cyclist ringing, the unequivocal smell of rubbish—all are there to keep this city from falling into a deep and probably very comfortable sleep. But being amongst constant alarm creates its own lethargy—people living here remain impassive while visitors get caught up by the anxiety of the constantly honking cars. Unlike me, the locals have become immune to these signals of danger, incorporating them as background noise in their dreams. If not the usual alarms, if not the usual surprises, what can now wake the dreamer from this state of sleep?

I am riding home in a cab. It has become dark awfully soon and quickly, the meter is not on, but the driver and I prearranged a price before commencing the journey. We are driving on an empty road, fairly fast as there is nobody around and the lane is long and grand. I have closed my window, and for the first time today I am experiencing something which sounds like silence. My head is starting to become heavy, millions of impressions flash through my mind when I close my eyes. I am about to fall asleep when, abruptly, the driver breaks the silence by honking, an impulsive response to the extensive absence of noise. I jump up and look around, and there is absolutely no other car around for which this signal could have been meant. We are all alone. The driver is honking to himself. It's an automated signal to prevent him from transgressing to another state. A silent state. A state I call sleep, but he probably calls wakefulness. I imagine the alarms he is using are somniferous, they give him a warm, blissful feeling; they are his medicine. Just like the old opium eaters, you can see him doze off—surrounded by alarms, drowsy from their effects, until they fade out of consciousness. The silence is a crude intruder in this world of noise, a ruthless waking call, to which the dreamer quickly responds by injecting an antidote into his ears, shooting it directly to his brain. Honk. This world is upside down. I love it.

Yakshas are clever, dangerous, fickle, wise, capricious and generous beings. They are known to lurk in wait for unsuspecting travellers whom they invariably test with an ordeal of demanding questions. Yakshas, condemned to long hours of keeping vigil over hoards of money, will do anything to make the passing traveller tarry.

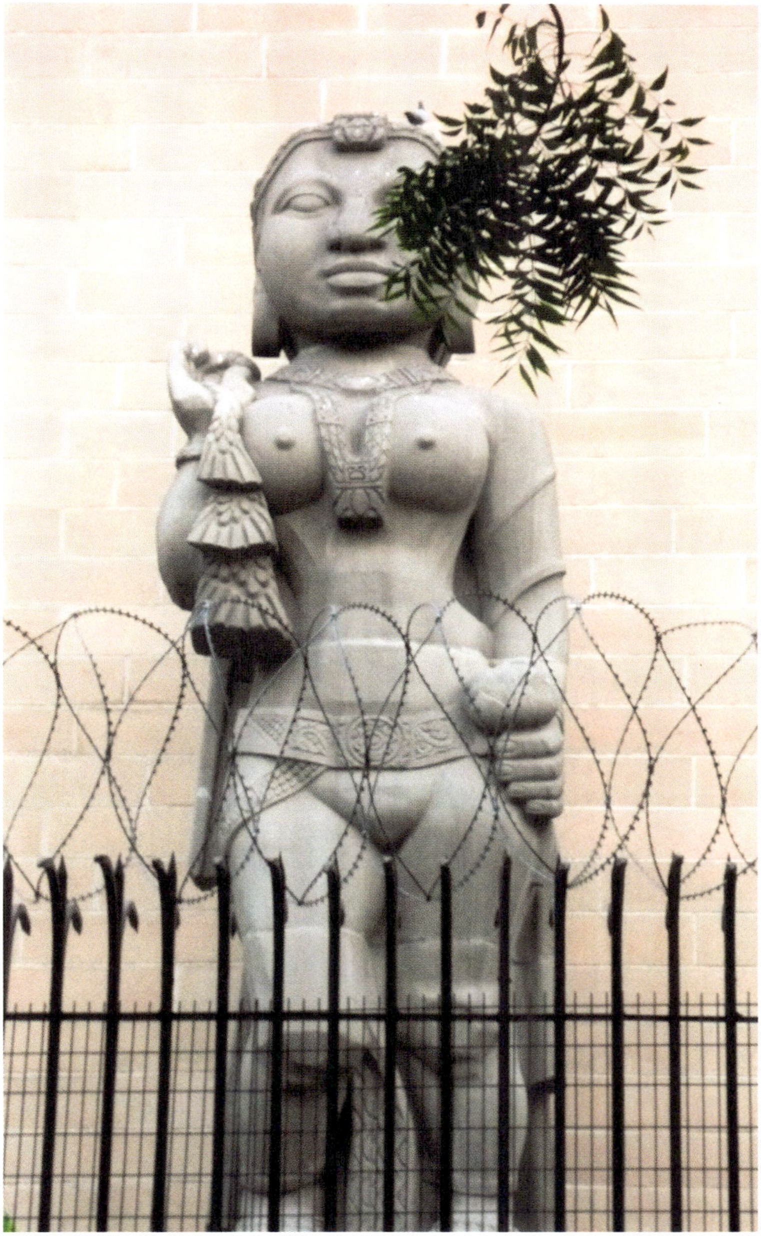

YAKSHI

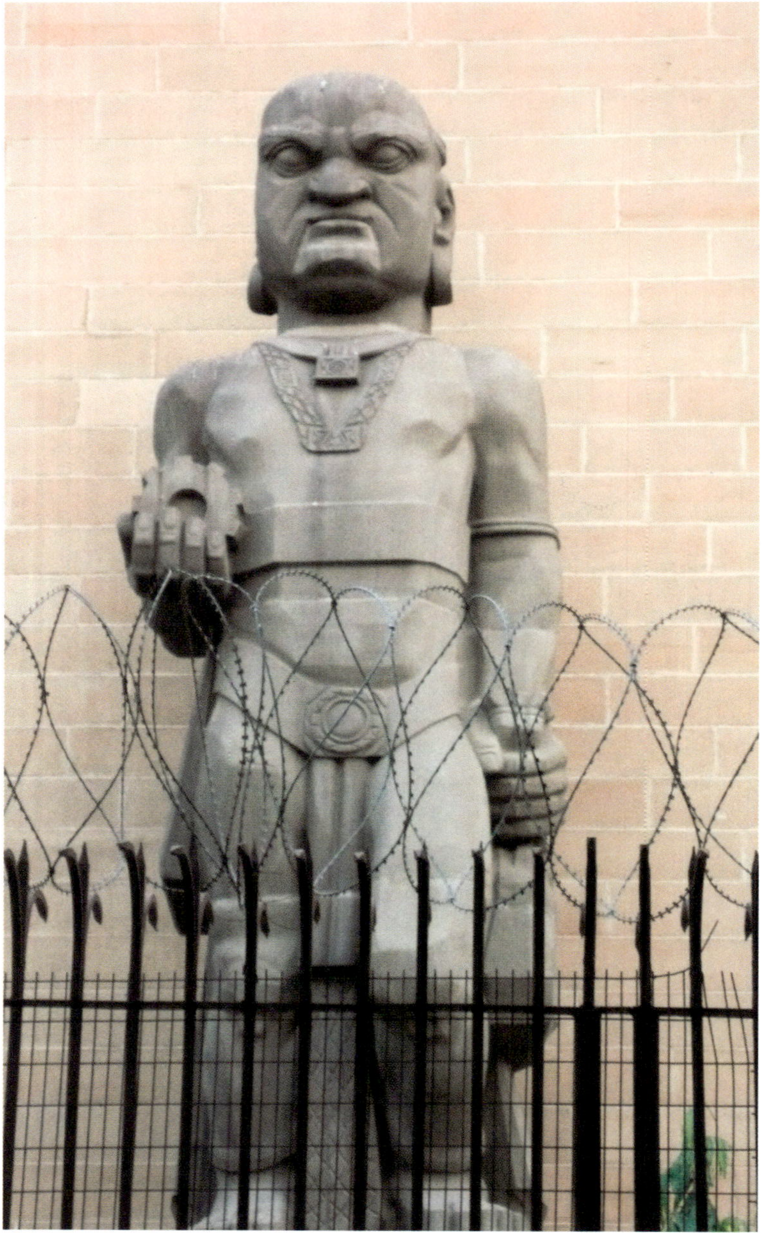

YAKSHA

Yaksha Prashna/The Yaksha's Questions

Yaksha: *Mrtah katham syaat purushaha?*
When is a man as good as dead?

Yudhishtira: *Mrto daridrah purushoh.*
A poor man is a dead man.

The Yaksha's Questions, *Aranya Parva (The Forest Canto)*, *Mahabharata*

Yakshi: Why does the road to the parliament pass by the central bank?

Raqs: Because a citizen without a bank account is as good as a dead man without a funeral, or a monument without a martyr.

Yaksha: What is more precious than gold, as worthless as a scrap of paper, heavier than stone, faster than the wind, slower than a turtle, lighter than a feather, as deadly as poison and as welcome as a blessing?

Raqs: A bank note. Because it can be valuable and worthless. Because it can be sluggish and volatile. Because it can weigh you down with debt or set you free. Because it can kill you and save you, and because it can kill you by saving you.

Yaksha: Why does a bank have to have guards, guns and barbed wire fences?

Raqs: To protect people from money.

Yakshi: When money talks, who listens?

Raqs: The deaf hear, the blind see, the wise man goes mad, the mad woman comes to her senses, the gossip turns silent, the spy reveals all, money lenders dance, misers become poets, artists become mathematicians, thieves pray and holy men babble.

Yaksha: Why do bank notes carry portraits?

Raqs: Because the promise to pay the bearer can have no meaning if it is not backed by a picture of the head of a king, a dowager, a dictator, a dead prophet or at the very least a magnificent wild beast. Because a bank note without a picture is like a security guard without a uniform.

Yakshi: In that case, why did Ram Kinkar Baij sculpt me naked?

Raqs: Because he knew the answer to the previous question. And because, though everyone knows that the emperor has no clothes, it is less well known that his treasury is actually empty, and that its guards keep their vigil, naked and alone.

Yakshas are the primordial, aboriginal guardian spirits of Indic mythology. They foster the health and well being of communities, bestow fertility on women and livestock, protect forests and water bodies, guard cities, homesteads, gold and hidden treasure and act as the minions, minders and foot-soldiers of the vast reserve army of Kubera, the Hindu god of wealth. Yakshas are clever, dangerous, fickle, wise, capricious, generous and given to lurk in wait for unsuspecting travellers whom they invariably test with an ordeal of demanding questions.

See: *Yakshas* by Ananda K. Coomaraswamy, Munshiram Manoharlal, New Delhi, 2001

Yakshas, condemned to long hours of keeping vigil over hoards of money will do anything to make the passing traveller tarry. Sometimes a solitary Yaksha, serving time in a remote forest will even inveigle a passing rain cloud into carrying messages to distant places.

See: 'Meghadootam' by Kalidasa, in *Kalidasa: The Loom of Time*, translated and edited from the Sanskrit and Prakrit by Chandra Rajan, Penguin Classics, Penguin Books India, 1990

The "Yaksha Prashna" or 'Yaksha's Question' is a well-known device for diversion, entertainment and moral instruction in the Sanskrit canon. It usually features a man or a woman providing illuminating answers to a series of riddles posed by a Yaksha as a means to fulfilling a quest, continuing on a journey, passing a threshold, obtaining a boon, clarifying a philosophical or ethical conundrum or resolving a vexed predicament. Failure to answer a Yaksha's questions usually results in a terrible curse or a horrible death.

See: *A Hindu Primer – Yaksha Prashna* by A.V. Srinivasan, a Parijata Publication published by IND-US Inc., Connecticut, 1984

In the Aranya Parva (Forest Canto) of the Mahabharata for instance, Yudhishtira, the exiled Pandava prince has to furnish answers by an enchanted lake to a particularly demanding set of questions in order to win back the lives of his brothers, which, in their haste to slake their thirst with the lake's water, they had forfeited when they had refused to be quizzed by the lake's guardian Yaksha.

See: *The Aranya Parva: The Book of the Forest* in *The Mahabharata*, Vol. II, edited and translated by J.A.B van Buitenen, The University of Chicago Press, 1975

Yakshas turn up. When forests are cleared, roads widened, land surveyed, or a riverbank mined for sand, digs reveal buried Yaksha figurines, often crude, sometimes exquisite, always enigmatic. Each excavated Yaksha brings in its wake a host of questions. Does it foretell an omen? Is there buried treasure? Are there reasons to dig deeper? Do they trigger repressed memories of fertility cults and esoteric magick? Usually, the questions cease when the excavated Yaksha or Yakshi is transported into a museum as an iconic exemplar of 'national treasure'.

See: 'The Endangered Yakshi: Careers of an Ancient Art Object in Modern India' by Tapati Guha Thakurta, published in *History and the Present*, edited by Anjan Ghosh and Partha Chatterjee, Orient Longman, 2002

Ram Kinkar Baij, who took more than ten years to complete his commission to sculpt the monumental Yaksha and Yakshi figures had to endure his own set of ordeals. Questions were raised in parliament about the propriety of immodest sculptures adorning the streets of the capital. Newspapers campaigned against what they saw as the 'obscenity' of the Yakshi's nakedness. The rumour mill gossiped about the resemblance that the female figure had to a leading woman-capitalist of the day. Costs mounted, and the project soon became the most expensive public art commission in Independent India.

See: *Of Art, Central Banks, and Philistines – Anecdotes and Trivia*, The Reserve Bank of India, Miscellany http://www.rbi.org.in/scripts/mis_anec3.aspx

Ram Kinkar Baij's Yaksha and Yakshi figures stand guard outside the gates of the Reserve Bank, India's central bank on Parliament Street in New Delhi. Their monumental presence is the secret of their invisibility in the discourse around Ram Kinkar Baij and his so-called subaltern modernity. As lasting reminders of the most expensive public art commission in independent India, their stony New Delhi metropolitan bulk is an uneasy intrusion into the mythology of the neglected and indigent artist in the idyllic pastoral Bolpur bosom of his Santhal Family.

They can neither be resolved into a celebration of the mythic category of the 'people', nor be seen as homage to the state. We could speculate that the Yakshi's impassive blank stare, and the Yaksha's barely disguised contempt for what he sees embody Ram Kinkar Baij's own 'Yaksha Prashna' to the Indian Republic. As of now, we do not know of any answers that have a satisfactory purchase on Ram Kinkar's sculpted question marks.

IRIT ROGOFF IN CONVERSATION WITH ANSHUMAN DASGUPTA

The following conversation took place on 16 November 2007 in anticipation of the exhibition Santhal Family: Positions Around an Indian Sculpture *at MuHKA. The exhibition team, represented by Anshuman Dasgupta, wished to gather the impressions of cultural theorist Professor Irit Rogoff, who had travelled to Santiniketan in February 2006 to attend the Ramkinkar Baij Centenary Seminar. The conversation was recorded at the RIBA Café, London.*

IR: Now, tell me the story you were telling... into the microphone!

ADG: Yes, I was wondering how [Rabindranath] Tagore's project had come to interest you... and how you see Ramkinkar [Baij] featuring in that project?

IR: ... one of the things that interested me—and remember that this was my first visit to India and to Santiniketan, that it was an extremely brief visit and that I was extremely ignorant about India—was how I could perceive Tagore as somebody who operated with what we call a self-organised politics, in a contemporary sense. The encounter with Santiniketan despite its being configured now as the site of tradition had a certain aura of contemporaenity and the Tagore that one encounters there is not just a modernist figure but one that feels quite contemporary. Now, I know that he came from a highly privileged position, I know that he had a lot of money, but that is not what is interesting about him. What interests me is that that he wished into being something that had never existed before, and not just in India, but hardly anywhere in the world—this model of a hugely progressive university that was really an international modernist community. He was willing to make this colossal personal effort of travelling and raising money, in order to support these projects. In some way, I find this personally very inspiring! Because you wonder, what is the worth of these vast amounts of work that you are always doing, which is not really supported by the institutions, which never really fits into mainstream existing structures... And I also found inspiring the ability to start from Bengal, and also from provincial Bengal—he had the ability to start from provincial Bengal in the 1920s, to recognise the emergent modernist world in the West and draw from it. For instance, I found it very interesting that, in the early twenties, the very first exhibition of Bauhaus took place in Santiniketan...

ADG: in Kolkata...

IR: ... in Kolkata? So, in Kolkata, but it was connected to Tagore.

ADG: Yes. It was because of his intervention, that the Bauhaus, or people in Germany supporting this project, were able to lend to the exhibition. He provided the guarantee... in a sort of symbolic way.

IR: The other thing that I found very interesting was that, on the one hand, Tagore was clearly steeped in not just the local art and craft tradition, but local thought, local literature and language, and on the other hand he was looking to the most progressive kinds of (granted some mainstream and established) things that were happening in the West. And the final thing that interested me was that Santiniketan was a real home for the refugees—people who were from the West and who, for political, ethnic or other reasons, found themselves unacceptable in Europe, discovered a home for their pursuits in the 20s, 30s and 40s in Santiniketan, in provincial Bengal. In conjunction with all of these encounters, I read the novel *The Home and the World*, where I got a broader sense of this. Santiniketan built specific relations between something like the home in the world—between something very international and something very local, with this internationalism as itself something rather small, unrecognised, unacknowledged, or possessing the qualities of an avant-garde movement…

ADG: Here, one is tempted to consider Tagore's ideas and his admonition or advice to his younger colleagues as to what comprised their national commitments—he suggested that, if you are serving your immediate surroundings, you can *better* serve the greater circumstance you call 'nation'. Nationalism was in the air, so it was quite natural for the idealist youngsters to join the enthusiastic nationalist league. But Tagore's advice to his younger colleagues was that if you serve your surroundings better then you will be a better nationalist than those who think in larger terms. Thus he urged the social workers to concentrate on the village developments, to look into the problems existing in the surrounding villages, to look at how they could solve them in a certain pragmatic way; meanwhile, he wanted the artists to evolve their ideas *from their locale*. He was not proposing this through his own works, perhaps because he was not a trained artist, but he was perhaps enacting his own advice at a more suggestive level. In his own works, he wanted art to lay bare the inexpressible deeper psychic material, that he thought lay suppressed deep under the skin—which itself was a very modern attitude. However, at the institutional level, for the organisation of Santiniketan, he relied on others—his younger and more capable colleagues—to handle the daily aspects of translating his ideas into practice. And perhaps we can now trace Ramkinkar in the loop of such a grand and simultaneously micro or modest project.

IR: This relationship of nationalism and localism which is so clear in Tagore's life's work, of speaking simultaneously for two different and largely incompatible perspectives is very interesting and again I find that very contemporary. It begins to explain what I really found interesting about Ramkinkar Baij's work—or those works that were on display on the campus grounds of Santiniketan, which were maybe four large pieces of sculpture. If you come from a really traditional art historical trajectory, then there is a link between the emergence of modernism and what in Western art history is called 'primitivism'. In the past two decades, there have been heated debates about the huge borrowing from other cultures, the scarce understanding of contexts, and how these so called 'primitivisms' operated within their own countries and cultures of origin; how the borrowing of formal properties was seemingly poised to reenergise and renew and to step out of frustrating limitations of much academically grounded Western art in the early part of twentieth century. At the same time, there was a complete disregard for the so-called primitive cultures. They were used as an instrument, in the process of pillaging properties. If you are reanimating and reenergising art through another culture, you are in no way addressing the problems of your own culture, even if you are using your own language. I think this is a key factor in the very early twentieth century, and especially of the works of the Parisian avant-garde, which had defined the early modernist project. One might say that these artists could not express their dissatisfaction with a stifling tradition, could not overthrow academicism, could not achieve their own sexual liberation, or sexual visibility, except by using the language of African sculptures or Indian paintings or a kind of South Pacific visual language. One of the problems for me with the general veneration of this early modernism, is that it is based on a formal borrowing, which is very different from lets say the early project of the Bauhaus, which is innovating within its own culture and language. In comparison, what I saw in Santiniketan felt very different. I am recalling the two big pieces depicting the Santhal family and the peasant family, which were the two big pieces in the yard…?

ADG: There are two sculptures on the campus: one is *Santhal Family* (1938), the other one is called the *Mill Call* (1956), both of them are in the shade, the latter has the women running to catch up with their duties...

IR: Aside from the two peasant groups, there is also a very overtly expressive sculpture of Gandhi, which was modernist in a particular way. This type of modernism was a modernism that understood itself as a kind of composite language with a lot of internal difference. I appreciate this difference in Santiniketan, where it seems important to be able to look at the inside from outside of yourself, to formulate an outer language, a visual language, a kind of formal language, in order to look at this internal difference within India. So it seemed to me to be a kind of modernism that was far more attenuated in terms of understanding the culture that it was inhabiting. What came from the West was not a formal language, but a host of contemporary industrialised concerns. The formal languages are kind of local. As I see it, what is new about the modernism of Ramkinkar is not its look, but its concerns; concerns with bringing difference into vision, and that makes it different from the modernism of the Western avant-garde.

ADG: To my mind, it is paramount to recognise the place of the very local elements in the context of Santiniketan. The practices of many artists there were generally seen to be very localised and to have certain generic values—often seen together as the local 'freakish', 'idiosyncratic' practices, done by a few mad men who were not generally related to an urbanity, like Tagore's, that is more easily recognised by the world travellers. And in a way, this was fruitful. Anecdotally, we can recall a situation with Ramkinkar that shows the affinities of Tagore for this particular idiom, a tale which is part of the oral lore of Santiniketan: One fine morning, after Ramkinkar made his first outdoor sculpture, *Sujata* (1935), which is slightly more personalised than his other sculptures, a stick-like figure, which he had erected on the campus, Tagore noticed it and summoned the maker. All of a sudden, Ramkinkar was on alert, along with the entire campus. They were all apprehensive and thought that they were going to be scolded, while the opposite happened. In no uncertain terms, Tagore encouraged Ramkinkar, and suggested that he should fill the campus with more such sculptures.

IR: Actually that sounds like a classic modernist, artistic patron, embracing the new in the face of any kind of conventional concern!

The issue of bringing together the familiar and the deeply unfamiliar that the art works in Santiniketan instantiate was also very evident for me in quite a personal way during this first visit to India. It was on the one hand very familiar having for many years read contemporary Indian fiction both diasporic and from the subcontinent, having steeped myself in postcolonial theory, having shopped on Brick Lane in London and eaten in countless Indian restaurants, watched countless Bollywood and art house films, tuned into the ambient sound of London, which so resonates with speech cadences and sounds from India. But on the other hand, India is entirely unexpected. It feels like a continent and it is vast, it has a long and complicated history, it is enormously nuanced internally, in terms of different groups of people and localities. In short, it presents this kind of hugely rich internal structure of difference! And exactly like in the classical phase of 'primitivism' in modernism, these nuanced structures of difference, which are matters of life and death within India, are entirely erased outside of it.

It may seem hugely familiar from literature, but it is an altogether different thing, on the one hand, to embody the preoccupations and the enormous internal complexities of this place, and, on the other hand, to be seamlessly part of the world. And being part of the world may take radically different forms. I have become very interested recently in the works of Amitav Ghosh, books like *In an Antique Land* (1992), *The Hungry Tide* (2004) and *The Glass Palace* (2000). His writing addresses the enormity of Indian diaspora, its global mobilities, its entanglements with so many other peoples and places beyond itself, and now with the global economies of new technologies and new markets. In his work, these hundreds of years of diasporic presence, moments that come out of colonialisms and empire, have actually become spaces wherefrom to inhabit the world. Mutual entanglements are important on so many levels: there is the shared language, which means that Indian literature is a part of English language literature, but it also means that English language literature is a part of Indian literature. All these kinds of complex entanglements are reflected in Santiniketan, and not in a kind of old modernist way of 'how do you bring progress from outside', but also through institutions and in this very contemporary model of self-organisation, where people get together, they have a set of aspirations and they work unbelievably hard to organise themselves and fund themselves.

It was a huge surprise—in coming from London, to this totally unfamiliar world—to feel at home in what are just vestiges of structures that I recognise to be run down. But even, if it is short on resources and is under-funded, if it is this mystical, musical, oddly self-important place, I found elements in it that really spoke to me of their contemporariness.

ADG: You have identified the internationalism in the locality of Santiniketan, a facility and intent that is not immediately available to many viewers as they look at the works from a distance, in their photographic or whichever form. Perhaps they can't recognise these internal dynamics unless they achieve a certain contact with the context and the interpellation of various factors—subjectivities and politics and the moments in history which one may relive through the works. It's a tough job. Unlike the novelistic material, which may have a certain apparent immediacy even in translation, visual culture presents one with another set of problems of cultural translation. Given this, how do you perceive today's context for Indian art? Do you see any of the forces or factors we've noted about Santiniketan as active or present?

IR: Well, you know that this is not the art world that I know intimately, but through you, I encountered this organisation called Khoj and, in my own world, I encountered the woks of Raqs Media Collective and at the conference that you organised on the legacy of Ramkinkar I encountered a lot of artists of younger and middle generations. I saw that contemporary art in India seems to be unfolding in different directions. On the one hand, there is a clear energy for making things that are sellable in the local and the international art market. I understood during my visit that a local art market is relatively new and very dynamic at present. This attempt to make things that are sellable in a 'hot' market, has an internationalist tinge to it, but in the least interesting way to me. A lot of it consists of just picking up artistic and visual trends, styles and fashions. On the other hand, I was interested in the way in which a group like Khoj brings in foreign artists to encounter the local in a way that stretches their perspective and makes them develop a practice in a very different way. For myself, a practice is always more interesting than objects; it is more complex, it allows for unfolding encounters and it is not reducible to pure commodification.

There is this issue that I was mentioning before—the illusion of familiarity—that has to be broken, though it does not have to be broken down into an estrangement. This is one of the notions, one of the reasons I absolutely hate the mythical or the mystical, for it assumes that estrangement—it assumes the inability to gain an insight into another culture. In contrast, I saw quite a lot of works that attempt to access several cultures at once and try to update the local traditions, which I am never entirely sure about, but I saw quite a few works, like the work of the Khoj people that seems to me to bring out the elements of both sides, by facilitating or staging encounters between people from outside of India and situations inside of India. Meanwhile the work of the Raqs Media Collective, from within the Sarai organisation, produces works that are familiar to me, in the sense that they understand art as more than an object, but as research, as investigation, as collaboration, as publishing; Raqs really understands art as a field of knowledge. And they take very sophisticated theoretical tools from everywhere—from India as well as elsewhere—and apply these to very specific local situations in a highly theorised, investigative mold. I had a chance to see quite a range during this visit, largely thanks to your conference, but what always appeals to me are the situations that bridge worlds in an interesting way and avoid awful binarisms between the local and the global, for that seems to me to be unproductive at every possible level.

In Delhi, our friend Suddha [Shuddhabrata Sengupta of Raqs Media Collective] took me to a conference at the Delhi University. It was a conference on masculinity. We only went for one afternoon. But there was a film by Rahul Roy, called *The Beautiful City*, about the slums at the edges of Delhi, which are constantly being bulldozed by developers, and it focused on two small families. One of the things that was absolutely fantastic about that film was that it didn't use these people as objects. It didn't try to do ethnography on them, it didn't try to record the difficult conditions of slums in Delhi; it allowed these people to use the film in order to speak to each other and to speak about the situation, in ways that are not usually available to them. We spoke to Rahul Roy afterwards, particularly about this young woman at the centre of the film. This was really an abject situation—she had an unemployed husband and very little employment of her own and absolutely no resources. During the film she is very dressed up, wearing a lot of jewellery and make up and looks wonderful. And Roy said that she understood that she could use the film in order to say something to her husband, which she wouldn't be able to say to him in the normal course of events. Which to me is the workings of art at its best—not to objectify, not to pretend to speak to some international audience, nor to pretend to be doing some kind of social work, or reporting, or ethnography—it's an understanding that art is a kind of multifaceted tool, and one can never understand whose hand it ends up in or whose hand it is most useful for. So that film was one of the things that really interested me in my brief encounter with Indian art, in its marriage of documentary tradition and very sophisticated narratology and sense of agency, not social work but empowerment that comes out of affording dignity. But I spent such a short time there that I should not really be speaking... certainly not drawing all these grandiose conclusions!

ADG: Maybe to wrap up, we could compare what you saw in India to what you recognise as your locality...

IR: I could note a certain set of contradictions that became apparent during this visit. On the one hand, what I found heartening was the enormous amount of care for people—family members or colleagues or friends. I saw this care for people in difficulties shown at the level of human interaction. Which brings forth a duality between the care and concern about other people and the lack of similar care in the social and organisational levels, or in the institutions. In human relations, in interactions and discussions everywhere I sensed a cultural ability to encounter very abstract questions at very personal levels, but not at institutional levels. I recognise an ability to sustain abstractions *in details*. I must say that this impressed me because I have never seen that in any other parts of the world.

What I found really devastating were some of the institutions. I have not encountered such horrible institutions, I mean official public institutions, in a country that is so developed and sophisticated—institutions that are abandoned by governmental powers, or powers that run institutions, and are in turn abandoning everybody that comes to them. So it seems that the fact that there is so much brilliant thinking and brilliant work going on in India, is *absolutely not* because the institutions are fostering this. It is because of people's energy, people's creativity, people's needs, people's ability to organise by themselves. Amidst the public institutions like the museums or universities, which are devastating, the people inside are so much better than these institutions. It was interesting to see how little support these institutions gave their people and how much support people gave each other, for that is something we are not used to. Maybe because in Europe and in the United States people depend on institutions; they are institutionally dependent and they think that's what facilitates and enables their work. And this is almost the opposite in India—institutions do nothing but hinder. And people somehow support one another in order to get to do good work. Somehow they self-organise. The contemporaneity of those models struck me and, in Santiniketan, in the relationship between Tagore and Ramkinkar Baij, I saw a kind of historical beginning of that.

126

MATTI BRAUN
German Dhaba

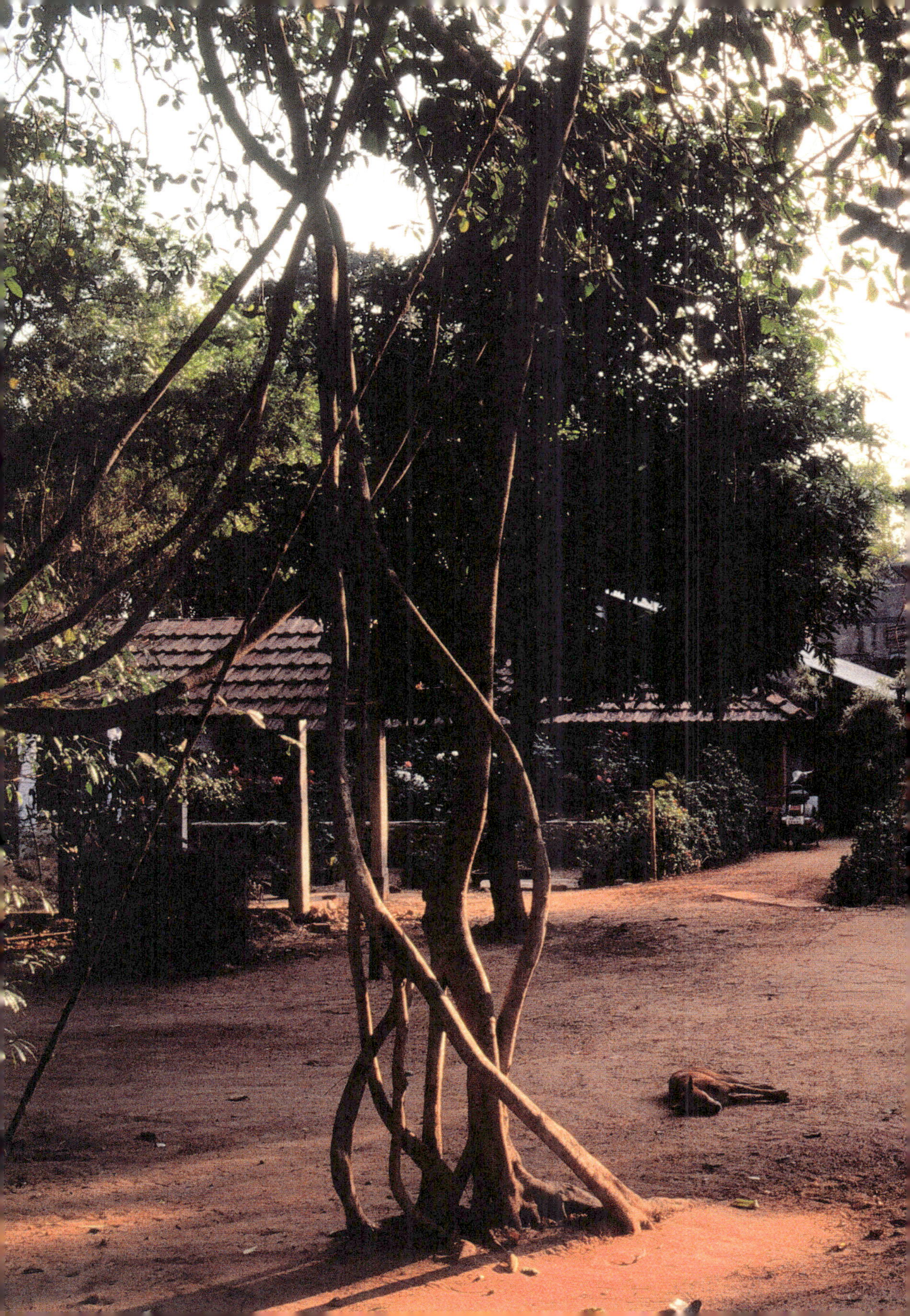

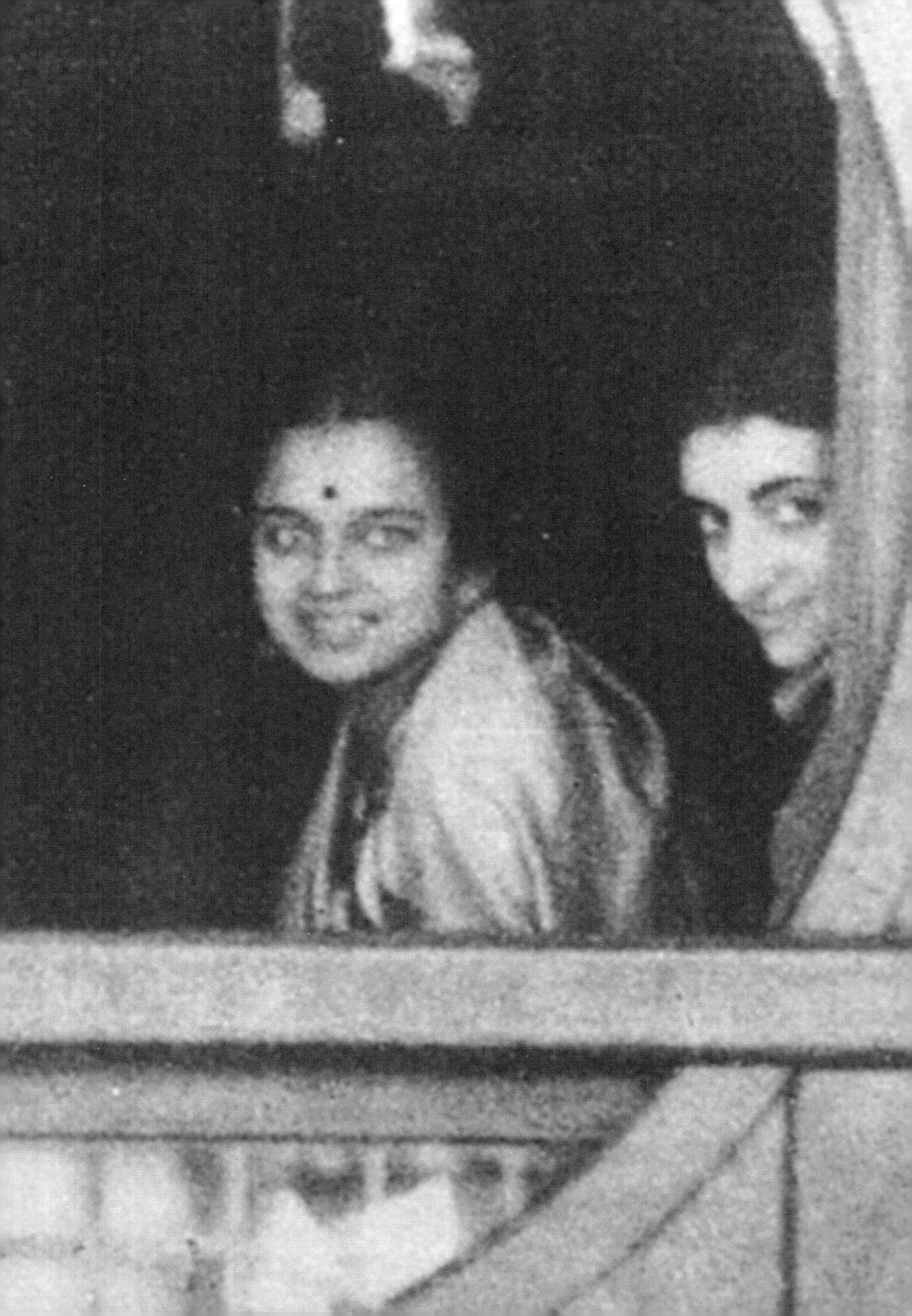

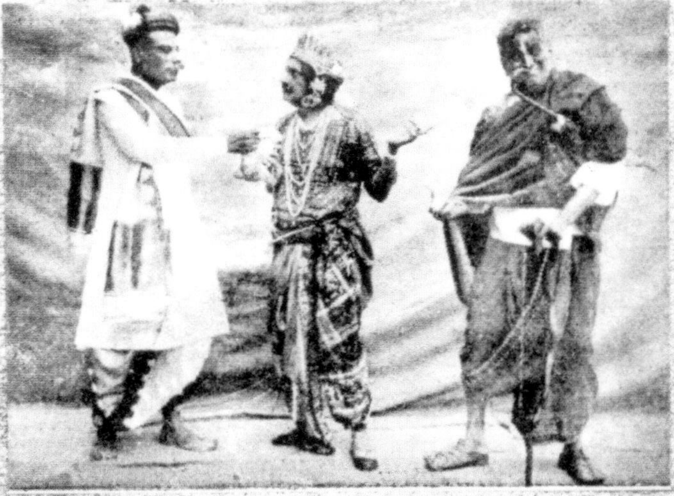

Three brothers in the play Phagune from left to right Sri Samerendranath Tagore, Sri Gaganendranath Tagore, Sri Abanindranath Tagore.

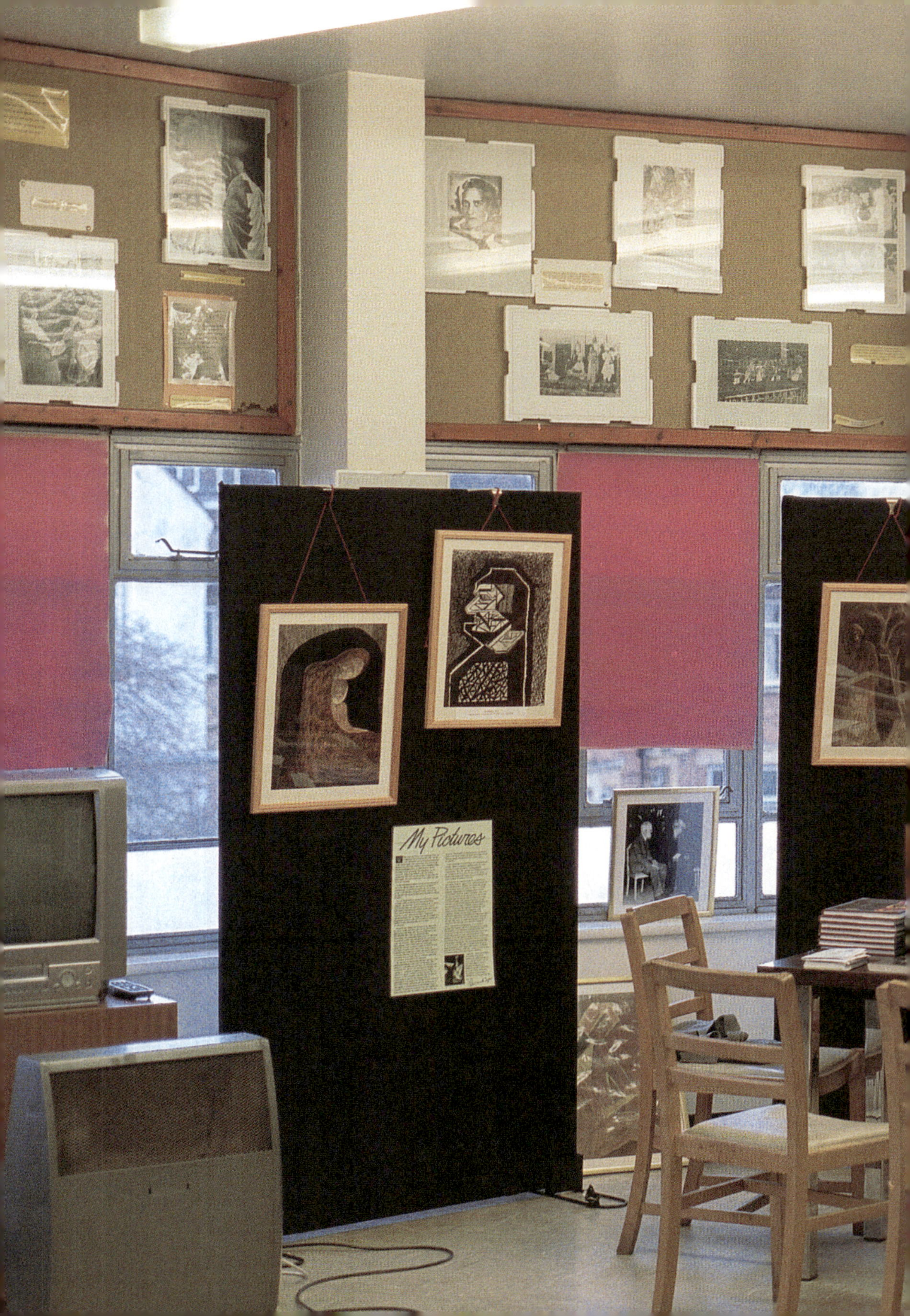
My Pictures

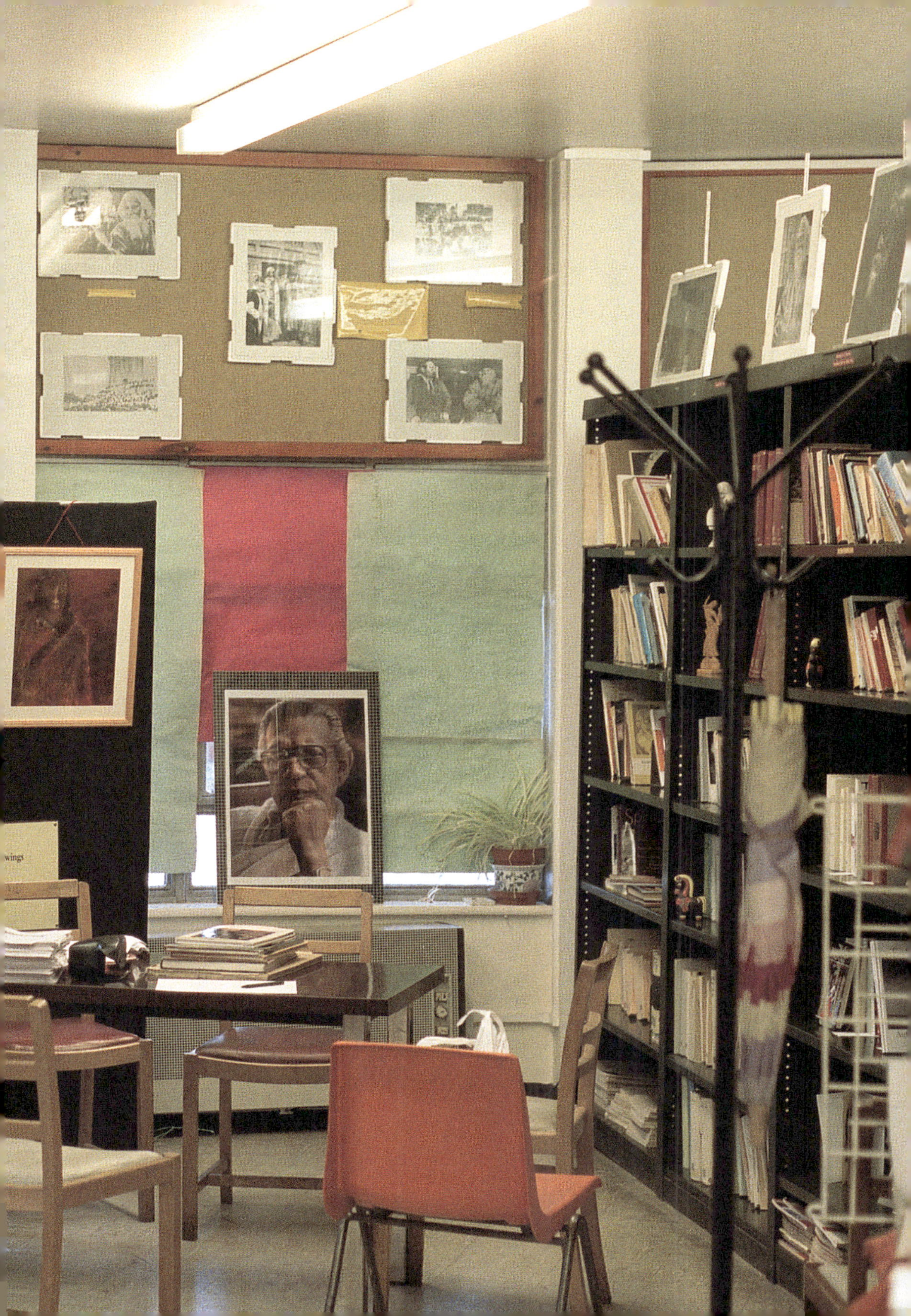

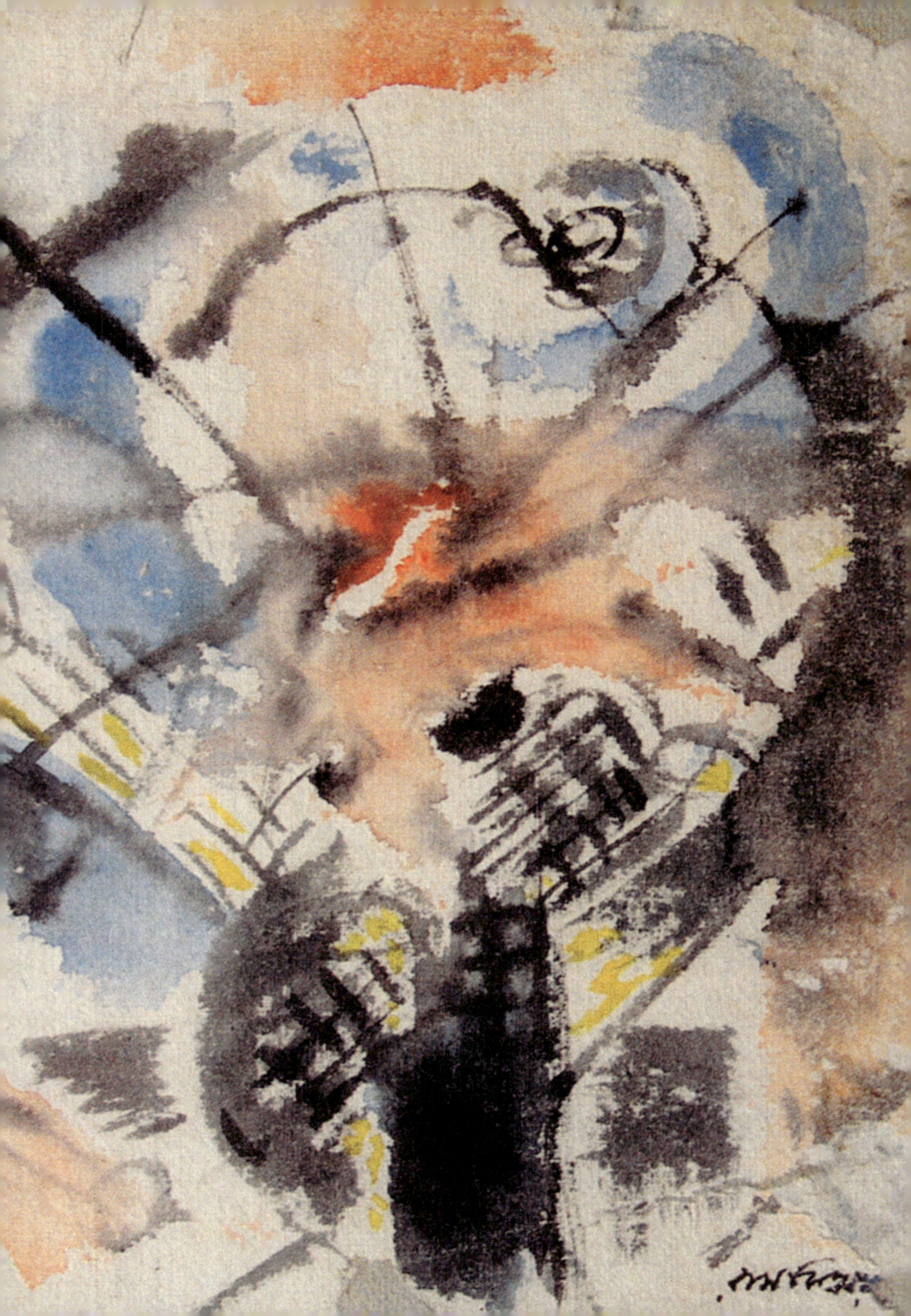

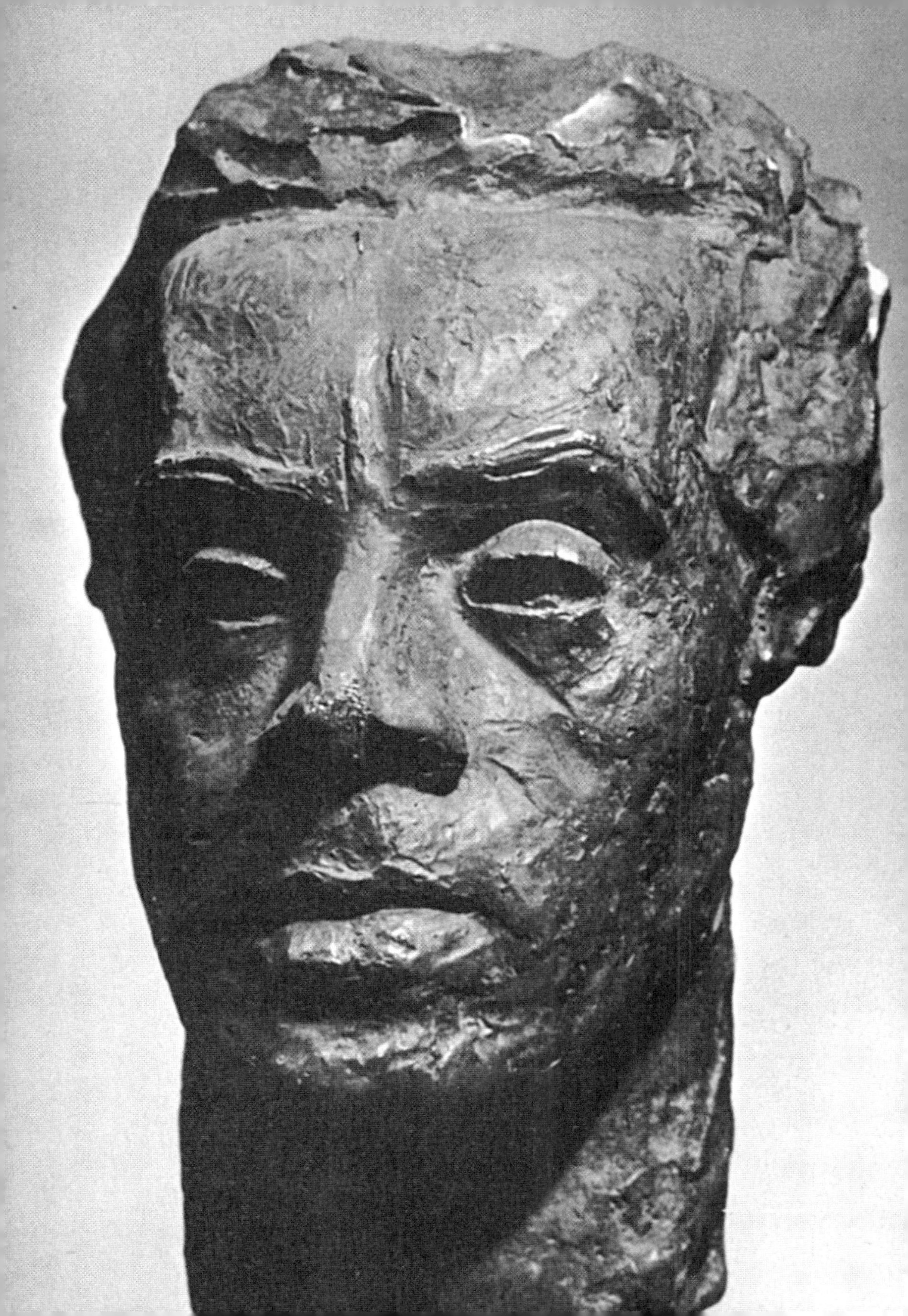

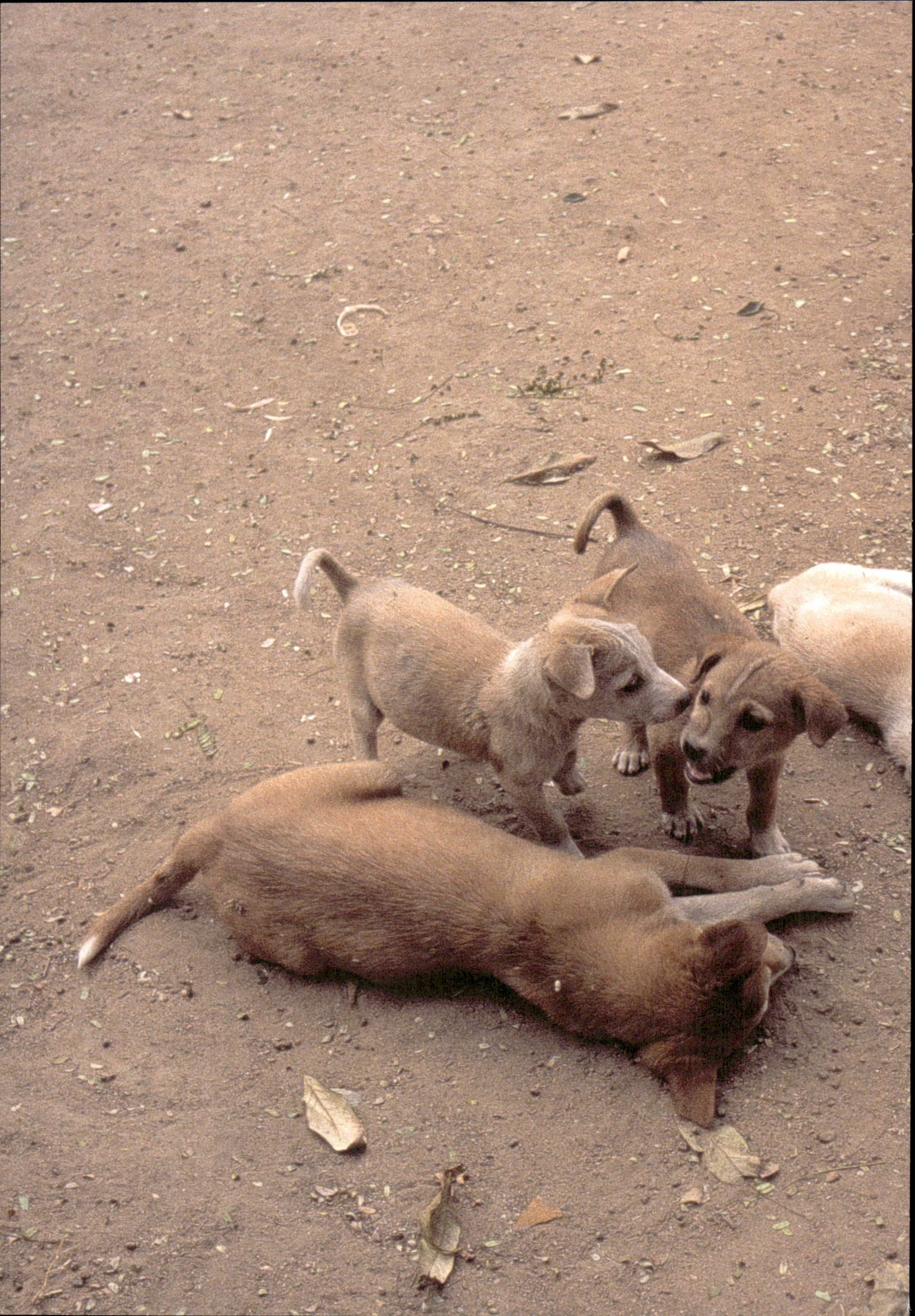

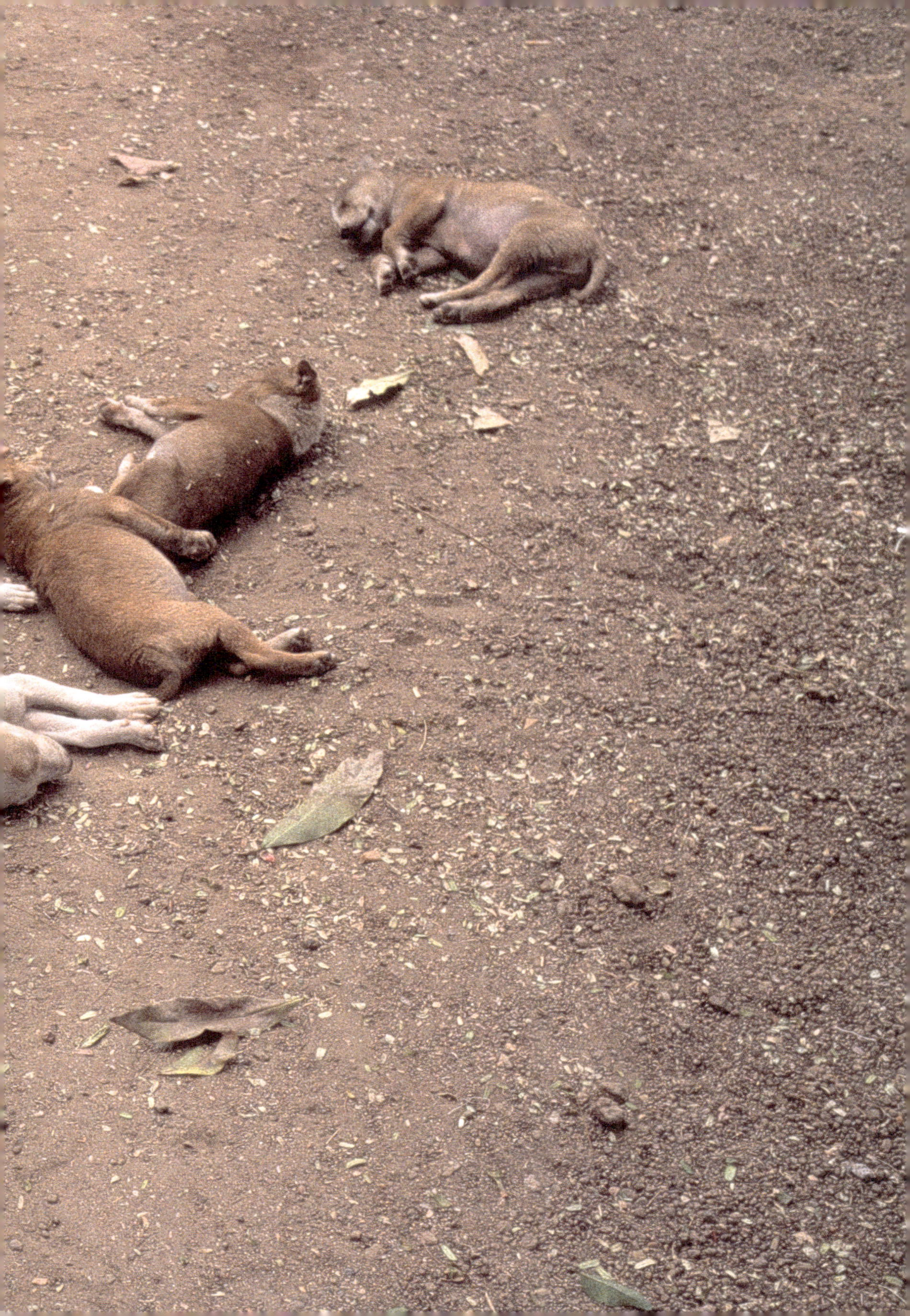

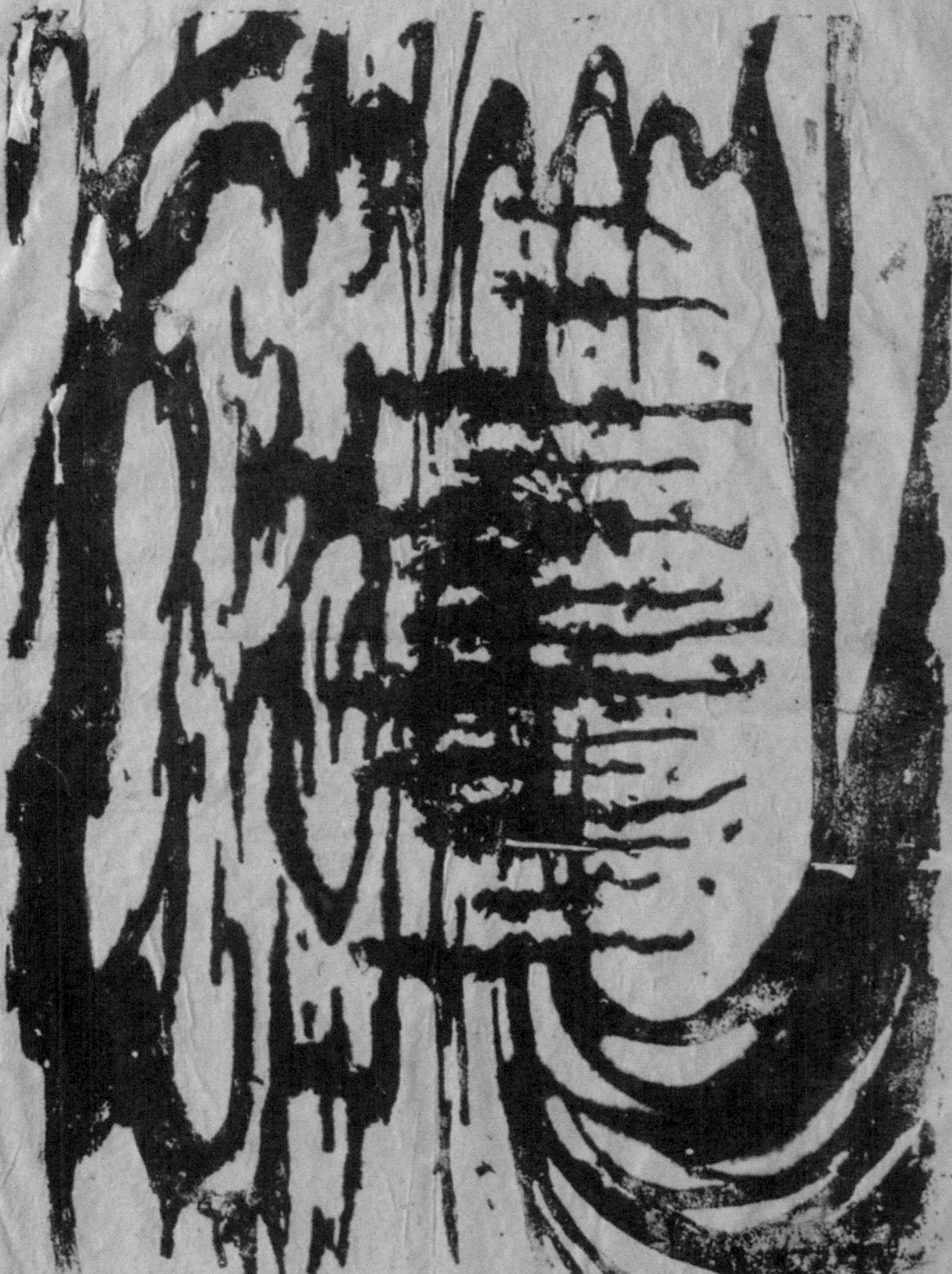

Notes

Goshka Macuga's photographs of Khala Bhavan, Santiniketan (pp. 8-13) were taken by the artist during a research trip in September 2007. Macuga was invited to India in preparation for her development of the exhibition design for *Santhal Family: Positions Around an Indian Sculpture* and to make a new work for the exhibition. All images © Goshka Macuga.

Anshuman Dasgupta's art historical image/text essay (pp. 20-33) was prepared for this publication in order to situate Ramkinkar's practice in a broader art historical context.

Juan Pérez Agirregoikoa's series of watercolours (pp. 35-42) were specially commissioned for this publication as the artist's response to the work *Santhal Family* by Ramkinkar Baij. A selection of these images also appear in the exhibition *Santhal Family: Positions Around an Indian Sculpture.* All images © Juan Pérez Agirregoikoa.

Sheela Gowda's images (pp. 48-55) were selected by the artist from her own photographic documentation of an artwork/site specific intervention located on the outskirts of Bangelore that she completed in 2001. The artist was invited to revisit this work in relation to the themes of this book—as a 'walking sculpture' which pays attention to the material qualities of a particular site. Sheela Gowda has also been commissioned to make a new work for the exhibition *Santhal Family: Positions Around an Indian Sculpture.* All images and text © Sheela Gowda.

Stephen Morton's essay commissioned for this publication (pp. 56-61) builds on some of the arguments presented in his study *Gayatri Spivak: Ethics, Subalternity and the Critique of Postcolonial Reason* (Cambridge, UK and Malden, MA: Polity Press, 2007).

Mahasweta Devi's short story, *Statue* (pp. 62-86), is reprinted with kind permission from Seagull Books, Kolkata.

Sunil Gupta's series of photographic portraits (pp. 88-97) entitled *Mr. Malhotra's Party* (2007-ongoing) have been selected for this book from a portrait project of the same name, of which the artist has written: "In the 1980's I made constructed documentary images of gay men in architectural spaces in Delhi (*Exiles* series). Now people are meeting less in parks etc., and more on the net, and in places like "private" parties. I am trying to visualize this latest virtual queer space by a series of portraits of real people who identify their sexuality as 'queer' in some way. This time they are willing to identify themselves. They are guests of an imaginary party, I'm calling it Mr. Malhotra's Party." He notes that: "Gay nights at local clubs are always signposted as private parties in a fictitious person's name to get around the law; Section 377, a British colonial law, which still criminalizes homosexuality in India. Mr. Malhotra is the ubiquitous Punjabi refugee who arrived post partition and contributed to the development of the city." Images (in order of appearance in this publication): *Diepriye, Khiyanur, Pavitr, Chapal, Bikram, Kaushiki, Priya, Akshara, Anokhi, Gautam*, all © Sunil Gupta.

Sudeep Dasgupta's essay commissioned for this publication (pp. 98-105) builds on arguments developed for a paper presented at a workshop on "The Migratory Aesthetic and Encuentro" in Murcia, Spain, organized by ASTA and CENDEAC.

Melvin Motti's project (pp. 107-114) was produced in Kolkata during a research trip to West Bengal in October 2007 coordinated by the MuHKA and Calcutta Art Research. The artist's project in this book is one version of a commissioned work which also appears in different form in the exhibition *Santhal Family: Positions Around an Indian Sculpture.* All images and text © Melvin Motti.

Raqs Media Collective's image/text essay *Yaksha Prashna/The Yaksha's Questions* (pp. 114-119) is a commissioned work by Raqs in response to the exhibition/publication's thematic. Designed here specifically for the pages of a book, this work is shown in a three dimensional format in the exhibition *Santhal Family: Positions Around an Indian Sculpture.*

Matti Braun's image essay (pp. 127-136) commissioned for this book responds to the thematic of the *Santhal Family* project and the specific context of Santinketan. It draws on extensive research undertaken by the artists on this subject including a trip to West Bengal in 2007 coordinated by Calcutta Art Research with the generous support of the Goethe Institute Max Mueller Bhavan, Kolkata.

Will Bradley is a writer and curator based in Oslo. His recent publications include *Art and Social Change: A Critical Reader* (co-edited with Charles Esche, Tate Publications, London 2007) and *Self-organisation/Counter-economic strategies* (co-edited with Mika Hannula, Cristina Ricupero and Superflex, Lukas and Sternberg, New York 2006); recent curatorial projects include *Forms of Resistance* at the Van Abbemuseum, Eindhoven, 2007 (with Phillip van den Bossche and Charles Esche) and *Radical Software: art, technology and the Bay Area underground* at the CCA Wattis Institute, San Francisco, 2006.

Matti Braun was born in Berlin. He studied at the Academy of Fine Art, Braunschweig and in Frankfurt am Main. He has exhibited widely in Europe, among others with solo projects at Museum Ludwig, Cologne (2008), Galleria S.A.L.E.S, Rome (2007), The Showroom, London (2003) and Stedelijk Museum Büreau Amsterdam (2002), and group exhibitions at Tate Liverpool (2004), Witte de With, Rotterdam (2004), and Kiasma, Helsinki (2001). Matti Braun's theatre project *The Alien*, a production that combines visual art and theatre disciplines in the staging of a version of the unrealised screenplay by Indian film director Satyajit Ray, was presented by The Showroom, London at the Laban Centre (2006), at the Bonner Kunstverein (2005), Project Arts Centre, Dublin (2005) and de VeenFabriek, Leiden (2005). He lives and works in Cologne and is represented by Gallery BQ, Cologne and Esther Schipper, Berlin.

Born in Kolkata, **Anshuman Dasgupta** completed undergraduate studies in the History of Art at the Department of Art History Kala Bhavan, Visva Bharati Universtity, Santiniketan and a master's degree from the M.S. University of Baroda. He taught at various institutions in India, including the National Institute of Design in Ahmedabad, the National School of Drama and the Jawaharlal Nehru University in New Delhi before assuming the post of Lecturer at his alma mater in Santiniketan in 1997. He has co-organized international artists' workshops like Khoj Kolkata (2006) and the Ramkinkar Baij Centenary International Seminar at Visva Bharati University, Santiniketan (2007). The latter was part of a set of year-long centenary activities starting in 2006, which also included the Ramkinkar Baij Centenary Exhibition and an extensive catalogue on Ramkinkar's work, organized/edited by Dasgupta. An active member of international platforms for curators such as the 4th International Berlin Biennale (2006), Dasgupta is currently affiliated with the Goldsmiths College, University of London as a PhD candidate in Curatorial/ Knowledge.

Sudeep Dasgupta is Assistant Professor in Media & Culture at the University of Amsterdam. His research interests and publications cover a range of topics from: aesthetics and the politics of migration, postcolonial studies, film and television studies and globalisation. His recent publications include an edited volume, *Constellations of the Transnational: Modernity, Culture, Critique* (Editions Rodopi, 2007).

Mahasweta Devi is an author and activist based in Kolkata. Her first book, *Jhansir Rani* (The Queen of Jhansi) was published in 1956. What followed was a prolific literary career, which includes publications of over twenty collections of short stories and close to one hundred novels, primarily in her native language of Bengali. As a chronicler of oppressed communities and tribal life in India, she is a regular contributor to several literary magazines such as *Bortika*. Devi has been awarded the Jnanpith in 1995, India's highest literary honour and was the recipient in 1997 of the prestigious Magsaysay Award for Journalism, Literature and Creative Communication.

Born in Bhadravati, **Sheela Gowda** lives and works in Bangalore. She studied painting at Ken School of Art, Bangalore, Visva Bharati University, Santiniketan and the Royal College of Art, London. Having worked in oils, mostly in an exploration of female representations influenced by her mentor K.G. Subramanyan, and later by Nalini Malani, in 1992 Gowda incorporated symbolically charged materials, such as cow dung, kumkum, paper, printed textiles and charred wood into her practice—a lasting concern of her work has been to negotiate a reflection on women's lives in specific geographic and economic circumstances in India with an engagement in a transnational modernism. Recent exhibitions include: documenta 12, Kassel (2007), Bose Pacia Gallery, New York (2006), Gallery Ske, Bangalore (2004), Walker Art Center, Minneapolis (2003).

Sunil Gupta is an artist, curator, writer, and cultural activist. Born in Dehli, Gupta emigrated with his family to Montreal when he was a teenager. He earned an MA at the Royal College of Art in London, England, in 1983, and was based there until 2005, when he moved to India to pursue artistic projects. He was diagnosed HIV positive in 1995. In 1988, he co-founded Autograph: the Association of Black Photographers, a publicly funded coalition of photographers of Asian and African descent. In 1992, he started OVA: the Organization for Visual Arts, a curatorial initiative dedicated to promoting a new internationalism in the production and consumption of art. In 2000, Sunil Gupta received a Creative and Performing Arts Research Fellowship from the British Arts and Humanities Research Council, which culminated in the book and photographic/video exhibition *Pictures From Here*.

Goshka Macuga was born in Warsaw and studied in London where she currently lives and works. Her artistic practice often exists in dialogue with the roles of the curator and collector, museological conventions and more esoteric forms of display. Recent exhibitions include *Objects in Relation* for the Art Now series of solo exhibitions at Tate Britain, London (2007), *Sleep of Ulro* for the Furnace Commission, A Foundation, Liverpool (2006) as well as participation in the 27th São Paulo Biennale (2006) with the presentation *Mula sem Cabeça* [Headless Mule].

Stephen Morton is a lecturer in English at the University of Southampton. He is currently working on a monograph titled *Colonial States of Emergency in Literature and Culture 1905-2005*. His published writings include *Salman Rushdie: Fictions of Postcolonial Modernity* (Palgrave, 2007), *Gayatri Spivak: Ethics, Subalternity and the Critique of Postcolonial Reason* (Polity, 2006), as well as articles in *Public Culture*, *New Formations*, *Ariel*, *The Year's Work in Critical and Cultural Theory* and *Interventions*.

Melvin Motti is an artist who lives and works in Rotterdam. A solo exhibition of his work will be organized by the FRAC Champagne-Ardenne, Reims in the Spring of 2008.

Juan Pérez Agirregoikoa was born in Donostia-San Sebastian and lives and works in Paris, where he studied with Alain Badiou at the University of Paris VIII (1993-1997) and with Peter Halley at the Ecole Nationale Superieur des Beaux Arts (1991-1992). Recent exhibitions, which featured his experiments with banners, watercolours and collage include: a solo presentation at the 2007 Lyon Biennale (commissioned by Peio Aguirre), the touring group exhibition *Populism* (2005, curated by Cristina Ricupero, Lars Bang Larsen and Nicolaus Schafhausen) and a solo exhibition at the Sala Rekalde in Bilbao (2004).

Raqs Media Collective (Jeebesh Bagchi, Monica Narula & Shuddhabrata Sengupta) have been variously described as artists, media practitioners, curators, researchers, editors and catalysts of cultural processes. Their work, which has been exhibited widely in major international spaces and events, locates them squarely along the intersections of contemporary art, historical enquiry, philosophical speculation, research and theory, often taking the form of installations, online and offline media, objects, performances and encounters. They live and work in Delhi, and are based at Sarai, Centre for the Study of Developing Societies, an initiative they co-founded in 2000. They are members of the editorial collective of the *Sarai Reader* series.

Irit Rogoff is a writer, theorist and curator who works at the intersections of the critical, the political and contemporary artistic practices. As Professor of Visual Culture at Goldsmiths College, London University, Rogoff has been Director of "Translating the Image—Cross Cultural Contemporary Arts" (AHRC Research Project 2001-2006) from which two volumes will be published by König Verlag in 2008. She is currently heading the PhD program Curatorial/Knowledge at Goldsmiths. Recent and upcoming publications include: *Terra Infirma: Geography's Visual Culture* (Routledge 2001), as well as *Unbounded* and *Looking Away - Participating Singularities - Ontological Communities* (both forthcoming in 2008). Recent curatorial projects include *De-Regulation with the work of Kutlug Ataman* (Antwerp, 2006; Herzylia, 2006; Berlin, 2008); *Academy: Learning from the Museum* (Van Abbemuseum, Eindhoven, 2006); and *SUMMIT: Non-aligned Initiatives in Education Culture* (Berlin, 2007).

R. Siva Kumar was born in Kerala and educated in Kerala and Santiniketan. He is presently Professor of Art History at Visva Bharati, Santiniketan. He has curated several important exhibitions and written extensively on Modern Indian Art. His publications include: *The Santiniketan Murals* (1995); *Santiniketan: The Making of a Contextual Modernism* (1997); *K.G. Subramanyan: A Retrospective* (2003); *A. Ramachnadran: A Retrospective* (2004); *K.S. Radhakrisnan* (2004); *My Pictures: A Collection of Paintings by Rabindranath Tagore* (2005) and *K.G. Subramanyan: The Painted Platers* (2007). He has also co-curated with Gulam Mohammed Sheikh *Benodebehari Mukherjee: A Centenary Retrospective* and co-edited the accompanying publication.

Monika Szewczyk is a writer, editor and curator based in Brussels. She is Head of Publications at Witte de With Center for International Contemporary Art, Rotterdam, and a contributing editor of *A Prior* Magazine, Ghent.

Grant Watson is a writer and curator based in Antwerp working at the Museum van Hedendaagse Kunst Antwerpen (MuHKA), where he is involved in curating exhibitions and artist projects as well as organising an ongoing lecture series. He was previously the Curator of Visual Arts at Project Arts Centre, Dublin, where his programme included artists such as Gerard Byrne, Martha Rosler, Goshka Macuga, Sheela Gowda, Enrico David, Seamus Harahan, Klaus Weber and General Idea, the group exhibition *Communism* and 'Enthusiasm' at Frieze Art Fair. He recently co-edited the book *Make Everything New: A Project on Communism* (London: Book Works, 2006) and was Visiting Curator for Documenta 12. He studied Curating and Visual Cultures at Goldsmiths College London. He has been researching and working with contemporary Indian art since 1997, including curating the exhibition *Room for Improvement* at the Crafts Museum, New Delhi and *Drawing Space: Contemporary Indian Drawing* with inIVA, London.

Acknowledgements

The editors thank: Autograph ABP (London), John Callow (Marx Memorial Library, London), Mandira Chaterjee (Bodhi Art, Delhi), Dinas Cooper, Louisa Dare (Courtauld Institute, London), Phalguni Desai (Bodhi Art, Delhi), Anubha Dey (Bodhi Art, Delhi), Arnaud Dusaucy (Belgian Embassy, New Delhi), Joseph Francis (Indian Embassy, Brussels), Rajeev Garg (Garg Tents, Ambala City), Ritaban Ghatak, Sanchayan Ghosh, Arnab Ghoshal, Ratan Gopinath, Katherine Hacker (University of British Columbia, Vancouver), Marjolijn Hendrix, Amit Judge (Bodhi Art, Delhi), Kala Bhavan Faculty of Fine Art (Visva Bharati University, Santiniketan), Geeta Kapur, Naveen Kishore (Seagull Foundation for the Arts, Kolkata), Kalyan Kundu (The Tagore Centre UK, London), Katharina Lepper (Lehmbruck Sammlung, Duisburg), Rajeev Lochan (National Gallery of Modern Art, New Delhi), Maja Lozic, Geetha Mehra (Sakshi Gallery, Mumbai), Palash Mondal, Pushpamala N, Nandalulal Mukherjee, Samiran Nandy, Anath Nath Das, Natarang Pratishthan Archive (New Delhi), Natyasodh Samstha Archive (Kolkata), Pankaj Panwar, Rabindra Bhavan Archive (Santiniketan), Claudia Schmid (Tate, London), Praneet Soi (Calcutta Art Research), Ranjana Steinruecke (Gallery Mirchandani, Mumbai), Ritwik Memorial Trust (Kolkata), Sonal Singh, Vivan Sundaram, Dorrie Younger (Kashi Art Gallery, Cochin), all the authors and artists.

MuHKA Team: Raoul Amelinckx, Katrien Batens, Maya Beyns, Carine Bocklandt, Els Brans, Edwin Carels, Marcel Casneuf, Tom Ceelen, Ann Ceulemans, Celina Claeys, Christine Clinckx, Rita Compère, Leen De Backer, Bart De Baere, Raphaël De Bois, Martine Delzenne, Luc Delrue, Frederic De Vos, Jan De Vree, Liliane Dewachter, Gustaaf Dierickx, Pierre Dufond, Kamil El Djebouri, Sophie Gregoir, Pascale Haerens, Ria Hermans, Sabine Herrygers, Brigitta Jacobs, Joris Kestens, Helena Kritis, Hughe Lanoote, Ben Lecok, Viviane Liekens, Djo Moembo, Geertrui Pas, Alexandra Pauwels, Ghislaine Peeters, Joost Peeters, Anne-Marie Poels, Aïcha Rafik, John Reiff, Dieter Roelstraete, Iris Roevens, Gustaaf Rombouts, Peggy Saey, Rita Scheppers, Rolf Schuurmans, Vincent Stroep, Hester Struben, Dominique 't Jolle, Margot Thysens, Georges Uittenhout, Chris Van den Broeck, Ria Van den Broeck, Frank Van der Kinderen, Carine Van Dyck, Willy Van Gils, Roel Van Nunen, Gerda Van Paemele, Lutgarde Van Renthergem, Kris Van Treeck, Harm van Zwol, Zeger Verbist, Sofie Vermeiren, Nine Verschueren, Jan Vertommen, Rebekka Wauters, Grant Watson, Magda Weyns, Kathleen Weyts, Hans Willemse.

Santhal Family: Positions Around an Indian Sculpture
The Exhibition

Artists
Ramkinkar Baij
Santanu Bose
Matti Braun
Calcutta Art Research
Ritwik Ghatak
Sheela Gowda
Boran Handsa
N.S. Harsha
Reba Hore
Indian People's Theatre Association
Valsan Koorma Kolleri
Goshka Macuga
Melvin Motti
Meera Mukherjee
Otolith Group
(Kodwo Eshun & Angelika Sagar)
Sudhir Patwardhan
Juan Pérez Agirregoikoa
Ashim Purkayastha
Kerala Radicals
(incl. Jyothi Basu, Anita Dube K.R. Karunakaran, K.P. Krishnakumar, Alex Mathew, C.K. Rajan, Reghunadhan K)
Raqs Media Collective
(Jeebesh Bagchi, Monica Narula, Shuddhabrata Sengupta)
N. Rimzon
Ravi Shah
Vivan Sundaram
Klaus Weber

Curated by
Grant Watson in collaboration with Anshuman Dasgupta and Suman Gopinath

Exhibition Design
Goshka Macuga & Grant Watson

Project Documentary
Julien Gastelo

IPTA Exhibition Graphics
Julie Peeters

Production
Ghislaine Peeters & Georges Uittenhout

Colophon

Santhal Family: Positions Around an Indian Sculpture

This publication has been produced in conjunction with the exhibition *Santhal Family: Positions Around an Indian Sculpture* curated by Grant Watson in collaboration with Anshuman Dasgupta and Suman Gopinath at the Museum van Hedendaagse Kunst Antwerpen (MuHKA) 1 February to 5 May 2008.

- **Concept:** Grant Watson
- **Editors:** Anshuman Dasgupta, Monika Szewczyk, Grant Watson
- **Proof Reading:** Rebecca Fortey
- **Contributors:** Will Bradley, Matti Braun, Anshuman Dasgupta, Sudeep Dasgupta, Mahasweta Devi, Sheela Gowda, Sunil Gupta, Goshka Macuga, Melvin Motti, Stephen Morton, Juan Pérez Agirregoikoa, Raqs Media Collective, Irit Rogoff, R. Siva Kumar, Grant Watson
- **Graphic Design:** Michaël Bussaer
- **Cover Image:** Samiran Nandy
- **Printer:** Die Keure (Bruges, Belgium)

ISBN: 978-907282-8323

Published by the Museum van Hedendaagse Kunst Antwerpen

M HKA

In association with Bodhi Art

BODHI ART

With support from the British Council and the Kunststiftung NRW

BRITISH COUNCIL

KUNSTSTIFTUNG NRW

MuHKA is an initiative of the Flemish Community (Vlaamse Gemeenschap)

With the support of the Province of Antwerp, the City of Antwerp, Nationale Loterij and Klara

PROVINCIE ANTWERPEN

STAD ANTWERPEN

Nationale Loterij

Klara